An Essay on Shakespeare's Sonnets

An Essay on Shakespeare's Sonnets

Stephen Booth

New Haven and London Yale University Press 1969

Library of Congress catalog card number: 69–15440

Designed by Marvin Howard Simmons, set in Baskerville type, and printed in the United States of America by The Carl Purington Rollins Printing-Office of the Yale University Press, New Haven, Connecticut. Distributed in Great Britain, Europe, Asia, and Africa by Yale University Press Ltd., London; in Canada by McGill University Press, Montreal; and in Latin America by Centro Interamericano de Libros Académicos, Mexico City.

Published with assistance from the foundation established in memory of Philip Hamilton McMillan of the Class of 1894, Yale College.

For Douglas Bush

Contents

Preface ix

1. The Critical Dilemma 1
   Finding a Structural Principle for the Sequence 1
   Finding a Structural Principle for the Individual Sonnets 15

2. Structures versus Structure 29
   Formal, Logical, and Syntactical Patterns 29
   False Starts and Changes of Direction 51

3. Multiple Patterns 61
   Rhetorical Structure 61
   Phonetic Structure 66
   Patterns of Diction 79
   Multiplicity 82

4. Unity and Division, Likeness and Difference 86
   Phonetic Unity and Division 87
   Antanaclasis 90
   Paradoxical Style 96
   Unity and Division as a Theme 110

5. Motion of the Mind 116
   Time's Continual Haste—Sonnet 73 118
   The Comfort of the Couplet—Sonnet 60 130

6. All Forwards Do Contend 144
The Thrust of the Sonnets 144
The Progress of Sonnet 94 152

7. Recapitulation and Conclusion 169
Shakespeare and the Essence of Verse 169
Shakespeare and the Sonnet Form—Sonnet 15 174
Shakespeare and the Sonnet Tradition—Sonnet 15 177
The Value of the Sonnets 186

An Appendix of Supplementary Notes 189

Index of Sonnets Discussed 215

Preface

The history of criticism opens so many possibilities for an essay on Shakespeare's sonnets that I must warn a prospective reader about what this book does and does not do. To begin with the negative, I have not solved or tried to solve any of the puzzles of Shakespeare's sonnets. I do not attempt to identify Mr. W. H. or the dark lady. I do not speculate on the occasions that may have evoked particular sonnets. I do not attempt to date them. I offer neither a reorganization of the sequence nor a defense of the quarto order. What I have tried to do is find out what about the sonnets has made them so highly valued by the vast majority of critics and general readers. On the assumption that the source of our pleasure in them must be in the line-to-line experience of reading them, I have set out to determine just what kind of reading experience that is.

I have tried to demonstrate that a Shakespeare sonnet is organized in a multitude of different coexistent and conflicting patterns—formal, logical, ideological, syntactic, rhythmic, and phonetic. The first chapters describe and illustrate the various kinds of patterning systems that coexist and overlap in the individual sonnets. The rest of the book is largely devoted to analyses of representative sonnets in terms of the reading experiences they evoke, reading experiences that result from the multiplicity of organizations in which, over the course of fourteen lines, the reader's mind participates.

I do not intentionally give any interpretations of the sonnets I discuss. I mean to describe them, not to explain them. That is to say, my concern is not to give a reading of the poems but to discover what in them or about them results in the reading experiences they evoke. I am sure that some of my descriptions will seem to be interpretations; they are better called errors—either of ignorance or insensitivity—than interpretations. My purpose and method exaggerate a danger that is always present in criticism: the responses I attribute to my hypothetical reader of the sonnets cannot ultimately be more universal or other than my own. I have attempted to demonstrate that the responses I describe are probable in a reader accustomed to Elizabethan idiom. I have also quoted at length from the responses of the critics and editors who have preceded me in the study of the sonnets; their comments, glosses, and emendations provide the best available evidence that the responses I describe are not idiosyncratic.

Readers of this book may well be made uneasy by the nonscholarly way I talk about phonetic patterns in the sonnets. I do not talk about the patterns either in technical language or with technical precision. The most obvious reason for not doing so—that I lack the necessary scholarship—is not the determining one. I have not sought the precision and convenience of phonetic symbols because I do not envision an audience to whom such descriptions are readily meaningful. (Note 3 of the Appendix presents an object lesson in the folly of challenging such an audience with scientific machinery.) Moreover, even though we have the tools to describe sounds precisely, we cannot know precisely what sounds to describe, because we do not know how Shakespeare's readers heard the words he wrote. Although there has been considerable study of Renaissance pronunciations, the evidence is often contradictory. To espouse one scholarly theory and argue for it would be to stand or fall on a reader's faith in that theory. To save myself from vulgar errors and to minimize the handicap to my readers that my innocence of formal training in phonetics might present, I have occasionally referred to conclusions in Helge Kökeritz' *Shakespeare's Pronunciation* (New Haven, 1953). I chose Kökeritz not because I mean to imply that he is the ultimate authority or the only one, but because his book is more widely known than any other among readers who are specialists in Renaissance literature and not in phonetic history. For such readers my unscholarly method has one prime advantage: whatever its drawbacks, it is not likely to lead to the most dangerous kinds of errors, those that are not easy to see, errors tricked out in scholarly trappings, errors that awe.

Renaissance pronunciation is not, however, so relevant here as it might seem to be. I do not attempt to describe sounds but to point out patterns. In most cases a pattern perceptible to a modern reader in his own dialect is perceptible in another dialect even though the particular sounds vary. The same is probably true between modern dialects and those of the Renaissance, as well as among the Renaissance dialects themselves. The evidence for such conclusions is that good Renaissance poems sound good in all modern dialects. They presumably sounded good in the various Renaissance dialects. From this I also conclude that, although the particular sounds in which the harmony of a line or a poem is made vary widely from dialect to dialect, the *patterns* of the phonetic harmony remain *generally* constant. Essentially, I am guessing that almost all the changes made in a poem by its translation from dialect to dialect are roughly comparable to the changes made in a tune by its translation to a variety of keys and instruments. That is a dangerous thing to say, but the most obvious evidence against it—the numerous instances in Renaissance poetry of irregular metrics, rhymes, and puns that seem once to have been regular—appears to me in fact to support the generalization because each irregularity surprises us—each intrudes in a phonetic harmony that has survived 400 years of change.

If my readers will agree to the wisdom of pointing out sound patterns rather than describing them, they may still object that some of the patterns I talk about do not exist in some modern English dialects and may not have existed either in Shakespeare's or in the various dialects of his readers. Some objections should be answered if I insist that, when I say that the sounds in a series resemble one another, I mean that they are similar, not identical. Even so, some of the patterns I observe will be inaudible in the dialects of some of my readers and were probably inaudible in some dialects of Renaissance English. Take, as an example, the patterns that involve the most problematic of all topics in phonetic history, what I casually label *r* sounds. Very evidently the sound indicated by an initial or intervocalic *r* differed in late sixteenth-century dialects from the sounds of final and preconsonantal *r's,* which in turn probably differed from each other. The degrees of difference seem to have varied from dialect to dialect just as they do in modern English. I am inclined to think that in Shakespeare's own dialect all the various sounds indicated by *r* were audibly recognizable, though sometimes distant, relatives of one another. It also appears probable that a London-born reader would not have pronounced the second *r* of *riper* in anything like the way he pronounced the first. This suggests that, as they do in the twentieth century, some of the patterns I describe would have existed for some of Shakespeare's readers and not for others. I had best leave it at that. As the validity of my particular arguments nowhere depends upon the particular sounds that are patterned, so my general thesis about sound patterns does not depend upon the eternal or universal existence of any particular pattern.

I should also attempt to justify one other of my questionable tactical decisions: I quote the sonnets in a modern text (the Pelican Shakespeare edition, ed. Douglas Bush and Alfred Harbage, Baltimore, 1961), and not in the 1609 quarto. The quarto is the closest thing we have to an authoritative text for the sonnets, but it is a careless printing, almost surely unauthorized by Shakespeare. Its errors are many but, for the most part, evident and easily repaired. Otherwise, spelling and punctuation reveal more about the accidents of the printing house and the idiosyncrasies of the printer than they do about the poet or the poems. I have decided, therefore, that persistent citation of the 1609 quarto can only add gratuitous complications to an already mazelike subject.

The strongest arguments in favor of quoting the 1609 text are for its punctuation. Two of the best commentaries on the sonnets, the discussion of their "fluid unity" in William Empson's *Seven Types of Ambiguity* (rev. ed. 1947, pp. 50–56) and the graceful Introduction to the Elizabethan Club facsimile of *Shakespeare's Poems* (ed. James M. Osborn, Louis L. Martz, and Eugene M. Waith, New Haven, 1964), both demonstrate that the modern, logically directive punctuation provided by editors can deny or attempt to deny some of the syntactic identities that Shakespearean sentences assume in passage. I agree wholeheartedly. However, even though in many cases the old punctuation reveals the multiplicity of structure that I argue for, I am not persuaded that the advantages of quoting the 1609 quarto outweigh the disadvantages.

When I say that using the quarto text can only add gratuitous complications to an already complicated subject, I do not mean to suggest that a reader prepared to take on a book like this one will be unprepared to handle old spelling and punctuation. On the contrary, I fear that the invitingly erratic text of 1609 will encourage a reader to form a distracting hope that its punctuation will furnish clues for solutions to the poems. Although Renaissance punctuation is not logical but rhetorical, a modern reader is likely to read rhetorical punctuation *as if* it were logical. Therefore, where the old punctuation accidentally shows a modern reader the syntactical fluidity of some poems, it accidentally denies the fluidity of others because the modern reader does not drop his usual assumptions about the significance of punctuation marks like semicolons, colons, and periods, all of which now give strict logical instructions to their readers. Modern editors have diminished or tried to diminish some sonnets by overpunctuating them. Modern readers can diminish some others by overreading the 1609 punctuation. Moreover, like Robert Graves and Laura Riding in their notorious essay in defense of the old spelling and punctuation of sonnet 129 (in *A Survey of Modernist Poetry,* London, 1927), a modern reader can ask the old punctuation to provide a key to interpretation, to make the old punctuation do what modern editors have made their new punctuation do—tell which of the several things a sentence says it "really" is saying. Such a reader, coming to poems that have spent their literary career as unsolved puzzles, will be as likely to overread the old punctuation as he is to overtrust the interpolated logical and limiting punctuating of an editor. Where he doesn't do that, he will be likely to duplicate casually and quickly the steps by which modern editors will already have seen and filled a need to fix or repair a poem. In short, we have a choice between two different kinds of misleading text: that of Thorpe's printer and that of a modern editor. Both—one directly and one indirectly—are made misleading by the literary conditioning and reflexes of a modern reader.

Since the fault is not in our texts but in ourselves, I have found it efficient to use an already modernized text rather than undertake the time-consuming double task of first anticipating the twentieth-century editing job that each modern reader does on an old text as he reads it, and then arguing down the limited reading to which my reader has worked his own way. I have, however, kept the 1609 text always in mind, and I have tried to inform my reader wherever its testimony is relevant to my discussion.

❧ ❧ ❧

I am surprised and embarrassed that I have needed so much help to turn out such a little book. A concise accounting of my debts to Douglas Bush would be longer than the book. William Alfred—who raised me from a footnote—introduced me to the Renaissance sonnet tradition and spent unthinkable amounts of time and trouble patiently teaching me most of what I know. Philip Finkelpearl not only designed my life for me but also casually gave me the best part of Chapter 5 in ten minutes over coffee. My debt to Archibald MacLeish will probably be apparent; I have stolen his critical method, though not his grace in using it. A great many real and specific debts will not be apparent, and, because the list is so long, can not be made so. I thank Theodore Morrison, Alan Lutkus, Boyd Berry, Steven Joseph, Julian Boyd, Wayne Shumaker, and Ulrich Knoepflmacher. They will recognize their contributions. I assure them that I too remember what and how very much they gave me. Some of them, notably Mr. Morrison, Mr. Boyd, and Mr. Shumaker, gave more advice than I took; no reader should think ill of them because their names appear here. I omitted four of my Berkeley colleagues from the list because I wanted to put each name last and preface it with "and especially." I have no choice but to thank them helplessly in alphabetical order; I am especially grateful to Paul Alkon, Stanley Fish, Jay Ludwig, and Josephine Miles. My wife is so far coauthor of this book that it is as presumptuous to thank her as it was to leave her off the title page; her name is Susan Patek Booth.

S.B.

BERKELEY, CALIFORNIA
MAY 3, 1968

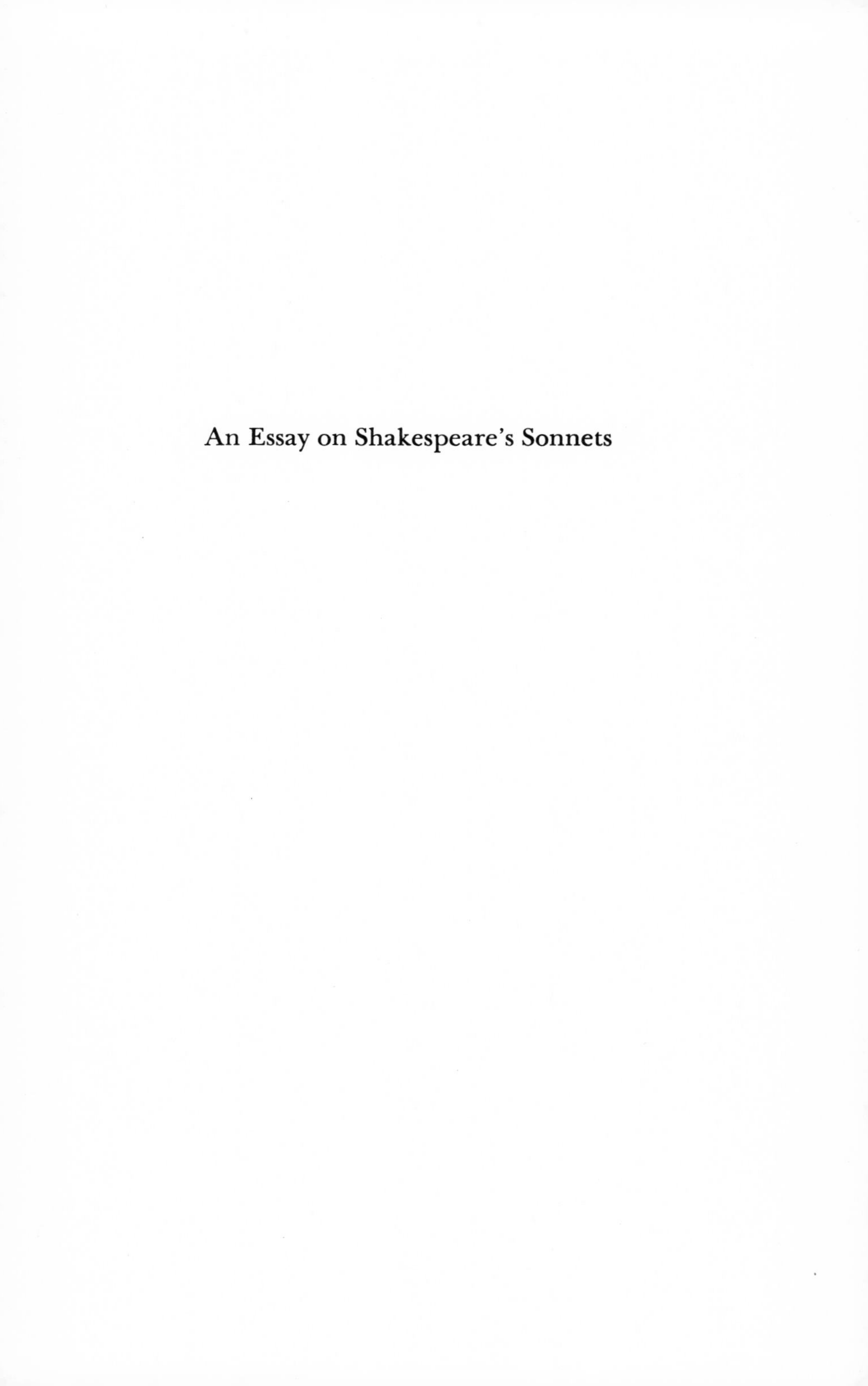

An Essay on Shakespeare's Sonnets

Chapter 1

The Critical Dilemma

Finding a Structural Principle for the Sequence

Shakespeare's sonnets are hard to think about. They are hard to think about individually and they are hard to think about collectively. In the chapters that follow, I will argue that the individual poems are multiply ordered, that the elements of each poem exist in more than one internal order. Since there is so surprisingly little written about the sonnets themselves, since there are so very many published efforts to demonstrate or restore logic in the 1609 sequence, and since I see a likeness between the lengthy experience of reading through the collection and the brief experience of reading almost any particular sonnet, a discussion of the way the sequence strikes its readers may serve as a helpful introduction to what I will say about the individual sonnets. Most readers have wished somehow to define Shakespeare's sonnets—to put them into a category more satisfying than "love sonnets" or to divide them into groups by their subject matter or imagery or structure. I think it is not accidental that, even in the criticisms that are concerned with the sonnets themselves rather than the creation or solution of biographical problems, a very high percentage of all critical attention has gone to the so-called procreation sonnets, the sonnets about the rival poet, the sonnets on the dark lady, and, strangely, the apparently detached pair of sonnets on Cupid. Falling easily and automatically into groups and under headings, these sonnets are potentially graspable and are a comfort to a critic attempting to find some logic in the collection of 1609.

There are good reasons why a reader of Shakespeare's sonnets looks for an order in them. Two of the reasons are accidental but no less powerful for that. The first of these is the analogy of Dante and Petrarch which, however often it is found to be inapplicable to most of their followers, persists. Secondly, when a reader has read through the sonnets in their quarto order and failed to find a consistent ordering principle for them, he is offered some comfort by the implied license for curative rearrangement provided by the well-known absence of any evidence that Shakespeare had advance knowledge of Thorpe's edition or, therefore, perhaps of the quarto order of the sonnets. If, however, there had never been in English or in any other language a narrative sequence of sonnets, or if it were established that the 1609 order was Shakespeare's own, or if there were documentary proof that the 1609 order of the sonnets was the order of their writing, or if we had an indisputable statement by Shakespeare himself that the sonnets are an anthology and not a sequence, I doubt very much that the general tenor of the reaction they have evoked would have been very different. It would have been less comic, but although the privilege of publishing the sonnets in a new order would have been removed, there is so much promise of overall coherence within the collection in the quarto order that we would be likely to feel, as many readers have traditionally felt in the midst of all the doubts about Thorpe's text, that Shakespeare is saying something in the collection as a whole that the reader can almost but never quite hear, and that in a moment more or with a moment's more attention he will hear it, and that it will be a simple and satisfying sound.

The promise of overall coherence, of a graspable sense of the single statement of the whole book of poems, is encouraged by the coherence of the first seventeen sonnets. Each of them is specifically harnessed in support of the case for the marriage of the young man to whom they are addressed. After seventeen sonnets a reader will reasonably expect not only that the poems that follow will have the same sort of clear logical relationship to each other but that, if he will not ultimately hear whether or not the young man marries, he will at least hear of some progress, even if it is only in time. When he has finished reading sonnet 17, however, he has had no indication that the collection of procreation sonnets is over, and sonnet 18 gives him none. It takes up the theme of immortality in verse which has been fused with the argument for marriage in the preceding poems. The change of subject matter in 18 is all but imperceptible; because its elements have been the auxiliary elements of previous poems, the reader has no reason to pay particular attention to the absence of the point around which the preceding uses of the language of 18 have centered.

Additionally, there are, besides the poems that seem obviously grouped by subject matter, pairs of logically linked poems like 15 and 16, 27 and 28, or 44 and 45, in which the syntax gives a sense of forward progress from one to another. There are also poems, like sonnet 120, where the reference to a previous time when the beloved was "once unkind" encourages the assumption that the time in question is an earlier time in the reader's experience of the sequence—that, since apparent incidents of the beloved's unkindness, like 33–35 or 57–58, appear earlier in the quarto, one or all of the appropriate incidents are not only referred to in 120 but occurred earlier chronologically. The simple makeup of a book, the fact that one reads one poem after another, leads a reader to confuse the chronology of his reading with a chronology of writing and a chronology for the events that prompted the writing. It is odd that in poems so often concerned with time there should be so little evidence of its passage. There is indeed a pervading sense of relationship among the poems, but no consistent sense of progress.

It is not surprising that critics have tried to find a new

arrangement for the sonnets or that they should have attempted to force the bulk of the poems to fit into a plan arising from some insight into a few of them. It is no more surprising that none of the various rearrangements or keys to interpretation has been generally accepted. However critics may have attempted to find the order in the collection that they feel is there, they have always had twenty or more poems to argue into a category or to file under "miscellaneous."

It may be that the 1609 order is the most satisfactory yet suggested, but it is not satisfying. Critics have looked elsewhere to find a way to cope with the sonnets. They have attempted to define them by subject matter; the groups readily apparent in the sonnets (procreation, rival poet, and so on) suggest the comfort possible from such groupings. We therefore get discussions of the sonnets on time or sonnets on absence or sonnets "about" poetry or "about" religion. The trouble with such categories is that very few sonnets clearly belong in any one group. The sonnets defy equally definition or categorization.

The simplest and the usual relationship of incident to incident in a piece of writing that pertains to the actions of particular people is in terms of time. In the sonnets the poems relate to each other by different means. Those that talk about growing things suggest the others that talk about growing things. Those that talk about time suggest others that talk about time. Some talk about both. In which terms are we to think about them? A single poem may suggest a relationship—by diction or imagery or subject matter or physical proximity in the 1609 order—to as many different other poems as it has elements. Witness, for example, the relations of sonnet 35, first with the poems that precede and follow it in the 1609 sequence, and then with the collection at large.

Sonnet 35, which does not begin as 33 and 34 do by focusing its reader's attention in the metaphor of sunshine and storm, is not so clearly linked to the two poems that precede it as they are to each other, but readers have traditionally and reasonably taken number 35 as the third in a narratively coherent group of sonnets in response to an injury done the speaker by the beloved. Here are the three poems:

33

Full many a glorious morning have I seen
Flatter the mountain tops with sovereign eye,
Kissing with golden face the meadows green,
Gilding pale streams with heavenly alchemy;
Anon permit the basest clouds to ride
With ugly rack on his celestial face,
And from the forlorn world his visage hide,
Stealing unseen to west with this disgrace:
Even so my sun one early morn did shine
With all-triumphant splendor on my brow;
But, out alack, he was but one hour mine,
The region cloud hath masked him from me now.
  Yet him for this my love no whit disdaineth;
  Suns of the world may stain when heaven's sun
    staineth.

34

Why didst thou promise such a beauteous day
And make me travel forth without my cloak,
To let base clouds o'ertake me in my way,
Hiding thy brav'ry in their rotten smoke?
'Tis not enough that through the cloud thou break
To dry the rain on my storm-beaten face,
For no man well of such a salve can speak
That heals the wound, and cures not the disgrace:
Nor can thy shame give physic to my grief;
Though thou repent, yet I have still the loss:
Th' offender's sorrow lends but weak relief
To him that bears the strong offense's cross.
  Ah, but those tears are pearl which thy love sheeds,
  And they are rich and ransom all ill deeds.

35

No more be grieved at that which thou hast done:
Roses have thorns, and silver fountains mud;
Clouds and eclipses stain both moon and sun,
And loathsome canker lives in sweetest bud.
All men make faults, and even I in this,
Authorizing thy trespass with compare,
Myself corrupting, salving thy amiss,
Excusing thy sins more than thy sins are;
For to thy sensual fault I bring in sense
(Thy adverse party is thy advocate)
And 'gainst myself a lawful plea commence;
Such civil war is in my love and hate
That I an accessary needs must be
To that sweet thief which sourly robs from me.[1]

Sonnet 35 strikes the reader as a new poetic approach to the incident behind 33 and 34. The weather metaphor, which dropped away after line 6 of 34, is also absent in line 1 of 35, but, following upon the beloved's tears and the speaker's forgiveness in the couplet of 34, both the substance and the spirit of the opening of 35 seem to progress from sonnets 33 and 34. The link between 35 and the two poems that precede it is further strengthened by line 3—*Clouds and eclipses stain both moon and sun*—which recalls the metaphor for the

1. *Shakespeare's Sonnets,* ed. Douglas Bush and Alfred Harbage (Baltimore, 1961). Unless otherwise noted, all subsequent citations of the sonnets are in this, the Pelican Shakespeare, edition. Editorial emendation in a quoted passage is ordinarily passed over in silence wherever it is irrelevant to the particular topic under discussion; for example, in 34.12 the 1609 quarto prints *losse* where almost all editors have substituted *cross,* and in 35.8 *thy . . . thy* replaces *their . . . their* in the quarto. Where the quarto reading is relevant, I cite the Huntington-Steevens copy as reprinted in *A New Variorum Edition of Shakespeare: The Sonnets,* ed. Hyder Edward Rollins (2 vols. Philadelphia, 1944); hereafter cited as Rollins, *Variorum.*

crime of 33 and 34, and casually uses *clouds, stain,* and *sun,* which had been central to 34.

Sonnet 35 simultaneously adheres to and separates from its two predecessors; the reader's mind adapts itself to a change of poetic tactic at the beginning of 35, and in line 3 finds that it has overadapted: the weather metaphor is no longer the primary vehicle for communication, but it is not gone either. Similarly, in line 7, *salving* echoes both the word *salve* in line 7 of 34 and the medical metaphor introduced in that line to dominate the rest of the poem; in 35, however, the medical metaphor is muted and incidental, and in 35 the salve is offered by the speaker to the beloved, where in 34 it was the other way round. The method and effect of such simultaneously like and unlike elements are actually themselves like similar methods and effects of incidental likenesses and differences between 33 and 34: the sixth and eighth lines of 34 repeat the rhyme pair of lines 6 and 8 of 33, *face–disgrace;* in 33 the *celestial face* (in the metaphor of the sun) is the beloved's, as is the *disgrace* of being masked with clouds; in 34 both the *storm-beaten face* in line 6 and the *disgrace* in line 8 belong to the speaker. The rhymes are identical and identically placed. The incident to which they refer is constant, but their application is not. The simultaneous connection and division of the three poems that is made by simultaneously realized likenesses and differences among them is akin in its paradox to a general quality of the three sonnets that only becomes overt in line 10 of 35 *(Thy adverse party is thy advocate).* The relationship of the three poems is like the relationship they describe, and its operation is like the operation of the terms of the description. The metaphor of the sun for the beloved and its relationship to the storm-threatened and then storm-beaten lover is constant in 33 and 34, but when in 34 the beloved breaks through the clouds to smile on the speaker, the reversal of attitude is mirrored in a reversal of the application of terms in which the incident has been described: in the metaphor the beloved's displeasure fell upon the speaker as rain; at the end of the poem the beloved's contrition is demonstrated in tears. In another scale, the subject of guilt and shame remains constant to 33–35, but who is guilty and what is shameful do not.

The reader continues to sense connection and division, continuity and change as he moves from 35 to 36. The first phrase of sonnet 36, *Let me confess,* is in the spirit of 35 and seems to introduce an example of the self-accusation cited at the end of that poem, but contrary to the expectations aroused by the series 33–35, the confession is not of a crime: *Let me confess that we two must be twain.* The end of the line changes the limitation on the reader's understanding of *confess* from the criminal context presented by the preceding poems to one whose reference to the future all but removes the overtones that connected this poem with those that precede it. The confession *that we two must be twain* is not so much a confession as a grudging admission; moreover, neither what is confessed nor the substance of the rest of the poem grows from any suggestion in 33–35:

36

Let me confess that we two must be twain
Although our undivided loves are one:
So shall those blots that do with me remain,
Without thy help by me be borne alone.
In our two loves there is but one respect,
Though in our lives a separable spite,
Which though it alter not love's sole effect,
Yet doth it steal sweet hours from love's delight.
I may not evermore acknowledge thee,
Lest my bewailèd guilt should do thee shame;
Nor thou with public kindness honor me
Unless thou take that honor from thy name:
  But do not so; I love thee in such sort
  As, thou being mine, mine is thy good report.

As the sonnet progresses, it moves the reader farther and farther from the concerns of 33–35. On the other hand, although the focus of this sonnet is very different, there are incidental but insistent links in this poem to those that precede it. In line 3, *blots* echoes the idea of physical and moral stains and spots that runs through 33–35. *Borne alone* in line 4 echoes *bears the strong offense's cross* in sonnet 34. Line 8, *Yet doth it steal sweet hours from love's delight,* echoes the sound but not the meaning of *stealing* in line 8 of sonnet 33, *Stealing unseen to west with this disgrace; steal* does, however, suggest the sense of *To that sweet thief which sourly robs from me,* the last line of 35, while *sweet hours* in this context of robbery echoes *sweet . . . sourly* in that line. More importantly, the idea of theft here in the general context of various kinds of separation *(we two must be twain,* line 1; . . . *with me remain,* line 3; *take that honor from thy name,* line 12), continues a muted and logically unfixed metaphor of travel, masks, and ambush for profit in sonnets 33 (lines 1–8) and 34 (lines 2–5, 14). *Lest my bewailèd guilt* in line 10 returns the reader's mind to the context of weeping (34.13–14), which had itself grown out of a context of faces, clouds, and rain in both 33 and 34. Moreover, *bewailèd guilt* presents the self-accusation promised in 35 and falsely signaled by *Let me confess* at the beginning of this poem. Similarly, the shame the speaker might bring upon the beloved *(Lest my bewailèd guilt should do thee shame)* pertains, although imprecisely, to the shame described by *disgrace* and brought by the clouds upon the beloved personified as the sun in 33, to the shame described by *disgrace* and brought by the clouds upon the speaker personified as a traveler in 34, and to the catalogue of shames in the first quatrain of 35. Again, as in the relationship of the first three poems to one another, the relationship of 36 to 35 is one which emphasizes both a break from preceding patterns and a continuation of them.

Sonnet 37 is almost as firmly linked to 36 as 34 was to 33. It picks up the idea on which 36 ended and amplifies it.

Moreover, as in the case of *face* and *disgrace* in 33 and 34, 37 repeats rhyme words from 36 (*spite,* 36.6, 37.3, and *delight,* 36.8, 37.1):

37

As a decrepit father takes delight
To see his active child do deeds of youth,
So I, made lame by Fortune's dearest spite,
Take all my comfort of thy worth and truth.
For whether beauty, birth, or wealth, or wit,
Or any of these all, or all, or more,
Intitled in thy parts do crownèd sit,
I make my love ingrafted to this store.
So then I am not lame, poor, nor despised
Whilst that this shadow doth such substance give
That I in thy abundance am sufficed
And by a part of all thy glory live.
  Look what is best, that best I wish in thee.
  This wish I have; then ten times happy me!

Sonnet 37 does not relate directly to 35; it is incidentally concerned with shame, but, if the two were not near each other and connected by a direct relevance of 36 to both, I doubt that 35 and 37 would ever keep company in criticism.

That does not, however, mean that 37 is not connected with 35. In the 1609 order the two *are* near each other, and they *are* connected by the direct relevance of 36 to both. In the experience of a reader moving from sonnet to sonnet in sequence, one kind of link can be as strong as another. As a reader comes upon 37, he feels that it belongs where it is. Probably the same feeling could be aroused by its proximity to many other sonnets: in its usual position it suggests poems other than the ones near it in the 1609 sequence, and other poems remind a reader of it. A rearranger could reasonably put 37 next to 143 (*Lo, as a careful housewife runs to catch*) on the basis of a likeness of rhetorical construction and choice of simile. He could put it and 33 together with sonnet 60 *(Like as the waves make towards the pebbled shore)* on the grounds that they have a common thematic thread in royalty, sun, son, and ascension. The *shadow* and *substance* of line 10 suggest the pictures and illusions of 27, 28, and 53. In the last line *ten times happy* links 37 with *ten times more in worth* in 38 and links both poems with lines 8 through 10 of sonnet 6. Line 8 of sonnet 37, *I make my love ingrafted to this store,* suggests the couplet of 15 and thus strengthens a possible argument that both the simile and the logic of 37 obviously link it with sonnets 1–17. Similarly, in *Interpretations in Shakespeare's Sonnets*[2] Hilton Landry devotes a chapter called "The Civil War: Sonnets 33–35, 40–42, and 57–58" to establishing the links among the poems listed in its title. He also links 34 and 35 with 120. Sonnet 35 also links itself by likeness to the other poems that use metaphors of law (among them 49, 139, and 149, which are also poems of self-accusation), by likeness to the other poems that use the metaphor of the rose, and, as I have demonstrated, to sonnets 36 and 37.

The foregoing paragraphs are presumably hard to follow. They are not purposely so designed, but they are intended both as evidence that the number of frames of reference for a sonnet is bewildering, and as an illustration of the proposition with which I began: Shakespeare's sonnets are hard to think about. Although I arbitrarily limited myself to five poems, I did not limit my discussion by arguing that one or another relationship or kind of relationship is more important to a reader's perception of them than the others. I did not choose a frame of reference and subordinate all others to it. My failure to focus my discussion, to choose an organization for the sonnets and for my analysis, is the primary source of a reader's difficulty with my description of the interrelations of sonnets 33–35. A similar failure of the collection itself, both in its 1609 order and in any of the subsequent

2. Berkeley and Los Angeles, 1963.

substitute arrangements, is the source both of the multiple directions of my analysis and of the various arbitrarily espoused solutions to the riddle of the sonnets and thus to the intellectual discomfort evoked by the multitude of the different kinds of equally active relationships among them.

The perfectly appropriate word "riddle" has followed the sonnets through most of their critical history. The only problems one labels "riddles" are ones that have solutions: riddles sound as if they had solutions; they usually contain the clues necessary to their solution. Shakespeare's sonnets do not present a reader with a constantly dominant organizing principle, but as my discussion of sonnets 33–37 should suggest, it does provide an abundance of evidence of organization. At the point where readers finish the sequence and try to think about it whole, the professionals among them have traditionally wanted either to rearrange the sonnets to suit the terms of one of the systems in which the poems cohere or to demonstrate that one such system governs the sequence as it stands. A riddle tests its audience's intelligence. If a reader cannot see the answer to the riddle, if he cannot see the organizing principle for a collection so obviously and insistently coherent, he may feel like a dunce, and he may be panicked into what an early rearranger called "a pertinacious adherence to a principle of continuity," biographical, thematic, or stylistic.

Ample evidence of such panic and its results is readily available in Rollins' *Variorum,* and to add to it or review it is neither necessary nor generous. I want only to emphasize that the 1609 sequence seems to need interpretation or reorganization not because it is disordered but because it is so obviously ordered. Although none of the justifications or rearrangements of the 1609 sequence is satisfactory, all are provoked by the nature of the collection itself. The links and patterns that the speculators have arbitrarily exaggerated into answers to the riddle of the sonnets are there and so can impinge on a reader's consciousness. Even the most bizarre of the arbitrary keys to the sonnets have had some basis in a perceptible pattern in the collection. A good recent example is Allen Cabaniss' "Shakespeare and the Holy Rosary."[3] Cabaniss points out that the Rosary consists of 153 Hail Marys, that there are 154 of Shakespeare's sonnets, and that 154 is only one more than 153. He begins his examination of Rosary–sonnet relationship with sonnet 7 "in order not to be too arbitrary" (p. 119). In his demonstration sonnet 37 is examined for evidence of the fourth Joyful Mystery:

> Lines 11f. of Sonnet XXXVII, "That I in thy abundance am suffic'd, / And by a part of all thy glory liue . . . ," an expression of intimate union of the poet and the person to whom the poem was addressed, suggest a phrase and an idea from the Gospel account of the fourth Joyful Mystery. The aged prophet Simeon, speaking to the Blessed Virgin, assures her that her indissoluble union with her Divine Son will mean that whatever happens to Him will happen also to her, "et tuam ipsius animam pertransibit gladius." This thought and virtually these words reappear in the first stanza of the great medieval hymn, *Stabat Mater dolorosa.* (p. 120)

All of this seems ridiculous, and it is, but, although it is impossible to see how such theses as Mr. Cabaniss' can be sustained, it is usually possible to see what gave direction to them. For example, standing alone, sonnet 37 does not seem even vaguely religious, but if one has a particular interest (Mr. Cabaniss has a previous history of literary-liturgical analysis), and if one comes upon lines 11 and 12 of sonnet 37 after reading the four poems that precede it in the sequence, they certainly have religious overtones, although not so loud

3. *University of Mississippi Studies in English, 1* (1960), 118–28.

or distinct as Cabaniss would have them. Each of the four poems that precede 37 contains words and phrases that are familiar in religious contexts: in 33 *heavenly* (line 4), *celestial* (line 6), *Suns of the world may stain when heaven's sun staineth* (line 14); in 34 *repent* (line 10), *bears the strong offense's cross* (emendation for *losse,* line 12); in 35 *sins* (line 8); and in 36 *Let me confess* (line 1).

Although the multitudinous potential frames of reference and systems of interrelation for the sonnets can panic the mind of a reader into arbitrarily maintained distortions, the same qualities can be a source of great solace to the same reader while he is reading, before he demands a definitive statement from himself. A reader has a sense always as he reads through the sonnets that each poem, each line that he reads, is in a specific relationship to what has gone before and that he can know what that specific relationship is. He is always on familiar ground, but he never knows just what that ground is. For example, the great number of different kinds of phonetic and substantial connections made among the sonnets by repetition of the various ideas that can be expressed by *bear* and *bare,* and by repetition of all the various forms and senses of the words themselves, gives the whole sequence an illogically powerful aura of coherence.

Perhaps the happiest moment the human mind ever knows is the moment when it senses the presence of order and coherence—and before it realizes the particular nature (and so the particular limits) of the perception. At the moment of unparticularized perception the mind is unlimited. It seems capable of grasping and about to grasp a coherence beyond its capacity. As he reads through the 1609 sequence, a reader's mind is constantly poised on just such a threshold to comprehension. The source of that pleasurable sense of increased mental range is the same multitude of frames of reference that frustrate him when he looks for a single label or formula by which his mind may take personal possession of the sonnets.

Finding a Structural Principle for the Individual Sonnets

The critics who have attempted to cope with the sonnets in terms of their style have had the same general kinds of difficulties as the commentators on their sequence.

In 1575 Gascoigne made the only incontrovertible statement about the structure of the English sonnet that has been or probably can be made: "I can beste allowe to call those Sonnets whiche are of fouretene lynes, euery line conteyning tenne syllables. The firste twelve do ryme in staues of foure lines by crosse meetre, and the last two ryming togither do conclude the whole."[4] Gascoigne, of course, is only describing the formal pattern of meter and rhyme by which the general type is distinguished. For purposes of dividing Shakespeare's sonnets into groups handy to the human mind, it eliminates three sonnets—99, 126, and 145—and does nothing otherwise to differentiate Shakespeare's sonnets either from each other or from any sonnets in the same meter and rhyme pattern. Later efforts to define the structure of the sonnets have therefore been chiefly concerned with two other kinds of structure, logical and syntactical, and with their relationship to the formal structure as defined by Gascoigne.

Most commentators have given logical structure their chief attention. Some have taken the end of the sonnet, the couplet, as their starting point and have attempted to determine the logical relationship by which the last two lines "ryming togither do conclude the whole." Attempting to speak generally about the relationship of couplet to quatrains, the critics have usually hedged their bets. The expenditure of words like "commonly," "frequently," and "often" is greater in the literature about Shakespeare's sonnets than in any I know. Thus, when an anonymous writer in 1873 follows an

4. George Gascoigne, *Certayne Notes of Instruction* (1575), in *Elizabethan Critical Essays*, ed. G. Gregory Smith (2 vols. London, 1904), 1, 55.

elaborately vague statement about the quatrains with a more specific statement of the function of the couplet, he finds it necessary to qualify the statement three separate times:

> [Shakespeare's sonnets] are characterized in construction by a certain apposition of terms and ideas, in which, by the juxtaposition of contrasts, force and colour are given to the sentiment. . . . These appositions and contrasts are commonly summed up and enforced in the couplet, which frequently presents the result of them in some other light or aspect than that conveyed in the quatrains; often giving great piquancy and increased intensity to what has gone before.[5]

On the matter of structure, even the most impressionistic critics put brakes to their generalizations. Who would expect the word "average" in such a passage as the following: "An average Shakespeare Sonnet comes dancing in, as it were, with the effortless grace of a bird, which after a few easy runs takes to its wings for a still easier flight, then comes to ground with the concluding couplet."[6]

The critics who have attempted to determine specific kinds of logical structure and to divide the sonnets into groups have also had to pay their subjects the compliment of qualification and vagueness. R. M. Alden, whose comments are among the best that have been made, attempts such statements about the structure of the sonnets as will help the reader to grasp them:

> [The Shakespearean sonnet], consisting of three separately rimed quatrains, plus a final couplet, commonly produces a wholly different effect from that of the more intricately composed lines of the Petrarchans; it is rather more colloquial in tendency, more fluent, more sugges-

5. "The Sonnet," *Quarterly*, 134 (1873), 196; quoted by Rollins, *Variorum*, 2, 404.

6. J. M. Robertson, *The Problems of the Shakespeare Sonnets* (London, 1926), p. 189; quoted by Rollins, *Variorum*, 2, 415.

> tive of spontaneous utterance. On the other hand it rarely produces the exquisite sense of highly wrought perfection, as of an ivory carving, which the best specimens of the Italian type attain. It makes an impression of movement, of thought and feeling recollected and made permanent "in tranquillity." At its best the three quatrains seem like incoming waves of imagery, each following upon its predecessor and rising a little higher; then there is a pause, when the couplet more quietly sums up or comments on the meaning of the three. Of this the unsurpassed example is Shakespeare's 73rd: [quoted]. Sometimes, again, as in the equally well beloved 29th sonnet ("When in disgrace with Fortune and men's eyes"), the poet may be thought to combine the advantages of the Italian and the English types, adding to the quatrain structure the characteristic Italian stroke of a pause and change of thought at the end of the eighth line, whereby we pass into a second scene distinct from that of the octave. And many other variants of structure will be noted by the careful reader.[7]

One feels sorrier for Alden than for the critics whose efforts are pathetic. In the passage quoted he is walking a tight line. It is nearly impossible to fulfill his critical obligations. He must speak both generally and accurately. In the phrase, "unsurpassed example," he manages to say both that sonnet 73 is the poem that best fits his structural formula and that it is surpassingly beautiful. When he talks about sonnet 29, he must avoid the word "sestet." His "second scene distinct from that of the octave" is satisfactory but dangerous to paraphrase, as most of the passage is. If one does not read with the same care with which Alden writes, one will misunderstand. If one reads with the care that Alden demands, the analysis brings one no nearer possession of the sonnets

7. Raymond Macdonald Alden, *Shakespeare* (New York, 1922), pp. 126–27; quoted by Rollins, *Variorum, 2,* 412–13.

than one was to begin with. As for Alden's last sentence, it is as sad as it is true.

The great effort of the critics has been to decide the relationship between the structure determined by the form as described by Gascoigne and the logical structure. The unwarranted assumption has often been that the rhyme scheme dictated the organization of the content. Those who have made the assumption have usually attempted to define the structure of Shakespeare's sonnets by its failings. Chiefly, it fails to be Petrarchan. Despite critical assurance at regular intervals that there is little structural likeness between the English sonnet and the Italian, the suspicion has persisted that there is something like a Petrarchan octave in a good (but never identified) number of Shakespeare's sonnets.[8] In 1930 Enid Hamer took out after the idea that there is an octave and sestet in Shakespearean sonnets:

> Many of the sonnets are composed of a single sentence whose divisions correspond with the quatrains and the couplet. The most marked pause is generally at the end of the third quatrain, and quite often the long sentence ends there, and the couplet contains a bitter summary or comment. In a few of the finest, "When to the Sessions of sweet silent thought," and "Not mine owne feares, nor the prophetick soule," there is a definite pause at the end of each quatrain, but there is hardly ever a more marked break after the second quatrain than at some other place, or any separation of ideas, or renewal of poetic force at the ninth line, which would suggest the division into octave and sestet.[9]

8. T. G. Tucker found a sestet as well as an octave in the sonnets. In his edition (Cambridge, Eng., 1924) he says (pp. lxvii-lxviii) that the ninth line qualifies, answers, or amplifies the octave, and that the couplet sums up the situation or else concludes the third quatrain, "and so is an integral part of the sestet."

9. Enid Hamer, *The Metres of English Poetry* (London, 1930), p. 198; quoted in Rollins, *Variorum, 2,* 421.

Recent critics have given up trying to talk about the structure of all the sonnets at once and have followed Alden in trying to divide them into kinds. Tucker Brooke attempts to be specific. He does not try to say which sonnets belong in his categories, but he makes cautious steps toward saying how large the categories are. His caution negates his candor. Such phrases as "over two-thirds," "perhaps ninety," and the ridiculous "some twenty-seven" sum up the dilemma into which the sonnets throw a critic:

> A strong pause in sense and rhythm at the close of each quatrain is for Shakespeare the primary law of sonnet harmony, from which he hardly ever varies. In some twenty-seven sonnets the chief pause comes at the end of the eighth line. In a very few it comes irregularly. But in over two-thirds of Shakespeare's sonnets the chief pause is placed after the twelfth line, at the close of three quatrains which are themselves divided by distinct but less emphatic pauses. . . .
>
> Normally, the couplet in a Shakespearean sonnet gives the moral or conclusion toward which the previous twelve lines have been pointing, and compacts into itself the true essence of the poem. This is true in perhaps ninety of the sonnets. Less often the couplet introduces a surprise or negation which suddenly swings the reader into a point of view antithetical to that developed in the quatrains. The cases are very few in which the couplet is content merely to add another idea or illustration.[10]

On structure Edward Hubler follows Brooke almost word for word. He removes "over" from "two-thirds" and "some" from "twenty-seven," but he doesn't attempt to say which two-thirds or which twenty-seven he means. He does, however, take up Brooke's "Less often the couplet introduces a surprise or negation," and identifies those sonnets as thirteen

10. Tucker Brooke, *Shakespeare's Sonnets* (London and New York, 1936), pp. 3–4; quoted in Rollins, *Variorum, 2,* 429–30.

in number—those being 19, 30, 34, 42, 60, 84, 86, 91, 92, 131, 133, 139, and 141.[11]

Only T. W. Baldwin has attempted an all-inclusive statement of the logical structure of the sonnets and its relationship to the formal structure. If it were accurate, it would answer perfectly the persistently felt need for the general statement about the sonnets that most readers feel could be made if only someone could find it. Baldwin quotes most of the criticisms that I have quoted above and attacks the commentators on the structure of Shakespeare's sonnets for concerning themselves at all with the structure of Italian sonnets, which were written by poets who did not attend Stratford grammar school. Baldwin asks his reader

> to remember that in the literary composition of Shakspere's day logic was inseparably intertwined with rhetoric. Upon logic various rhetorical forms were based, which were not themselves necessarily in our sense logical. There were certain basic types from which variants were evolved. Learned grammarians were taught by *Ad Herennium* that the most absolute and perfect *argumentatio* consisted of five parts, (1) *propositio,* (2) *ratio,* (3) *rationis confirmatio,* (4) *exornatio,* (5) *complexio.* But either *exornatio,* or *complexio,* or both might be omitted, thus giving from three to five parts. Erasmus, in a textbook for grammar school consumption, bases his most perfect *argumentatio* upon *Ad Herennium* and Cicero as follows: (1) *propositio,* (2) *ratio,* (3) *propositionis assumptio,* (4) *assumptionis ratio,* (5) *complexio.* Brinsley phrases this framework for a theme as (1) *exordium,* (2) *narratio,* (3) *confirmatio,* (4) *confutatio,* (5) *conclusio.* Shakspere was, of course, familiar with and used these basic forms. In the sonnets, the first quatrain is always *propositio,* the couplet is always intended

11. Edward Hubler, *The Sense of Shakespeare's Sonnets* (Princeton, 1952), pp. 17–18, 27.

> to be some form of *complexio* or *conclusio.* The second quatrain is regularly some form of *ratio.* The third quatrain then has its choice from the numerous possibilities of the other two sections, whether we call them *rationis confirmatio* and *exornatio* with *Ad Herennium,* or *propositionis assumptio* and *assumptionis ratio* with Erasmus, or *confirmatio* and *confutatio* with Brinsley, or still other terms employed by anyone else. This is the literary-logic of Shakspere's day and this is what he uses in his sonnets.[12]

There is not much point in illustrating from the sonnets themselves that the first quatrain is not always *propositio,* that the second quatrain is not regularly a form of *ratio,* or that, no matter whom we follow, the third quatrain chooses from many more possibilities than *rationis confirmatio* or *confutatio* can offer; this is the literary logic of Shakespeare's day, but it is not always or often what he uses in his sonnets.

Much more interesting than Baldwin's error is the state of mind that seems to have evoked it. One of the commonest sources of error is our natural inclination to define an object we value in the terms by which we are accustomed to define value. That is to say, if something is good, we are likely to say that its characteristics are the characteristics of other good things of the same general sort. George Rylands, for example, says that, for a reader of the sonnets, "what was faint, confused and half-realised becomes precise, acute, ordered, permanent."[13] Rylands was extremely sensitive to and fond of both Shakespeare's sonnets and poetry in general. What he says here of the sonnets is an excellent statement of the qualities by which most good lyric poems have their excel-

12. T. W. Baldwin, *On The Literary Genetics of Shakspere's Poems and Sonnets* (Urbana, 1950), p. 350.

13. George Rylands, "Shakespeare the Poet," in H. Granville-Barker and G. B. Harrison, *A Companion to Shakespeare Studies* (Cambridge, Eng., 1934), pp 109–10; quoted by Rollins, *Variorum, 2,* 428.

lence, but without vast qualification it will not serve for Shakespeare's sonnets. Baldwin has taught us to see that Shakespeare's knowledge of rhetorical theory contributes to the nature of his writing. Shakespeare valued rhetorical theory, and Baldwin values its effect on the poetry. Baldwin also values the sonnets. Baldwin is a patient and painstaking scholar, but, in closing his eyes to the dizzying structural complexity and variety of the sonnets as they actually are, he is, in his way, doing what Rylands did in his.

There is good reason for Baldwin to close his eyes: an accurate and thorough description of the structure of the sonnets will send one running in circles—and to no useful purpose. The one solid, accurate, and complete analysis of the structure of Shakespeare's sonnets is that of Claes Schaar.[14] Unfortunately, it is the best proof there is of the futility of attempting to help the reader to a satisfactory comprehension of Shakespeare's sonnets by classifying them. Schaar founds his accurate analysis on Baldwin's inaccurate formula. That he should do so suggests as much about the nature of the sonnets as his analysis itself. Schaar's purpose in analyzing the structure of the sonnets is not to refute Baldwin; he does so only incidentally. His exhaustive chapter on structure is part of the meticulous comparison of Daniel's *Delia* and Shakespeare's sonnets, which is his purpose in the study as a whole. He probably organizes his structural analysis around Baldwin's formula because without some sort of general hypothesis he would have no place to start. Baldwin may be wrong, but he or someone like him is a prerequisite to Schaar's effort to be orderly as well as accurate in classifying the sonnets. Classifying them according to structure is (as is their classification according to any other of their stylistic features) like trying to classify a snowstorm flake by flake. No two snowflakes are alike, but they all look alike as they fall and they have features in com-

14. Claes Schaar, *An Elizabethan Sonnet Problem,* Lund Studies in English, 28 (Lund, 1960), pp. 27–37.

mon under a microscope. One has arbitrarily to decide in what part of the flake one will look for the determining characteristic—whether one will classify by edges or corners or centers or angles. The edges of one snowflake may look like several formations at the center of another or at both the edges and the center of a third. There is no obvious place to start.

Schaar starts with Baldwin. He determines how many (fourteen) and which of the sonnets fit Baldwin's formula. He then proceeds to classify the sonnets according to the nature and extent of their variations from the structure as Baldwin defined it. When Schaar finishes, he has done something that no previous commentator ever did: he has managed to place within four groups, with nine subgroups and four subdivisions of subgroups, every one of the 154 poems in the 1609 quarto, and to tell his reader which poems belong in which groups. One must admire Schaar for doing the job so many people have only said they were doing, but one must also ask what good his distinctions and lists are. In suggesting the question, I do Schaar a disservice. In the context of his own purposes his proliferation of distinctions is a warranted and useful step toward his conclusions about the literary relationship of Shakespeare and Daniel. Still, Schaar will have contributed significantly to our understanding of the nature of Shakespeare's sonnets if we learn from his analysis of their structure that scholarly accuracy in dividing the sonnets into groups will bring us no closer than did the vague general groupings of Alden and Brooke to a satisfying sense that we know what Shakespeare's sonnets are.

If one can find no other way to come to grips with the nature of the sonnets, one can always blame the sonnets and dismiss them. There is a suggestion of this approach in the work of some of the critics who measured the Shakespearean form against the Petrarchan and found it wanting. They, however, could not dismiss the sonnets outright. They settled for beauty. In the last three centuries there have been only three truly great dismissers. In the eighteenth century George Steevens said of the sonnets that "the strongest act of Parliament that could be framed, would fail to compel readers into their service."[15] The nineteenth century never forgave him. In the nineteenth century itself, Henry Hallam, whom Rollins calls "a covillain to Steevens," defended heterosexuality against imagined insult from the sonnets and found it "impossible not to wish that Shakespeare had never written them."[16] The twentieth century has not forgiven Hallam. The chief contribution of the present century to the list of demons has been John Crowe Ransom, whom no one so far has forgiven. His self-conscious eagerness to enrage his reader might excuse him from serious consideration here. His "Shakespeare at Sonnets" is an ostentatiously red flag, and at this late date, when the field has been well trampled,[17] I cannot feel obliged to charge. In the course of his display, however, Ransom makes incidental comments on the style of the sonnets which are among the most helpful that have been made; their usefulness justifies some summary of the cause in which they were mustered. Essentially, Ransom objects because Shakespeare wasn't Donne. He prefaces his objections with a heroically inflexible discussion of the structure of Shakespeare's sonnets:

> I begin with a most unhappy feature: generally they are ill constructed.
>
> They use the common English metrical pattern, and the metrical work is always admirable, but the logical pattern more often than not fails to fit it. If it be said that you do not need to have a correspondence between a

15. Rollins, *Variorum, 2,* 337.

16. Ibid., p. 359.

17. The gentlest but most thorough of those who have taken the offense offered by Ransom is Arthur Mizener in his review of *The World's Body* (in *The Southern Review, 5* [Autumn 1939], 376–82), and in "The Structure of Figurative Language in Shakespeare's Sonnets" (*The Southern Review, 5* [Spring 1940], 730–47).

> poet's metrical pattern and his logical one, I am forced to observe that Shakespeare thought there was a propriety in it; often he must have gone to the pains of securing it, since it is there and, considering the extreme difficulty of the logical structure in the English sonnet, could not have got in by a happy accident. The metrical pattern of any sonnet is directive. If the English sonnet exhibits the rhyme-scheme ABAB CDCD EFEF GG, it imposes upon the poet the following requirement: that he write three coordinate quatrains and then a couplet which will relate to the series collectively.
>
> About a third of the sonnets of Shakespeare are fairly unexceptionable in having just such a logical structure. About half of them might be said to be tolerably workmanlike in this respect; and about half of them are seriously defective.[18]

Ransom's contribution to our understanding of Shakespeare's sonnets is his complaint that the logical pattern of the sonnets "fails to fit" the formal pattern. In the majority of the sonnets, he says, "we can find the standard metrical organization, and then some arbitrary logical organization which clashes with it" (p. 535). In the following chapters I propose to implement Ransom's complaint, to expand it, and to redefine the failure as a strength.

I expand Ransom's complaint by bringing into play more kinds of structure than Ransom considers. He treats only of formal and logical structure, and thereby gets to keep an unspecified third of the sonnets within the pale of his requirements. The addition of syntactical structure to the other two would, I think, have removed most of these. To formal, logical, and syntactical structure Arthur Mizener has added "the structure of figurative language in Shakespeare's Son-

18. John Crowe Ransom, "Shakespeare At Sonnets," *The Southern Review, 4* (Winter 1938), 533; reprinted in *The World's Body* (New York, 1938).

nets; "[19] C. S. Lewis has added what he calls rhetorical structure;[20] and David Masson has pointed out "free phonetic patterns in Shakespeare's sonnets,"[21] which, although they are free of the formal phonetic pattern of the rhyme scheme, are nonetheless structural patterns in their own right. These last three kinds of structure are better taken up in later chapters after the more basic problem of the interrelation of form, logic, and syntax has been considered. For now, it will suffice to say that, when all the coexistent structural patterns in the individual sonnets are examined, there is no sonnet in which the correspondence Ransom demands between Shakespeare's formal pattern and his logical one exists between those two patterns and all the other patterns in the poem. In other words, if Ransom were to follow his own rules to their logical extreme, he would be left, perhaps gladly, with none at all of Shakespeare's sonnets to admire.

As to my own admiration for the sonnets and grounds for attempting to redefine as a strength what Ransom calls a structural weakness, I have safety in numbers for the first and a critical authority not inferior to Ransom for the second. I think, and I hope to demonstrate, that the multiplicity of structural patterns in Shakespeare's sonnets is the means by which they qualify under the standard of poetic excellence quoted below. In fairness, I must admit that Keats is the critical authority and that Keats is a Romantic poet. I do not, however, think that even the embattled Ransom of 1938 could have followed his avowed inclination and disposed of Keats' good sense "a little distastefully as 'romantic' " (p. 537). Keats said, "Poetry should be great and unobtrusive, a thing which enters into one's soul, and does not startle it or amaze it with itself, but with its subject.—How beautiful are the re-

19. *The Southern Review, 5* (Spring 1940), 730–47.

20. C. S. Lewis, *English Literature in the Sixteenth Century* (Oxford, 1954), pp. 506–08.

21. David I. Masson, "Free Phonetic Patterns in Shakespeare's Sonnets," *Neophilologus, 38* (October 1954), 277–89.

tired flowers! how would they lose their beauty were they to throng into the highway crying out, 'admire me I am a violet! —dote upon me I am a primrose!' "[22]

I must also admit that some criticism has been directly concerned to point out Shakespeare's sonnets as examples of the kind of poetry exactly opposite to the sort Keats recommends. Keats himself is among the critics who have admired the "beauties," the purple patches, in the sonnets, but deplored their effect on the entity of the poem: "One of the three Books I have with me is Shakspear's Poems: I neer found so many beauties in the Sonnets—they seem to be full of fine things said unintentionally—in the intensity of working out conceits. Is this to be borne?"[23] Keats then quotes the second quatrain of sonnet 12.

One cannot be sure just what Keats wanted Reynolds to notice about the quatrain or how we are to take the question, but it is certain that line 4 *(Borne on the bier with white and bristly beard)* is a notably unshrinking violet. The line is as audacious an exhibition of craftsman's proficiency as Shakespeare makes in the sonnets. Later I will have something to say about the sound patterning in this line and in sonnet 12 as a whole. Here I can only suggest what I hope satisfactorily to demonstrate later, that this and less mechanical "beauties" of the sonnets are considerably less obtrusive than they could be if the formal structure, logical structure, syntactical structure, rhetorical structure, patterns of diction, and extraformal phonetic patterns were aligned in a concerted phalanx.

The chapters that follow are an effort to demonstrate the various kinds of structural patterns in the sonnets and the effect of their interaction. The establishment of one or another kind of structure in a particular number of sonnets

22. John Keats to John Hamilton Reynolds, February 3, 1818; *The Letters of John Keats, 1*, ed. Hyder Edward Rollins (Cambridge, Mass., 1958), 223.

23. John Keats to John Hamilton Reynolds, November 22, 1817; *Letters, 1*, 188.

is not intended to be significant in itself, but is only a step in demonstrating the means by which the multiplicity of kinds of structure within the individual sonnets is achieved. The nature of the means is not significant, but the nature of their effect is.

An ultimate purpose of this essay is to establish that the sonnets fit Keats' word "unobtrusive" and his demand that a poem amaze the soul not with itself but with its subject. There are many tedious steps to this goal. I must ask a reader with patience enough to make his way through the mass of detail that follows to have faith that it will come to something. Most people like the sonnets and think they are good. If they are good, they must be good because they are as they are. Establishing their nature is not easy, but it is the only way we are likely to get an indication of what it is that has given the sonnets their peculiar hold over their admirers. Even critics who have thrown off the hold have had difficulty. They sound like Christians who have lost faith. Consider this strange footnote to Yvor Winters' essay on the sonnets: "John Crowe Ransom antedates me by quite a few years in this heresy. . . . Ransom's objections and my own are similar in some respects and different in others. My own tardiness in seeing Shakespeare's weaknesses is evidence (a) of the effect of established habit on critical judgment and (b) of the curious way in which a shifting mixture of the good and the bad can produce a result which it is difficult to judge objectively."[24]

Winters had twenty years in which to come to terms with (a) and (b). Something in the sonnets held Winters' attention and presumably gave him some pleasure during those years. It may be worth the effort that follows to find out what it was.

24. Yvor Winters, "Poetic Styles, Old and New," *Four Poets on Poetry*, ed. Don Cameron Allen (Baltimore, 1959), p. 47n.

Chapter 2

Structures Versus Structure

Formal, Logical, and Syntactical Patterns

The most important thing about a sonnet is that it is a sonnet: that is true because the sonnet form is, like the sonnet tradition, a peculiarly urgent factor in a reader's experience of the particular sounds and substances of particular sonnets. By its structural nature, any sonnet stresses simultaneously both its unity and its disunity. The unity of a sonnet is the first thing that a reader sees about it. A sonnet is a tight little block of print on a page. The reader sees the whole poem at once; he can read it in less than a minute. On the other hand, if, as it must be to justify the classification at all, a sonnet is to be distinguished from any fourteen-line rhymed poem, it must be on the basis of the characteristics common to the various particular rhyme patterns that sonneteers use. The rhyme scheme of any poem that we label a sonnet is such as to make several kinds of internal division within a single fourteen-line unit.

The Petrarchan rhyme schemes and their continental variations accentuate the division between an octave and a sestet. The two rhymes in the paired quatrains (usually *abba, abba* or *abab, abab)* divide the octave phonetically from any one of several common patterns of two or three different rhymes in the sestet. With such a rhyme scheme, if a poet conforms to Ransom's requirement that the logical and syntactical structures of the sonnet conform to its formal structure, the effect upon an otherwise successful poem is likely to be pleasing.

The logical and syntactical reinforcement of the division between the two physically dissimilar parts of the sonnet centers the energy of the poem inside it. When, as is often the case in such sonnets, the sestet contradicts or modifies the statement of the octave, and when the division is simultaneously enforced by rhyme and syntax, the whole energy of the first eight lines is directed forward, while the energy of the last six is directed backward in formal, logical, and emotional contradiction to the octave. The division at line 9 not only heightens the contrast but turns the poem in upon itself, asserting unity by division. The continental sonnet, a vehicle for paradoxes, is itself paradoxical.

The rhymes of an English sonnet divide it into four parts —three separated quatrains and a couplet. Although, since each has its exclusive pair of rhymes, the quatrains are phonetically cut off from each other, the chief phonetic break is between the three separate but equal quatrains and the formally unexpected final couplet. Such a rhyme scheme, if it is not countered with rhythmical and syntactical devices, invites a writer to make a stairlike progression of statements in which the reader moves from one quatrain to the next toward culmination in the couplet. If the structure of the argument and the poetic structure are made identical, the English form can become a liability. The energy of the reader can be directed onward to nothing but an abrupt stop in a final spastic epigram:

> Ffrom Tuscan cam my ladies worthi race;
> Faire Fflorence was sometime her auncient seate;
> The westerne ile, whose pleasaunt showre doth face
> Wylde Chambares cliffes, did geve her lyvely heate;
> Ffostred she was with mylke of Irishe brest;
> Her syer an erle, hir dame of princes bloud;
> From tender yeres in Britaine she doth rest,
> With a kinges child, where she tastes gostly foode;
> Honsdon did furst present her to myn eyen;

Bryght ys her hew, and Geraldine shee highte;
Hampton me tawght to wishe her furst for myne;
And Windesor, alas! doth chace me from her sight.
Bewty of kind, her vertues from above,
Happy ys he that may obtaine her love.[1]

This particular Surrey sonnet is an exaggerated illustration of the propensity of the English sonnet form for mastering the poet. Surrey elsewhere holds his own more successfully against his medium, but as a device to exemplify the form rather than the poet, this sonnet is invaluable. Here the coincidence of syntactical, rhythmical, and logical points of division with those inherent in the rhyme scheme contribute to the general vapidness of the poem.

Surrey's poem is a journey through space and time toward the poet's present physical and psychological situation. The three quatrains are phonetically distinct; the third line of each of the first two quatrains runs on into the fourth, adding rhythmical finality to the finality of the completed rhyme pattern in lines 4 and 8. Similarly, the word *and,* which links lines 11 and 12, and the double caesura in line 12 give rhythmical completeness and separate unity to the third quatrain. The couplet is formally and rhythmically unexpected. Moreover, its substance is relevant to the expectations that the sonnet convention rather than this particular poem has evoked. The couplet has nothing whatever to do with the geographical progression that the reader has followed. Whether one chooses to think of the action of the poem as three starts and a stop or as a twelve-line progression in three revolutions arrested by a couplet, all the thrust of the poem is forward and it is frustrated by the couplet in which a new sentence, a new rhythm, and a new diction align themselves with the natural divisiveness of a new rhyme pattern. A case

1. *The Poems of Henry Howard Earl of Surrey,* ed. Frederick Morgan Padelford, University of Washington Publications: Language and Literature, 1 (rev. ed. Seattle, 1928), p. 83.

could be made for the aesthetic validity of a frustrating vehicle for a frustrating experience, but to do so for a poem as self-consciously slight as the sonnet to Geraldine would be a wanton expense of ingenuity. In this instance, Surrey's romantic and artistic frustrations are regrettably independent of each other.

Stranger than his wish that Shakespeare had aligned his logical and syntactical structure with the formal structure is Ransom's apparent surprise that Shakespeare failed to do so. If it is a failing, it is a failing for which Shakespeare had impressive precedents among his English predecessors. Surrey himself several times surmounted the obstacle of the couplet simply by using it to complete a sentence left unfinished at the end of the third quatrain. Throughout the following Surrey sonnet large syntactical units and the overriding rhythmic unity corollary to them counteract the divisiveness inherent in the rhyme scheme:

> When Windesor walles sustained my wearied arme,
> My hand, my chyn, to ease my restles hedd,
> Ech pleasaunt plot revested green with warm,
> The blossomed bowes, with lustie veare yspred,
> The flowred meades, the weddyd birdes so late,
> Myne eyes discouered. Than did to mynd resort
> The ioily woes, the hateles shorte debate,
> The rakhell life, that longes to loves disporte.
> Wherwith, alas! myne hevy charge of care,
> Heapt in my brest, brake forth against my will;
> And smoky sighes, that over cast the ayer;
> My vapored eyes such drery teares distill,
> The tender spring to quicken wher thei fall;
> And I have bent to throwe me downe with all.[2]

This poem presents the reader with a stalemate quite different from the one in the sonnet to Geraldine. Here the various

2. Padelford, p. 83.

devices for dividing the poem do not coincide with the divisions between quatrains or between the three quatrains and the couplet. The poem falls clearly but unobtrusively into octave and sestet. The primary reason that the division does not obtrude is that it is not supported by the rhyme scheme; the division by rhyme between the first quatrain and the second is just as strong as that between the second and third. Syntax, tone, and rhythm intensify the division at line 9, while the completion in the first line of the second quatrain of the sentence begun in the first quatrain minimizes the finality of the completed rhyme pattern at the end of line 4. The run-on line and the syntactical stop in the middle of line 5 superimpose the prose rhythm of the syntax upon the concurrent rhythmic unit of the line. The iambic pentameter quatrains are still heard, but they do not govern the poem any more than they are governed by the syntax and the prose rhythm.

There is a similar sort of stalemate between poetic forces inside the sestet. The rhyme scheme divides the third quatrain violently from the couplet. Syntactically, however, the same six lines are divided into two three-line sentences. Here, as in the octave, there are separate concurrent patterns—one rational, with its own prose rhythms, and one phonetic and metrical.

Moreover, countering both the patterns of division, the argument of the poem progresses in such a way as to assert the unity of the whole. As the division into quatrains and couplet is muted by the syntax, so the sharpness of a potential division between a joyful octave and a sorrowful sestet is averted by the progression within the octave toward the contrasting emotional state in the sestet. The diction *(hateles shorte debate, rakhell life)* and the miniature paradox of the oxymoron *ioily woes* reinforce the contrast between sight and thought introduced during the second quatrain. The octave leads up to and into the otherwise too violent break in tone at the beginning of line 9. Similarly, the separateness of the last six lines is lessened by a reminder in line 14 of the bending posture with which the poem began.

I have been at such length about this poem because its multiple patterns demonstrate a source of potential stylistic energy, energy that is available from the nature of the English sonnet. The couplet presents an aesthetic obstacle. In surmounting the obstacle by such means as Surrey used in the sestet of *When Windesor walles,* a poet could give positive virtues to his poem which, because they do not offer a necessity from which to make a virtue, the continental sonnet forms rarely have.

The integrated couplet in *When Windesor walles* is almost unique among seven-rhyme sonnets, but mastery of final couplets in other rhyme schemes is not. Sidney, although he used continental octaves and so restricted himself to five rhymes, usually used a final couplet, and probably his chief technical accomplishment is that he usually mastered it. *Astrophel and Stella* set the English sonneteering vogue in motion, and it is of some importance that the sonnets which were the models for a whole generation of poets have the extrarational complication that results from the superimposition of prose rhythm and syntax upon the metrical and rhyme patterns of the English sonnet. This is sonnet 2 of *Astrophel and Stella:*

NOT at first sight, nor with a dribbed shot
  Love gave the wound, which while I breathe will bleed:
  But knowne worth did in mine of time proceed,
Till by degrees it had full conquest got.
I saw and liked, I liked but loved not,
  I loved, but straight did not what *Love* decreed:
  At length to *Love's* decrees, I forc'd, agreed,
Yet with repining at so partiall lot.
  Now even that footstep of lost libertie
Is gone, and now like slave-born *Muscovite,*

I call it praise to suffer Tyrannie;
And now employ the remnant of my wit,
  To make my self beleeve, that all is well,
  While with a feeling skill I paint my hell.[3]

Syntactically and logically, the last six lines fall into two three-line units. The rhyme scheme divides them into quatrain and couplet. The superimposition of the syntactical pattern upon the formal pattern is a simple and effective way both of avoiding the dangers of the couplet and of maintaining the division at line 9, that between time past and time present, as a principal division in the poem. To the ear, however, the couplet still has its identity: the last two rhymes give finality to the poem and to the speaker's despair of a change for the better. Sidney gives his poem the structural advantages of both the Italian and English sonnets. The discrepancy between the formal structure and the syntactical structure also makes for a slight but energizing tension between the pattern of the sounds the reader hears and the pattern in which they have their meaning.

Sidney's disciples seldom attempted to imitate the simple device by which he integrated the couplet with the body of his poem. Shakespeare is no exception. In only two of his sonnets, 35 and 154, is there a similar effort to run the syntax of the third quatrain on into the couplet, and of those 154 is so generally atypical of his usual practice that a case has been made for excluding it altogether from the Shakespearean canon. However, although he fails to use multiple, coexistent, antipathetic patterns at the end of the sonnet, where the device is most obviously appropriate, Shakespeare does take up the device itself, and the bewildering number of kinds of patterns inside the individual sonnets contributes largely to the bewilderment with which they have traditionally been read.

3. *The Poems of Sir Philip Sidney*, ed. William A. Ringler, Jr. (Oxford, 1962), pp. 165–66.

The emotional response evoked by the structural conflict within the sestet as Sidney uses it is analogous to the logical response evoked by paradox. Shakespeare, by multiplying the number of kinds of pattern within a sonnet, is refining, expanding, and intensifying the kind of response which, however far it may get from simple paradox, is essentially a response to the paradoxical. He takes the principle of the paradox into the smallest stylistic elements of the presentation of the paradoxes of the lover's condition. The most easily demonstrated manifestation of the principle is in the opposition of logical patterns to syntactical patterns and of both to the metrical pattern and to the rhyme scheme.

In nearly two-thirds of Shakespeare's sonnets there are vestigial remains of the octave of the continental sonnet.[4] The octave in a Shakespearean sonnet can, of course, never be as distinctly a unit as it is in sonnets where its unity is supported by rhyme, but Shakespeare can counter the pattern of his rhyme scheme to achieve a sense of greater division between the second quatrain and the third than between the first two. In the continental sonnet the effect is automatic, an unavoidable bonus of the introduction in line 9 of the first new rhyme since the first quatrain. On the other hand, in Shakespeare's sonnets whatever the device by which he makes the division at line 9 more momentous than that at line 5, the device is always working to contradict the never obliterated pattern of the rhyme scheme. When it is present, Shakespeare's octave is muted, and instead of increasing the reader's comfort by asserting the pattern in which the paradox may be grasped, it diminishes the symmetry of the loose pattern to which the reader has begun to accustom himself.

The number of Shakespeare's devices and combinations of

4. There is a perceptibly distinct octave in 96 of the 152 fourteen-line sonnets. The 56 in which I find *no* distinct octave are 4, 6, 25, 30, 31, 34, 35, 38, 40, 42, 51, 53, 57, 59, 60, 64, 66, 67, 69, 73, 75, 80, 86, 87, 89, 92, 93, 95, 96, 97, 98, 100, 101, 103, 105, 108, 111, 112, 113, 116, 124, 130, 131, 132, 133, 134, 135, 136, 137, 140, 144, 147, 149, 150, 151, 152.

devices to effect his muted octaves is almost as great as the number of sonnets in which a suggestion of an octave appears. In some of the sonnets the first two quatrains are held together syntactically, but in only three of all the sonnets that have definable octaves is the division between quatrains 1 and 2 so diminished by an overriding syntax that the three-quatrain pattern becomes only incidentally perceptible. As units, the first two quatrains of 63, 145, and 154 qualify in Puttenham's terminology as "merely auricular in that they reach no furder then the eare." This is sonnet 63:

> Against my love shall be as I am now,
> With Time's injurious hand crushed and o'erworn;
> When hours have drained his blood and filled his brow
> With lines and wrinkles, when his youthful morn
> Hath travelled on to age's steepy night,
> And all those beauties whereof now he's king
> Are vanishing, or vanished out of sight,
> Stealing away the treasure of his spring—
> For such a time do I now fortify
> Against confounding age's cruel knife,
> That he shall never cut from memory
> My sweet love's beauty, though my lover's life.
>   His beauty shall in these black lines be seen,
>   And they shall live, and he in them still green.

Here the octave is made continuous by a clause that has its subject in line 4 and its predicate in line 5. The first two quatrains flow together; they are logically and syntactically a single unit. On the other hand, the division between the second and third quatrains coincides with an emphatic logical and syntactical division. The whole of the octave is subordinated to the adverbial phrase that begins line 1. At the end of the second quatrain the main subject and verb, the actor and the act promised syntactically in line 1, are still lacking. The sentence is left incomplete. Line 9 begins with an appositive phrase and makes a complete new syntactical start: *For such a time do I now fortify.*

In most Shakespearean octaves the first quatrain has some sort of syntactical identity to correspond with its identity as a unit in the rhyme scheme. The quatrain need not be an independent logical unit. In sonnets 23, 32, 47, 94, 106, 118, 128, and 143 the first quatrain is not a complete sentence, but, unlike the first quatrain of 63, the unity of the first quatrain is more than auricular.

In 32, for example,[5] the first quatrain is an *if* clause, and the second is the main clause of a conditional sentence. The coincidence of the two clauses with the two quatrains accentuates the independence of the two logically interdependent clauses:

If thou survive my well-contented day
When that churl Death my bones with dust shall cover,
And shalt by fortune once more resurvey
These poor rude lines of thy deceasèd lover,
Compare them with the bett'ring of the time,
And though they be outstripped by every pen,
Reserve them for my love, not for their rime,
Exceeded by the height of happier men.
O, then vouchsafe me but this loving thought:
'Had my friend's Muse grown with this growing age,
A dearer birth than this his love had brought
To march in ranks of better equipage;
  But since he died, and poets better prove,
  Theirs for their style I'll read, his for his love.'

The formal division between quatrains, the syntactical division between protasis and apodosis, and the logical division between condition and proposition reinforce each other. The break between quatrains is efficient and sharp.

5. The establishment of the octave in 23, 47, 94, 106, 118, 128, and 143 is described in Note 1 of the Appendix, p. 180.

That this is a single sentence helps to define it as an octave rather than two quatrains, but essentially the octave has its identity because the break between the second and third quatrain is simply greater in degree than that between the first and second. The third quatrain begins a new sentence. It accentuates the finality of the preceding line, and thus the unity of the octave, by beginning in a large summary gesture and a new vigorous tone: *O, then vouchsafe me but this loving thought.*

There are eleven other sonnets in which the octave is a single sentence, in which the first clause coincides with the first quatrains, and in which one of the two halves of the sentence cannot stand without the other. The distinction between these octaves and those just discussed is slight but important: at the conclusion of the first quatrains of 23, 32, 47, 94, 106, 118, 128, and 143 the reader knew from grammatical necessity that the thought he had been following in the first quatrain would be continued into the second; in numbers 20, 21, 26, 29, 33, 68, 72, 114, 117, 129, and 153 the first four lines are logically complete in themselves and could stand alone; it is a surprise to the reader when the syntax carries over into line 5.[6]

This is the first quatrain of 33:

> Full many a glorious morning have I seen
> Flatter the mountain tops with sovereign eye,
> Kissing with golden face the meadows green,
> Gilding pale streams with heavenly alchemy

The second quatrain unexpectedly tacks another clause onto the previous construction:

6. See also 122, where, although the second quatrain turns out to be an independent syntactical unit, it seems until line 8 to be an appendage of quatrain 1. The interaction of the first two quatrains of 142 is also similar to that in the eleven described here.

Anon permit the basest clouds to ride
With ugly rack on his celestial face,
And from the forlorn world his visage hide,
Stealing unseen to west with this disgrace

The reader's sense of syntactical and logical completeness at the end of line 4 is so heightened by the completion of the rhyme scheme of the quatrain that at line 5 he must redefine the structural units of the poem. The syntax of the sentence is such that Shakespeare gives his reader both the sense of two quatrains and of a continuous unified octave. At the end of line 4 the reader takes in the logical, syntactical, and formal completeness of the first quatrain. After he has assented to the division between quatrains and to the quatrain as the operative logical unit of the poem, the syntax of line 5 requires that he revise his understanding of the first quatrain to accommodate its unexpected logical and syntactical fulfillment in the second quatrain.[7] The reader's sense of the completeness of quatrain 1, his readiness for a new logical step and syntactical start, and the delay in its coming all go to emphasize the importance of the later division, when the analogy finally is completed and the third quatrain applies it.

The syntactical division between the second and third quatrains is complete, and the break between quatrains coincides with a logical step in the argument:

Even so my sun one early morn did shine
With all-triumphant splendor on my brow;
But, out alack, he was but one hour mine,
The region cloud hath masked him from me now.

7. What William Empson says about the overlapping sentence structures in Donne and Shakespeare is also true of the overlapping of formal and logical structures in the sonnets: "The renewal of energy gained from starting a new sentence is continually obtained . . . without the effect of repose given by letting a sentence stop" (*Seven Types of Ambiguity* [rev. ed., 1947], p. 52).

The first two lines of this quatrain recapitulate the first quatrain, and the second two lines recapitulate the second quatrain. Formally, syntactically, and logically the third quatrain is balanced against the octave to make the division at line 9 stronger than that at line 5 and thus to complete the contradiction of the three-quatrain pattern of the rhyme scheme.

The break at line 13, however, is greater than either of the breaks between quatrains:

> Yet him for this my love no whit disdaineth;
> Suns of the world may stain when heaven's sun staineth.

The couplet is a new start syntactically, a new approach logically, and a new pattern in the rhyme scheme. Only in the couplet do all the logical and rhetorical devices work to the same effect. The couplet demands that the reader again redefine the structure of the poem. The unit of the poem was first the quatrain, then the octave and sestet, and now twelve lines and a couplet. As the reader moves through the poem, he has constantly to widen his vision, and, what is more important, he is constantly changing his idea of the relationship of one part of the poem to another. Each formal division is greater than the one before and each new section relates itself to all of what went before, so that each division acts to obliterate the one that precedes it.[8]

A less strenuous sort of syntactical unification of the octave after the fact of division between quatrains is made in 7, 28, 83, 91, 97, and 132, where the copula at the beginning of the second quatrain mechanically connects two otherwise independent syntactical units. In thirteen sonnets (3, 5, 10, 22, 24, 27, 37, 39, 45, 87, 120, 121, 127), where there is no mechanical link between the first two quatrains, the second quatrain begins with the conjunction *for* and is taken up

8. The ten octaves similar to the octave of 33 are described in Note 2 of the Appendix, pp. 191–92.

with the grounds upon which the statement of quatrain 1 is based.

Some few other octaves are also pulled together by devices in line 5 to assert a more than logical connection between a syntactically self-sufficient first quatrain and the quatrain that follows it: in 12 and 15 the second quatrain is in syntactical apposition to the first; in 9, 46, and 90 the first words of line 4 are repeated as the first words of line 5; and in 123, although there is no conjunction to indicate their relationship, the second quatrain states the basis for the assertion of quatrain 1. But the bulk of the sonnets that achieve a distinct octave do it not so much by minimizing the division between the first two quatrains as by heightening the division at line 9. Thus, although in eleven sonnets[9] the word *but* at the beginning of line 9 makes a division sharp enough to define the octave, in sonnets 1, 48, and 115 *but* begins line 5, has the same logical and syntactical function, and is simply superseded by an even more pronounced division at line 9. For example, sonnet 1:

From fairest creatures we desire increase,
That thereby beauty's rose might never die,
But as the riper should by time decease,
His tender heir might bear his memory;
But thou, contracted to thine own bright eyes,
Feed'st thy light's flame with self-substantial fuel,
Making a famine where abundance lies,
Thyself thy foe, to thy sweet self too cruel.
Thou that art now the world's fresh ornament
And only herald to the gaudy spring,
Within thine own bud buriest thy content
And, tender churl, mak'st waste in niggarding.
  Pity the world, or else this glutton be,
  To eat the world's due, by the grave and thee.

9. Sonnets 7, 14, 18, 41, 44, 54, 62, 138, 141, 151, 153.

The division at line 9 is not only sharper logically and syntactically than that at line 5, it is also sharper phonetically. Line 9 begins with a trochee, and the rhyme between the stressed syllables of *Thou that art now* emphasizes the metrical variation and thereby emphasizes the change of approach.

The number of different devices by which the change in line 9 is made clear enough to define the octave is almost endless and is endlessly complicated by the presence in most of the sonnets of several simultaneously divisive factors working in conjunction to impress upon the reader the distinction between what is said in the first eight lines and what is said after them. A few examples will suffice to indicate at least the range of Shakespeare's divisive resources.

In 18, 19, and 48 the octave is affirmative and is set off against a third quatrain in which the verb is governed by *not.* The opposite is true of 14 and 21. In 13 and 115 the octave is declarative and the third quatrain is interrogative; in sonnet 28 it is the other way round. In 61, 76, 114, and 125 the octave asks a question which is answered in quatrain 3. Sonnet 146 is interrogative in the octave and imperative from then on. In 22, 23, 24, and 27 the octave is declarative and the third quatrain is imperative. The octave of sonnet 5 is in the indicative mood; the third quatrain is subjunctive. The octaves of 68, 110, and 119 are defined by a change of tense in the third quatrain. In 43 and 71 the new start in the third quatrain is simply announced mechanically by the insertion of *I say* as the second foot of line 9. The octave of 56 is taken up with a metaphor of appetite; quatrain 3 takes up a new metaphor: *Let this sad int'rim like the ocean be.* Similarly, the break after the octave of 94 is marked by the first introduction in line 9 of the extended metaphor of the *summer's flower.*

Sometimes, as in 8 and 17, a change in tone alone is enough to emphasize the superiority of the break at line 9. In both 8 and 17 the change in tone is supported by a metrical variation in the first foot of line 9. Indeed, in twenty-one sonnets[10] an unexpected or unusually emphatic trochee at the beginning of line 9 either establishes or helps to establish the identity of the octave. Abrupt logical stops within the ninth line give rhythmical emphasis to a new start after the octaves of 58, 82, 121, and 148. There is a similar effect from the exclamation with which the third quatrains of 39, 41, 65, and 119 begin. After octaves in which the pauses in the sentences coincide with the ends of the lines, the prose rhythm of the syntax runs counter to the formal pattern in the third quatrains of 55, 79, and 90.

A syntactical pause coincides with the fulfillment of the rhyme pattern of the first quatrain of all the sonnets that have octaves except 63, 145, and 154. That division in each case is superseded by a fuller stop and a greater sense of finality at the end of quatrain 2. In each poem the finality of the second quatrain and the change at the beginning of the third is sufficient to demand that the reader accept the first eight lines as a single unit. In almost all of them the third break in the rhyme pattern, the break before the couplet, is the greatest of all and again redefines the structure of the poem, now as a unit of twelve lines set against a couplet.

Although nearly a hundred of the sonnets have octaves, only sonnet 154 really has both an octave and a sestet. All the rest also have a syntactical stop after line 12 which, in combination with the inherently divisive couplet rhymes, is sufficient to cut the last two lines away from the body of the poem. After the more leisurely rhyme pattern of the quatrains, a couplet following a quatrain which is not patently incomplete syntactically is bound to sound epigrammatic and summary, even if it is not an actual summary of the substance or the spirit of the poem. The couplets of 8, 44, 46, 71, 117, 121, and 153 are syntactically incomplete and are tacked on to third quatrains which are potentially complete syn-

10. Sonnets 1, 3, 8, 15, 16, 17, 27, 29, 48, 52, 53, 70, 85, 102, 105, 107, 109, 120, 127, 129, 139.

tactical units. The method here is the one that in 33 and the poems similar to it makes a sufficiently effective couplement of the first two quatrains to make them a single unit. When the dangling auxiliary is a couplet, however, the device is hardly more effective in unifying the last six lines into a sestet than the use of *and, for,* and *or* in the twenty sonnets which have octaves and in which only a conjunction ties the couplet to the third quatrain.[11]

Although the couplet of sonnet 8 is a relative clause dependent from the preceding line, it makes the largest logical step in the poem, harnessing the whole discussion of music to the general purpose of the first seventeen sonnets. The couplet sounds like a statement of the purpose of the poem, and it retroactively removes all formal and logical complexity from the first twelve lines. It reduces the whole body of the poem to a single unit easily comprehensible in the terms of the single argument the poem seems written to express:

> Music to hear, why hear'st thou music sadly?
> Sweets with sweets war not, joy delights in joy:
> Why lov'st thou that which thou receiv'st not gladly,
> Or else receiv'st with pleasure thine annoy?
> If the true concord of well-tunèd sounds,
> By unions married, do offend thine ear,
> They do but sweetly chide thee, who confounds
> In singleness the parts that thou shouldst bear.
> Mark how one string, sweet husband to another,
> Strikes each in each by mutual ordering;
> Resembling sire and child and happy mother,
> Who, all in one, one pleasing note do sing;
> Whose speechless song, being many, seeming one,
> Sings this to thee, 'Thou single wilt prove none.'

Similarly, in 71, where, although it is syntactically depen-

11. Nine couplets with *and:* 12, 15, 39, 48, 54, 68, 82, 90, 107, eight with *for:* 29, 50, 72, 76, 94, 104, 106, 109; three with *or:* 14, 47, 56.

dent, the couplet makes the major logical step in the poem, the couplet states the premise for the commands which take up the body of the poem. In doing so, the couplet erases the previous divisions and patterns of the sonnet and brings them into one:

No longer mourn for me when I am dead
Than you shall hear the surly sullen bell
Give warning to the world that I am fled
From this vile world, with vilest worms to dwell.
Nay, if you read this line, remember not
The hand that writ it, for I love you so
That I in your sweet thoughts would be forgot
If thinking on me then should make you woe.
O, if, I say, you look upon this verse
When I, perhaps, compounded am with clay,
Do not so much as my poor name rehearse,
But let your love even with my life decay,
  Lest the wise world should look into your moan
  And mock you with me after I am gone.

While the couplet of 46 is syntactically dependent from the sentence preceding it in quatrain 3, its substance is the final logical step of the poem. It does not make syntactical sense standing alone, but a pair of parallel statements, made more evidently parallel by rhyme, must act as a summary simplification of the jumble of syntactical relationships between *heart* and *eye* in the body of the poem. The couplets of 117 and 121 are general contradictions of the premises upon which the poems have progressed. And the very act of contradiction solidifies and simplifies the whole of what precedes it into a unit that cannot be more complex than the contradiction itself.

The couplet of 153 allows for more sense of a sestet than exists in most of the other sonnets. The first statement in the couplet is linked to the preceding sentence and is relevant only to that sentence; it is a real continuation rather than a break in the whole. The second statement of the couplet, however, is an overt summary of the whole and takes in both the rhyme words:

I, sick withal, the help of bath desired
And thither hied, a sad distempered guest,
  But found no cure: the bath for my help lies
  Where Cupid got new fire, my mistress' eyes.

Outside of 154 among the sonnets that have octaves, Shakespeare probably comes closest to a sestet in 29 and 44. The couplet of 44 is both a syntactical and a logical appendage of the third quatrain. It has direct logical relevance only to the sentence that it completes, and, because line 12 has a vagueness of diction and relationship unusual so late in one of Shakespeare's sonnets, this couplet seems less of an afterthought than most of the other syntactically incomplete couplets:

If the dull substance of my flesh were thought,
Injurious distance should not stop my way;
For then, despite of space, I would be brought,
From limits far remote, where thou dost stay.
No matter then although my foot did stand
Upon the farthest earth removed from thee;
For nimble thought can jump both sea and land
As soon as think the place where he would be.
But, ah, thought kills me that I am not thought,
To leap large lengths of miles when thou art gone,
But that, so much of earth and water wrought,
I must attend time's leisure with my moan,
  Receiving naught by elements so slow
  But heavy tears, badges of either's woe.

Even here, however, the poem cannot really be described as an octave and a sestet. Although there isn't much finality about the conclusion of quatrain 3, the four lines are a potentially complete logical unit. The pause after line 12, combined with the naturally divisive effect of the couplet rhymes, is enough to break the couplet from quatrain 3 and to make the division before the couplet at least as great as the break made by the exclamation after the octave. Moreover, in pointing to the four elements, the couplet summarizes, simplifies, and makes graspable the self-consciously helter-skelter interplay of insubstantial *thought* with *earth* and *water*. The couplet gives the reader the appropriate standard diction *(tears, woe)* for dealing objectively, at a distance, with the state of mind which he was temporarily forced to share while he followed the vague and extravagant imaginative jumps of the first twelve lines. Insofar as the couplet gives the reader distance, it lets him view the preceding three quatrains as a whole, and, insofar as it does that, it brings him, as all the other couplets do, to redefine the structure of the poem as one twelve-line unit and a couplet.

The division after the octave of 29 is the sharpest in the poem. The rhythm of the octave becomes increasingly agitated in the second quatrain as frustrated desires come quicker and quicker. The last line of the octave is perfectly regular, colorless, and, in the oxymoron of *most* and *least,* has a sound of final defeat:

> When, in disgrace with Fortune and men's eyes,
> I all alone beweep my outcast state,
> And trouble deaf heaven with my bootless cries,
> And look upon myself and curse my fate,
> Wishing me like to one more rich in hope,
> Featured like him, like him with friends possessed,
> Desiring this man's art, and that man's scope,
> With what I most enjoy contented least

The first foot of the next line is trochaic, and its first syllable pushes off into a long, sibilant, smooth, luxurious, eleven-syllable line. *Haply* in the next line is another trochee and pushes off again, this time into a succession of pushing sounds provided by the alliteration of *th* in the next three stressed syllables. Another trochee at the beginning of the next line makes the final push: *Like to the lark.* From there the words glide easily to the slow alliterating aspirates of *hymns at heaven's gate.* At the end of the quatrain the rhythm seems incomplete; the reader is left up in the air. The couplet seems rhythmically and emotionally necessary to the completion of quatrain 3:

> Yet in these thoughts myself almost despising,
> Haply I think on thee, and then my state,
> Like to the lark at break of day arising
> From sullen earth, sings hymns at heaven's gate;
>   For thy sweet love rememb'red such wealth brings
>   That then I scorn to change my state with kings.

The two lines are a summary in reverse order of the poem as a whole. Line 13 is a stolid restatement of the third quatrain, and line 14 is a revision of the now obsolete attitudes of the octave. The couplet restates the exaltation of quatrain 3 in diction appropriate to the octave: *wealth, scorn, change,* but in its metaphor and diction the couplet is neatly, epigrammatically, even elegantly, mundane. It brings the reader down to earth. It simplifies the whole experience and makes it graspable. In doing so, this couplet, like Shakespeare's others, breaks from the poem. Although the division between line 12 and the couplet is not as striking emotionally as the break after the octave, it does demand that the reader make still another revision in his idea of the relationship of the parts of the poem to each other.

The one sonnet in the 1609 quarto that has been an exception to all the generalizations I have made in this chapter is 154:

> The little Love-god, lying once asleep,
> Laid by his side his heart-inflaming brand,
> Whilst many nymphs that vowed chaste life to keep
> Came tripping by; but in her maiden hand

The fairest votary took up that fire
Which many legions of true hearts had warmed;
And so the general of hot desire
Was, sleeping, by a virgin hand disarmed.
This brand she quenchèd in a cool well by,
Which from Love's fire took heat perpetual,
Growing a bath and healthful remedy
For men diseased; but I, my mistress' thrall,
  Came there for cure, and this by that I prove:
  Love's fire heats water, water cools not love.

There are any number of ways of accounting for the vapidness of this poem; the diction is dull, the conceit is duller. I think its vapidity is also helped along by the relative absence of conflict between its formal and syntactical structures.

I say "relative absence," but, relatively to other Shakespeare sonnets, 154 might seem to present more rather than less conflict between its formal and syntactical structures: the broken quatrains and enjambments in lines 4 and 12 easily superimpose a syntactical octave and sestet upon a formal pattern in three quatrains and a couplet. The key word is "easily." Sonnet 154 shows the same skill at countering a formal break that Surrey showed in the sestet of *When Windesor walles* and that Sidney regularly shows in his sestets. It is not a skill to be scorned, but its results are quite different from those I have described in the rest of the sonnets among the 1609 collection that have octaves. The difference is in the action of the reader as he reads. The fusion of contrary structural principles in 154 demands minimal effort from its reader.

In the rest of the sonnets that have octaves, the reader, whatever else he is engaged with, is constantly revising his own conception of the poem before him. As he moves from the end of the first quatrain of the sonnets that have octaves, he finds the poem always divisible into two parts: the section being read at the given moment is one, and everything that has gone before is the other. At each succeeding break in the poem, the preceding unit becomes larger and more general. Reading one of these sonnets is something like looking up a city in a big atlas, where a single page may have separate maps of the center of the city, the county, and the whole state. One moves from one scale to another smoothly and gratefully, but the opportunity of seeing the same things three different ways at once demands considerable mental activity from the viewer. The adjustment of the scale and relationships of the parts of the sonnets does not require much effort or conscious effort from the reader, but it does demand constant effort. Where Shakespeare presents a formal pattern, a logical pattern, and a syntactical pattern that run simultaneously but not concurrently, he forces a reader subject to them all to give the poem some if its energy by the act of reading it.

False Starts and Changes of Direction

Those lips that Love's own hand did make
Breathed forth the sound that said 'I hate'
To me that languished for her sake;
But when she saw my woeful state,
Straight in her heart did mercy come,
Chiding that tongue that ever sweet
Was used in giving gentle doom,
And taught it thus anew to greet:
'I hate' she altered with an end
That followed it as gentle day
Doth follow night, who, like a fiend,
From heaven to hell is flown away.
'I hate' from hate away she threw,
And saved my life, saying 'not you.' (Sonnet 145)

Several generations of scholars have wishfully thought that this feeble little sonnet is spurious. Perhaps it is, but the effect for which it strives and the device by which that effect is achieved are of the same general sort as the effects and devices I have described in the first part of this chapter and will describe in the remainder of the essay. The adjustment that sonnet 145 describes in the speaker's own understanding is comparable to the less conspicuous adjustment that other sonnets demand of the reader.

Its meter aside, 145 is unusual among the sonnets only because its device and effect are so obvious. In 145 Shakespeare ostentatiously points to the shift in understanding that is necessitated by the addition of *'not you'* to *'I hate.'* Elsewhere he makes more subtle and more efficient use of his awareness that syntax and the reader's experience of it are chronological. In sonnet 145 he tells the reader that, although the chain of events that is a sentence may seem to lead in one direction, it can lead somewhere else entirely. Elsewhere he puts the reader through miniature but real experiences like the one that is described in 145 and thus made distant from the reader.

Sonnet 145 makes a good stepping-stone to the chapters that follow, because it is not only a crude example but an overt description of one way in which what I take to be the chief stylistic peculiarity of the sonnets can manifest itself: the sonnet actually describes a listener's active adjustment of his understanding of both the substance and structure of what he hears while he hears it.[12] The following further examples of the device of 145 provide a simple demonstration of the characteristic to whose further manifestations I will devote the rest of the essay: uneasiness in the relationship of object to object in all the details of the individual sonnets of a sequence whose substance is similarly unfixed relationships.

As he reads a Shakespeare sonnet, a reader is likely to make several false starts similar to the one made by the speaker in 145. The false starts are usually effected from the reader's

12. See the discussion of fluid syntax in the sonnets by William Empson in *Seven Types of Ambiguity,* pp. 50–56.

readiness to understand what he reads in any one of several contexts: the context of the sonnet convention, the context of this collection, the context of the particular sonnet he is reading, and the context of his own knowledge of English idiom. When a reader goes off on a wrong track, he usually returns from it without bringing his detour to consciousness. The false starts do not call attention to themselves because they do not usually involve the reader in misconceptions about the essential meaning of the sonnets in which they appear, and because the forward motion of the rhythm and syntax is not interrupted as it is in 145. In the examples that follow, nothing points up or otherwise confirms the validity of a reader's momentary experience of the multiplicity of the systems in which a given word or phrase or fact can be conceived.

This is the second sentence of sonnet 47:

> When that mine eye is famished for a look,
> Or heart in love with sighs himself doth smother,
> With my love's picture then my eye doth feast
> And to the painted banquet bids my heart (lines 3–6)

The word order here is not hard to follow, but neither is it the prose order in which these words would ordinarily be arranged to make the statement they make here. On the other hand, inside the unusual overall syntactical pattern are several common constructions, each of which is momentarily capable of impinging on the reader's understanding before being cast off by the syntactical necessity revealed by the subsequent development of the sentence. At the beginning of line 4, *Or* could introduce a noun alternative to *look*. It introduces a new subject for a new clause: *Or heart . . . doth smother*. As the line is read, the reader comes on the standard idiom *in love with,* in the context of a love sonnet, preceded by *heart* and followed by a potential object, *sighs*. As the line continues, *himself doth smother* suggests that *with* before *sighs* might have indicated agency, but the next line begins

With my love's picture; so that a reader to whom a probable reading of *with* in line 4 has just been suggested must now reject the possible similar construction "smother by means of my love's picture," because a picture is a less probable instrument for the purpose than sighs, and because, coming as it does in the context of *famished for a look,* the completed line, *With my love's picture then my eye doth feast,* carries the sense "feast on." The phrase "feast with," however, is a common one, indicating "feast in the company of." That meaning is impossible here, but as soon as the suggestion of a host entertaining a guest is brushed aside as irrelevant to line 5, it appears as the substance of line 6: *And to the painted banquet bids my heart.*

Such substantially gratuitous journeys in the mind are very common indeed in the sonnets:

The fifth line of sonnet 131 appears in the 1609 quarto as *Yet in good faith some say that thee behold.* Most editors have attempted to solidify the syntactical relationships of the line by setting off *in good faith* with commas. Even when the phrase is thus punctuated, its nearness to *say* and the commonness of the phrase "say in good faith" should be sufficient to evoke a reader's uneasiness about the syntactical relationship within the line. Moreover, punctuation is of no use whatever in doing away with the syntactical expectations set up in the reader by *some say that.*[13] Here the word *that* is a pronoun, but before he reaches *thee behold,* the reader should be well on his way toward accepting *that* as the conjunction ultimately appropriate but only elliptically present in the completed construction:

> Yet, in good faith, some say that thee behold,
> Thy face hath not the power to make love groan

13. See also the stock phrases *blame thee for, brass eternal,* and *wasted time* in the lines *I cannot blame thee for my love thou usest* (40.6), *And brass eternal slave to mortal rage* (64.4), and *When in the chronicle of wasted time* (106.1).

The first line of sonnet 15 is: *When I consider everything that grows.* The first sense the line gives is: "When I look at all growing things"; *everything* seems to be the direct object of *consider.* The next line requires that the reader understand line 1 as if it were "When I consider *that* everything that grows":

When I consider everything that grows
Holds in perfection but a little moment,
That this huge stage presenteth nought but shows
Whereon the stars in secret influence comment

As the sonnet progresses, the speaker so broadens the scope of his view that he seems indeed to consider everything. Thus here, as in 47 and 131, a rejected provisional meaning turns out to have relevance to an impression evoked later in the sonnet.[14]

I have already talked about the reader's obligation to reject a completed syntactical identity for the first quatrain of sonnet 33. As the action appended in line 5 changes the syntactic nature of the whole first quatrain, so the first line *(Full many a glorious morning have I seen)* presents the potential subject, verb, and direct object of a complete statement, and the second line *(Flatter the mountain tops with sovereign eye)* makes the reader reconstrue *Full many a glorious morning* as a member of the newly extant object clause. Each violation of the reader's confidence in his expectations about a syntactical pattern evokes a miniature experience for the reader that mirrors the experience of betrayed expectations which is the subject of the poem and which overconfident expectation of continued good weather metaphorically describes.

14. See also line 2 of sonnet 11, where, although *from that which thou departest* means "as a result of that which thou bestowest," the standard construction "depart from" appears in the midst of a continuing discussion of departure from this life.

Throughout the sonnets Shakespeare plays on momentary confusions between *my love,* meaning "the person I love," and *my love,* meaning "my affection." In sonnet 124 the adjective *dear* and the fact that a *child of state* is likely to be a person lead a reader toward an understanding of *my dear love* in line 1 that *It* in line 2 makes impossible:

> If my dear love were but the child of state,
> It might for Fortune's bastard be unfathered

As he moves from line 1 to line 2, the reader's experience is unsettling; the particular nature of the error evoked is such as to make his experience of the otherwise unambiguous statement that follows unsettling on a larger scale. Although the idea that *my dear love* in line 1 is the beloved has to be rejected, there is strong indication elsewhere in the collection that the beloved is indeed a child of state. As a result of the reader's momentary misconception in line 1, the speaker's account of the nature of his affection is colored by the reader's awareness from other sonnets of the not always admirable nature of the beloved.

In the first quatrain of 79 the poet speaks as an injured party:

> Whilst I alone did call upon thy aid,
> My verse alone had all thy gentle grace;
> But now my gracious numbers are decayed,
> And my sick Muse doth give another place.

This is line 5: *I grant, sweet love, thy lovely argument.* Following upon the tone of quatrain 1, the conjunction of *grant* and *argument* in a potentially complete sentence sends the reader off into a simple understanding of the line in the debater's terms it uses:

> I grant, sweet love, thy lovely argument
> Deserves the travail of a worthier pen

The completed statement makes it clear that *thy lovely argument* means "the theme of thy loveliness," but the process of reading this particular statement in this particular diction and syntax will have been such as to make the reader's state of mind as a reader similar to the speaker's state of mind as a lover. They have both experienced a sense that something is wrong.

Sometimes a provisional meaning emerges only when the poem is heard. For example, the phrase *the peace of you* in line 3 of sonnet 75 can be momentarily understood as "the piece of you": *And for the peace of you I hold such strife.* In his edition of 1924 T. G. Tucker actually suggested emending *peace* to read *piece.*[15] The syntax and the obvious relationship between *peace* and *strife* make his suggestion ridiculous, but that the meaning should have crossed his mind is not at all ridiculous. The phrase *the peace of you* appears in the company of the word *hold*—and in a sonnet that in the 1609 order follows immediately upon sonnet 74, which contains such phrases as *The very part* [*of me*] and *the better part of me.*[16] In quatrain 1 of sonnet 141 a listener may momentarily hear a similar pun in *of view*. Since the first three lines are chiefly concerned with *thee* and *eyes,* "in despite of you" is as

15. Similarly improbable emendations by other editors provide evidence that what I say goes on in the mind of my hypothetical reader does go on in the minds of actual readers. The minds of the editors have been demonstrably "like the dyer's hand." John Payne Collier, for example, read "money" for *many* in 67.12 (Rollins, *Variorum, I,* 177). What might seem to be only a vagary of the counterfeiting spirit becomes understandable (though of course still unacceptable) when one considers the financial context in which the word *many* appears:

> For she hath no exchequer now but his,
> And, proud of many, lives upon his gains

16. Sonnet 75 goes on to talk about *a miser and his wealth* in the next three lines. Into that context comes the word *counting* in line 7, where its only and obvious meaning is "accounting," "thinking."

appropriate and meaningful in line 4 as *in despite of view* and is a more idiomatic construction besides:[17]

> In faith, I do not love thee with mine eyes,
> For they in thee a thousand errors note;
> But 'tis my heart that loves what they despise,
> Who in despite of view is pleased to dote.

The rapid mental adjustments I have discussed are for the most part incidental to the substance of the poem, but they can occur on any scale and still not call attention to themselves or to the poet's cleverness. This is the first quatrain of sonnet 35:

> No more be grieved at that which thou hast done:
> Roses have thorns, and silver fountains mud;
> Clouds and eclipses stain both moon and sun,
> And loathsome canker lives in sweetest bud.

The second quatrain seems to be about to continue in the same vein: *All men make faults* . . . . As the sentence continues, the speaker's self-incrimination is in keeping with the attitude he exhibits in quatrain 1. That consistency sus-

17. For another pun of this kind see *The Troyan's trumpet* in *Troilus and Cressida* IV.5.53–64:

> *Diomedes.* Lady, a word. I'll bring you to your father.
> [Exeunt Diomedes and Cressida.]
>
> *Nestor.* A woman of quick sense.
> *Ulysses.* Fie, fie upon her!
> There's a language in her eye, her cheek, her lip;
> Nay, her foot speaks. . . .
> O, these encounterers, so glib of tongue,
> That give a coasting welcome ere it comes,
> And wide unclasp the tables of their thoughts
> To every ticklish reader, set them down
> For sluttish spoils of opportunity
> And daughters of the game.
> *Flourish. Enter all of Troy.*
> *All.* The Troyans' trumpet.

tains the reader's sense of continuity, while at the same time quatrain 1 turns out to be an instance of the crime for which the speaker blames himself:

> All men make faults, and even I in this,
> Authorizing thy trespass with compare,
> Myself corrupting, salving thy amiss,
> Excusing thy sins more than thy sins are;
> For to thy sensual fault I bring in sense
> (Thy adverse party is thy advocate)
> And 'gainst myself a lawful plea commence;
> Such civil war is in my love and hate
> That I an accessary needs must be
> To that sweet thief which sourly robs from me.

Like so many of his predecessors, Shakespeare compares the condition of a lover to that of a state in civil war. Unlike his predecessors, Shakespeare evokes in his reader something very like the condition he talks about.

One of my purposes in this essay is to support the thesis that in all their details the sonnets set a reader's mind in motion, demand intellectual energy as they are read, and that that effect, the effect of the actual experience of passing from word to word for fourteen lines, is unusual and valuable. Each reading of a Shakespeare sonnet is a peculiarly real experience for its reader. It is the experience not of recognizing the mutable nature of the human condition but of participating in an actual experience of mutability.

As he reads a Shakespeare sonnet, a reader's mind moves from one system of relationship to another just as it does when it contemplates physical experience. As most minds casually and imperceptibly shift their standards to admire both Robin Hood and Justice Holmes, to approve both "look before you leap" and "he who hesitates is lost," so in the sonnets, where the experience of imperceptible shifting is both scaled down to a size appropriate to the sixty-second experience of reading a fourteen-line poem, and exaggerated by the concentration and diversity of its manifestations, a reader's mind is constantly moving from one scheme to another in its perceptions of verse units, syntactical units, sound patterns, image patterns, and the relationships of word to word, object to object, person to person, and idea to idea in the course of reading a poem.

Art comforts the spirit by presenting experience selected and organized in such a way as to exhibit the sense of pattern that the human mind tries always to perceive in all experience. The experience of nature, so-called everyday experience, is haphazard; it never quite conforms to the patterns imposed upon it by its participants, who must think about it, talk about it, remember it, and predict it. From moment to moment a person engaged in such experience must relate sensations and ideas to one another; he is not thinking hard, but he is actively and totally engaged. In the sonnets Shakespeare does not achieve, and surely wouldn't want, the effect of natural experience, whose randomness prompts the imposition of artistic order in the first place. Shakespeare does, however, evoke in his reader the incessant intellectual motion which the controlled experience of art ordinarily precludes. There is nothing in a Shakespeare sonnet that does not pattern, but there are so many patterns that in moving from one system to another the reader's mind operates similarly to the way it operates upon unstructured experience. Shakespeare approaches the popular impossibility of having his cake and eating it too.

To the well-worn irony of Shakespeare's promise in sonnet 81 that the sonnets would make the name of the beloved immortal, I hope that this essay will add the humbler irony of his implied description of his style in sonnet 76:

> Why is my verse so barren of new pride?
> So far from variation or quick change?

Chapter 3

Multiple Patterns

Rhetorical Structure

In *English Literature in the Sixteenth Century* C. S. Lewis made stimulating but necessarily brief comments on the structure of Shakespeare's sonnets. His description of what he calls rhetorical structure concludes with a moving defense of critical concern for such minutiae as I am about to consider. I quote at length both to establish the sort of patterning I shall be considering in this chapter and for the comfort to be had from the support of a distinguished and articulate ally:

> The rhetorical structure is often that of theme and variations, as in *Lucrece*. The variations more often than not precede the theme, and there is usually an application which connects the theme of the particular sonnet with what may be called the 'running' theme of that part of the sequence to which it belongs. There are exceptions to this. In CXLIV, for example, we have something like a continuous progression in which each line adds to the thought. CXXIX ('The expense of spirit') starts as if it were going to develop in that way, but progression almost ends with line 5, 'Enjoy'd no sooner but despised straight.' The next seven lines are largely, though not entirely, variations on the fifth. To see the typical Shakespearian structure at its simplest we may turn to LXVI ('Tired with all these'). The theme occu-

pies the first line, the application, the final couplet: in between we have eleven instances of the things which produce weariness of life. This numerical equality between the different variations is very uncommon, and chosen, no doubt, to give a special effect of cumulative bitterness. More often it is contrived that the variations should be either unequal simply, or, if they begin by being equal, that they should presently grow longer. Thus XII ('When I do count the clock') is built on the pattern: variations—theme—application. The theme ('You too will pass') occupies the four lines beginning 'then of thy beauty do I question make,' and the application is in the final couplet. The preceding variations have the numerical pattern 1, 1, 1, 1, 2, 2; a line each for the clock, the nightfall, the violet, and the curls, then two lines each for the trees and the harvest. The effect on the reader is one of liberation just at the moment when the one-line *exempla* were about to produce a feeling of constraint. In XXXIII ('Full many a glorious morning') we have only one variation in the form of a continuous simile filling the first eight lines. But then this simile contains its own pattern: one line announcing the morning, three which catch each one aspect of its beauty, and four to tell the sequel. XVIII ('Shall I compare thee to a summer's day?') is exquisitely elaborated. As often, the theme begins at line 9 ('But thy eternal summer shall not fade'), occupying four lines, and the application is in the couplet. Line 1 proposes a simile. Line 2 corrects it. Then we have two one-line *exempla* justifying the correction: then a two-line *exemplum* about the sun: then two more lines ('And every fair') which do not, as we had expected, add a fourth *exemplum* but generalize. Equality of length in the two last variations is thus played off against difference of function. The same transition from variation by examples to variation by generalizing is found in LXIV ('When I

> have seen by Time's fell hand defaced'); theme in lines 1–2, first *exemplum* in line 3, second *exemplum* in line 4, the fourth *exemplum* triumphantly expanding to fill lines 5–8, generalization (9–10) passing into Application which occupies the last four lines. To some, I am afraid, such analysis will seem trifling, and it is not contended that no man can enjoy the Sonnets without it any more than that no man can enjoy a tune without knowing its musical grammar. But unless we are content to talk simply about the 'magic' of Shakespeare's poetry (forgetting that magic was a highly formal art) something of the kind is inevitable. It serves at least to remind us what sort of excellence, and how different from some other poetic excellences, the Sonnets possess.[1]

The preceding passage probably contains as many intriguing and suggestive statements as a single paragraph can hope to hold. To flesh them out and assess them individually would take many pages. I hope that this essay as a whole will go a long way toward doing so. For the moment, however, what is most pertinent about this paragraph is the suggestion it contains of the multiplicity of patterns within a given sonnet. To say that there is multiplicity of patterns in a sonnet is to say that it is ordered in several different schemes, that the poem coheres in several systems simultaneously. The investigation of structure is ordinarily the search for the system not the systems in which a poem coheres. The discovery of structures rather than structure does not make for a satisfying critical performance. Readers of criticism have learned to expect a critic to show them a way, *one* way, of looking at a poem, a viewpoint from which a reader can perceive the poem and in terms of which he can make it his own.

Lewis makes a courageous effort to serve his reader as his reader expects to be served. He sets out with the statement

1. Lewis, *English Literature in the Sixteenth Century,* pp. 506–08.

that *"the* rhetorical structure is often that of theme and variations," and he continues throughout to talk about *"an* 'arrangement,' " *"a* pattern," and *"this* pattern." At the same time, however, he has sufficient self-confidence to describe the sonnets he cites as they are rather than as they must be to fit his theory of their structure. As a result, the idea of theme and variations becomes decreasingly useful as the paragraph becomes increasingly informative. The paragraph is very hard to follow because it presents itself as a demonstration of the validity of "theme and variations" as the usual structural principle of the sonnets, and is largely devoted to demonstrating the incidental patterns emergent from the size of the units in which substance is presented. The paragraph, therefore, does not seem to be going anywhere. Nonetheless, although it turns out to be only a tantalizing hodgepodge of brilliant insights, this paragraph is, I think, the best work that has been done on the structure of the sonnets: when Lewis strays from theme and variations proper to the pattern produced by the amount of space given to the successive examples in the octave of sonnet 12, he directs his reader to a phenomenon that is not only more usual in the sonnets than theme and variations but also more efficient in determining their nature.

The pattern 1, 1, 1, 1, 2, 2[2] that Lewis observes is superimposed upon the octave just as the pattern 8, 4, 2 of "variations—theme—application" is superimposed upon the formal pattern 4, 4, 4, 2. Lewis' contribution to the criticism of Shakespeare's sonnets is the freedom he offers to those who follow him from the traditional, self-imposed requirement of arguing for one structuring principle over all others. If the size of the units devoted to exemplary objects in sonnet 12 can produce an efficient pattern, cannot patterns also be produced by the size of logical units, by the size of syntactical

2. I have adopted Lewis' system for defining the units of a sonnet numerically. It is not elegant, but it is efficient and clear.

units, and by the nature of the sentence structure? They can. Here, to continue with the same poem, is sonnet 12, in which three patterns (4, 4, 4, 2, the rhyme scheme; 8, 4, 2, the argument; and 1, 1, 1, 1, 2, 2, the *exempla* in the octave), have already been noted, and in which the catalogue of patterns manifested by different principles of organization is still incomplete:

When I do count the clock that tells the time
And see the brave day sunk in hideous night,
When I behold the violet past prime
And sable curls all silvered o'er with white,
When lofty trees I see barren of leaves,
Which erst from heat did canopy the herd,
And summer's green all girded up in sheaves
Borne on the bier with white and bristly beard;
Then of thy beauty do I question make
That thou among the wastes of time must go,
Since sweets and beauties do themselves forsake
And die as fast as they see others grow;
  And nothing 'gainst Time's scythe can make defense
  Save breed, to brave him when he takes thee hence.

The *when/then* construction divides the sonnet in two at line 9. Syntactically (and only syntactically) the poem thus is in two parts, octave and sestet. The *when/then* construction also produces a pattern similar in its effect to Lewis' liberating rhythm of examples; the pattern 1, 1, 1, 1, 2, 2, produced by *clock, day, violet, curls, trees, harvest,* coexists with a syntactical pattern 2, 2, 4 made by the three appositive *when* clauses beginning at lines 1, 3, and 5. Moreover, the pattern of progressively larger syntactical units is unlike the similar pattern of exemplifying units in that it carries over the whole poem and does not cease with the octave. The pattern runs *when/and* (lines 1–2), *when/and* (lines 3–4), *when/and* (lines 5–8), *then/and* (lines 9–14) and may be expressed numerically 2, 2, 4, 6; or 1 *and* 1, 1 *and* 1, 2 *and* 2, 4 *and* 2.

Lewis says that the pattern of examples has a liberating effect. So does the syntactical pattern. It is more to the point perhaps to call the pattern of progressively expanding units expansive. The expansion of the units is emotionally auxiliary to the increasingly expansive statements of the poem culminating in the sweeping generalization of the couplet. In the particular case of sonnet 12, then, the syntactical pattern gives direct support to the logical pattern of the sonnet. A similar progression from particulars in short syntactical units through particulars in larger syntactical units to generalization in the couplet is not uncommon in the sonnets. For example, in sonnets 15, 40, 53, 76, 77, 102, and 130 syntactical expansiveness similar to that of sonnet 12 has the similar effect of giving emotional validity to generalizations from minimal evidence. The presence of such effects in particular poems justifies attention to syntactical structure in those particular poems. However, although the pattern of the syntax may directly support the progress of the argument in some of the poems, that is not a sufficiently common function to be added to a general definition of style in the sonnets. On the other hand, the simple presence of multiple coexistent conflicting patterns, each evoked in its exclusive ordering system, is a distinguishing characteristic of Shakespeare's sonnets. Any word or phrase or line is likely to be simultaneously in several distinct relationships with other parts of the poem.

Phonetic Structure

Study of the sounds of the sonnets has from the beginning been the study of alliteration. It has not come to much because most critics who have touched the subject have put their energy not to demonstrating the effect upon the poems of sound patterns traditionally labeled alliteration but to deciding what sound patterns can and cannot be called alliteration, and, except for incidental comments (usually specious cases of onomatopoeia), to little more. A welcome exception to the rule is "Free Phonetic Patterns in Shakespeare's Sonnets" by David I. Masson.[3] Masson summarizes the work of his chief predecessors, frees himself from their concern for defining the device rather than its effect, and states his own intention of demanding critical utility for the knowledge for which his predecessors so valiantly counted and classified:

> We are concerned with sound-classes which are aesthetically important in a given passage . . . .
>
> This article will scan sound-patterns with the very flexible approach appropriate to unique individual entities. It will therefore have little concern with the statistical attack [by B. F. Skinner] on the sonnets in 1939–41. The sceptical psychologist seems to have restricted "alliteration" to initial consonants of words and proposed to ignore all cases in which the repeated element did not occur at least twice as often as the statistical probability which he estimated for chance occurrences in poetry . . . Common sense and a careful "ear" will do far more than mathematics. As to restricting our field to the initial sounds of words, this is nearly as irrelevant as the choice of a factor of 2. As implied or allowed by Stoll and U. K. Goldsmith, there is no need even to restrict the pattern either to stressed syllables, or (in the consonants) to syllable-initials; very often the counterpoint of rhythmic and phonetic pattern and the shift from initial to final position or *vice versa,* are important contributions to the aesthetic significance of the pattern. And as Stoll has well observed . . . alliteration "may involve the repetition of kindred consonants . . . instead of the same." To this we would add that vowel modulation or even dissonance at similar points in a pattern is also of importance. Both Stoll and Goldsmith appear to maintain that the poet's patterning is conscious,

3. Masson, *Neophilologus, 38,* 277–89. For a comment on Masson's tactics and readers, see Note 3 of the Appendix, p. 193.

> though Stoll agrees that it may become "second nature." How far the patterning was conscious is of less concern, however, to this article, than what was its nature and poetic significance.[4]

What Masson says has needed saying for a long time. It is, in effect, that if one hears a sound pattern in a sonnet one may say so, and that whether there is a term in formal rhetoric to describe a pattern, or what term to use, or how often the pattern is found in the sonnets as a whole, or whether Shakespeare knew how he achieved an effect that satisfied him has no effect whatever on the sound of a particular sonnet.

Masson goes on to talk about kinds of sound patterning, progressing from simple repetition through the true pun to paranomasia or jingle. He continues:

> The most solid kinds of jingle found are a rhyme, a rich rhyme with the wrong final consonant, or a rich rhyme with dissonance. But there are more attenuated jingles, in which the recurrent elements are spread out among several irrelevant sounds *(e.g. mount/minute,* or *yellow/meadow),* and/or inexactly echoed *(banners/pin us, loud/hide).* The order of recurrence may vary *(minute/mitten),* and intrusive repetitions of some sounds may occur *(loud/loaded).* The most attenuated echo of all is one of simple assonance or alliteration, particularly if some of the recurrences are unstressed. . . .
>
> What are their functions in verse? The most obvious is the *equivalence-trick,* if we may name it so disrespectfully. A resembles A′ in sound, therefore in meaning or in the author's attitude to them. On the other hand, we

4. Masson, pp. 279–80. The articles to which Masson refers are these: B. F. Skinner, "Alliteration in Shakespeare's Sonnets . . . ," *Psychological Record, 3* (1939), 186–92; and "A Quantitative Estimate of Certain Types of Sound-Patterning . . . ," *American Journal of Psychology, 54* (1941), 70–77; Edgar Elmer Stoll, "Poetic Alliteration," *MLN, 55* (1940), 388–90; U. K. Goldsmith, "Words out of a Hat . . . ," *JEGP* (January 1950), 33–48.

> find the *distinction-trick:* A resembles A′ in sound, but they are clearly opposites, and this likeness accentuates their polarity. Between the two effects we find all types of likeness in difference and difference in likeness. More generally, there is the *relation-trick:* A is related to A′ grammatically, dialectically, etc. More subtle and elaborate mechanisms occur. E.g.: A B C B′ C′ A′; therefore some process seems to have been undergone, leading us back to near our starting-point. The precise effect depends upon the details of the pattern and those of the significance of the words. (pp. 280–81)

The likeness of Masson's alphabetical notation and Lewis' numerical one is more than superficial. Like patterns of syntactical units, sound patterns can evoke the sense of an ordering in the poem that is independent of its argument or formal structure. For purposes of demonstration I propose to look again at sonnet 12 and to point out patterns additional to those already discussed. I do so with some trepidation—first, because the use of ordinary prose to dissect a poem into phonetic particles may make for clarity but is irritating and considerably more time-consuming than the same process done in signs and terms and symbols; and secondly, because, already irritated by a tortuous and tediously long exhibition of sound patterns, a reader is likely to jump to the conclusion that the exhibitor is trying to substitute his ingenious perception of minutiae for a perception of the poem. I therefore insist in advance that I mean to suggest neither that patterns of sound have meaning divorced from substance, nor that noises are the key to Shakespeare's sonnets. Despite the complexity of the demonstration, my point is simple and only a slight extension of the truism that verse is defined in terms of sound. The formal structure of the sonnet is determined by rhyme and meter. In Shakespeare's sonnets other and independent phonetic patterns evoke a sense of other and independent schemes of organization. Sounds that are similar are related; they belong together. The words in which they appear may have no other logical relationship to each other, and yet the pattern of sound will evoke a sense of rightness, a sense that the words belong together, a sense of an active organization independent of rhyme, meter, diction, syntax, or substance. In demonstrating sound patterns, I make no claims for them other than that they exist. I ask that the reader remember my promise in Chapter 1 to demonstrate that the effects on which these poems turn are not of the obtrusive sort to which Keats objected. In short, I hope to convince my reader that there are so many patterns in a given sonnet, so many effects that could be boisterous violets, that no single pattern or effect can divert the reader's attention from the whole to a part. It is therefore because sound patterns, like the other patterns I describe, are individually insignificant that I find it so important to describe them at all.

Here, then, again is sonnet 12. I give it this time as it was printed in 1609 (*u, v,* and *s* are normalized):

> When I doe count the clock that tels the time,
> And see the brave day sunck in hidious night,
> When I behold the violet past prime,
> And sable curls or silver'd ore with white:
> When lofty trees I see barren of leaves,
> Which erst from heat did canopie the herd
> And Sommers greene all girded up in sheaves
> Borne on the beare with white and bristly beard:
> Then of thy beauty do I question make
> That thou among the wastes of time must goe,
> Since sweets and beauties do them-selves forsake,
> And die as fast as they see others grow,
> And nothing gainst Times sieth can make defence
> Save breed to brave him, when he takes thee hence.

Within the ticking regularity of line 1, *count the clock* and *tels the time* are distinct phonetic units, one alliterating in *c* and the other in *t. Count* belongs with *clock,* and *tels* belongs with *time.* The mutually exclusive patterns of alliteration insist upon the separation of the two phrases. At the same time, however, the phrases are phonetically similar in their identical rhythms and in the presence in both of the word *the* as the unaccented syllable. Moreover, an overriding alliteration in voiced *th* in the unaccented syllables is provided by the word *that,* which indicates yet another relationship between the two phrases—their syntactical relationship.

This one line manifests in little the structural peculiarity of the sonnet as a whole and of the sonnets in general: its parts are simultaneously in several relationships to each other, and each relationship is established by a different distinct patterning factor. In this particular poem a pattern established phonetically in the first line is maintained by other means throughout the poem: first we hear *count* and *clock* as two units of a whole, then *count the clock* as one half of the unit *count the clock that tels the time;* then we see the whole of the first line as one half of the *when/and* construction of the first two lines; then we see those two lines as one half of the balance between them and the second *when/and* construction in lines 3 and 4. That balance is simultaneously made by the answering end-rhymes in the second pair of lines. The completed first quatrain is then balanced by the second quatrain, a four-line *when/and* construction. At line 9 the second member of the overall syntactical balance is introduced with *then.* Finally, at the couplet, the two kinds of rhyme scheme are set off against each other. The poem is in two parts throughout, each balance is of larger members than those that precede it, and balance is each time evoked by a different ordering principle.

To return again to the demonstration of the numerous and fleeting phonetic organizations in sonnet 12, the syntactical link provided in line 2 *(And see the brave day sunck in hidious night)* by the copula and second verb for the pronoun *I* is supplemented phonetically in line 2 both by the repetition in the "b" rhyme, *night,* of the vowel sound of the "a" rhyme, *time,*[5] and by the repetition in *sunck,* the sixth syllable of line 2 of the final consonant sound of *clock,* the sixth syllable of line 1. In line 2 itself, however, the repeated vowel sound in *brave day* and the combinations of *s* and *n* in *sunck in hidious night* give separate identities to the two phrases. Here, just as in the case of *count the clock* and *tels the time* in line 1, the phonetic individuality of the two phrases is denied by an overriding third phonetic pattern, a pattern in *d* and *s,* first together in *and see,* then separated by vowel sounds in *hidious.* In these two lines, then, different sound patterns pull the lines themselves, phrases within lines, and words within phrases together and apart simultaneously.

Line 3 *(When I behold the violet past prime)* connects with line 1 by anaphora in *When I* and by the completion of the first rhyme-pair *time/prime.* The *b* sound of *brave* and the *d* sounds in line 2 are picked up in *behold; brave* is also echoed in the labial-plus-*r* of *prime.* Internally, *past prime* coheres obviously by alliteration, and *I behold the violet* has a subtle unifying harmony in its *i, o,* and *l* sounds. Simultaneously canceling the individual unities of the two phrases is the equally subtle overriding pattern of labials in *behold, past,* and *prime* as well as the repeated *i* sound in *I, violet,* and *prime.*

In the fourth line *(And sable curls or silver'd ore with white)* the muted echo of *behold* in the combination of the *b* and *l* of *sable* provides some phonetic continuity with the preceding line; *s* and *l* sounds in various combinations in *sable, curls,* and *silver'd* give the three words an identity as a phonetic group; and slightly differing *w* sounds do the same for *with white.* It is, however, nearly impossible to say any-

5. In the final syllables of the first two lines a similar assonance occurs from the vowels in 7, 9, 18, 35, 45, 64, 71, 79, 127, and 145; and from the consonants in 11, 21, 22, 25, 27, 30, 36, 38, 53, 61, 70, 73, 77, 78, 85, 89, 101, 104, 111, and 152. For further examples of definable identity in the first two lines of Shakespeare sonnets, see Note 4 of the Appendix, p. 195.

thing meaningful about the phonetics of a line that is in obvious need of the emendation it has regularly received. Since Malone, most editors have substituted *all silver'd o'er* for *or silver'd ore.*[6] Malone said that *or* "was clearly an error in the press" for *all.* The emendation makes good sense and sounds good, but a two-inch square of small type in the *Variorum* testifies that it is not so obvious as Malone took it to be. What is most interesting in the context of the present discussion is that a careful study of the phonetics of the sonnet gives no support whatever to Malone's emendation or to any other. In his edition of 1898 George Wyndham said that "Malone's emendation is rendered probable by 'all girded up' " in line 7, but to draw conclusions from such evidence implies a knowledge of Shakespeare's principle of harmony in this particular instance that he gives us nowhere else in the sonnets. An emender can reasonably assume that the word Shakespeare intended related harmoniously to those around it, but there is no way in a poem of multiple harmonies to guess into which of the several harmonic schemes the lost word fitted.[7]

6. Rollins gives details of various emendations in *Variorum, 1,* 32–33.

7. As Malone emended the line, *all* fits in handsomely with the surrounding *l* sounds: *And sable curls all silver'd o'er with white.* The same is true of Verity's variation on the Malone emendation: *And sable curls o'er silver'd all with white.* In Malone's version the *l* sound drops away after the sixth syllable, and the *r* first introduced in *curls* becomes the dominant sound in the seventh and eighth syllables. Verity keeps the *l* through the eighth syllable and avoids a distinct pattern in *r.* This line is unlike the three preceding ones in that the phonetic identities of the alliterative phrase *with white* and the *sable-curls-silver'd* group are not muted by a third all-inclusive pattern. If we assume that, like those that precede it, line 4 was simultaneously unified and divided phonetically, it would seem reasonable, since no one has yet suggested any emendation that would replace *or silver'd ore* with a phrase that contains any of the sounds of *with white,* to prefer Verity's line to Malone's on the grounds that it comes closer to providing a pattern that runs over the whole line. We have, however, no grounds in this sonnet or in any of the

Line 5 *(When lofty trees I see barren of leaves)* is intricately patterned in *l,* in voiced and unvoiced *f,* and in the repetition of the same vowel sound in combination with *s* in *trees, see,* and *leaves.* The sounds of *when,* the first word in the line, and *barren,* the first word after the caesura, are notably absent from the overriding sound pattern of the line. *Barren* stands opposed phonetically as well as substantially to *lofty, trees,* and *leaves.* The line is linked to those that precede it by the reappearance in *barren* of *b* and *r* and by the reappearance in *of leaves* of the *v* sound from *brave, violet,* and *silver'd.*

In line 6 *(Which erst from heat did canopie the herd) heat* and the final syllable of *canopie* pick up the double *e* sound from *tree, see,* and *leaves* in the preceding line. Internally, division in the line is stressed by the alliteration—in *h* plus a dental consonant—of *heat,* the last word before the caesura, and *herd,* the last word of the line; at the same time, the widely separated but similar *r* sounds of *erst* and *herd* draw the two halves of the line together.[8]

In line 7 *(And Sommers greene all girded up in sheaves)* Lewis notes an "artful pattern *s, gr, g, sh*" which he calls "groups linked with simples and arranged chiasmically" (p. 506). He seems to have overestimated the effectiveness of

---

others for assuming any such continuing allegiance to a particular pattern of phonetic construction. The internal phonetic design of line 5, for example, is not at all that of the first three.

8. In lines 5 and 6 the caesura is stressed both by a phonetic link between the last words of the two half-lines and by a phonetic link between the first words of the two half-lines:

> Whe*n* lofty trees I s*ee*
> barre*n* of l*ea*ves
>
> Wh*i*ch erst from *h*eat
> d*i*d canopie the *h*erd

The phonetic link between the pairs of first words is barely perceptible, but each link is between a pair of sounds that are similar to each other but to no other sounds in the line.

the initial sounds of *Sommers* and *sheaves* as patterning factors; the similarity between *s* and *sh* is more evident to the eye than to the ear. It is actually the final *s* of *sheaves* that links itself with *Sommers* and gives unity to a line otherwise split apart by *greene all girded,* a tight phonetic entity made lively by *g* and two varieties of *r,* first together and then separated and modulated by an intervening vowel. Coexisting with the pattern of alliteration and in conflict with it is another phonetic organization for the line—that made by the caesura and its accentuation by identical vowel sounds in *greene* and *sheaves.* In addition to their various relationships to each other, the sounds in line 7 are in a remarkable number of unobtrusive relationships with the preceding lines. *Sommers,* for example, participates in a pattern of *and s . . .* in *and see* (line 2), *and sable* (line 4), and *and Sommers;* it is also a unit of a pattern of vowel-*r-s,* vowel-*r-d,* running through lines 6 and 7 in *erst, herd, Sommers, girded.* The vowel sound of *greene,* the fourth syllable of line 7, is identical with that of the fourth syllables of the two preceding lines (and of the line following). *Up* in line 7 echoes a similar sound in *canopie* in the preceding line. *Sheaves,* the end-rhyme, reasserts the *v* sound that has run through the poem.

The last line of the octave, *Borne on the beare with white and bristly beard,* is probably the source of Keats' dismay in this quatrain. Its heavy alliteration makes the line stand out to an extent unusual in the sonnets. The play on *b* and *r* in varying relationships to each other and to vowel sounds is heavy but differs only in degree from the effects made by sound play in earlier lines. As with such patterns as *d-s* in line 2, *s-l* in line 4, and *g-r* in line 7, the heavier alliterative pattern here is made on two consonants in a variety of relationships. As in the first three lines of the quatrain, the caesura is stressed by phonetic similarity between the final syllables of the two half lines; indeed, the two sounds *(beare, beard)* are nearly identical as pronounced in modern English. Here, however, although the consonantal similarity is valid enough, the modern pronunciation of the vowels is misleading: *beard* is rhymed with *herd,* and there is ample evidence that Shakespeare's reader would have pronounced it so.[9]

It is probable that had he seen "Borne on the beare with white and bristly *berd*" on the page before him, Keats' ear would have been less shocked by the line, but even if we allow that he might have been eased by a pennyworth of scholarship, something remains to be learned from his attention to this line as, because of an accident in the history of pronunciation, he heard it. What is genuinely remarkable about the line is that a modern reader feels no need to fulfill the rhyme pattern by adjusting his usual pronunciation of *beard;* he hears, in fact, too much music rather than too little. A modern reader is put regularly on edge by demands from the ear (such as that evoked by Spenser when he rhymes bowers and paramours), which he cannot allow his tongue to gratify. We pronounce Renaissance poetry as if it were modern poetry, making adjustments only for rhythmic requirements. The distortion is rarely perceptible, but when it is perceived, it does, as it does in the case of *bowers-paramours* in the first stanza of *Prothalamion,* impinge momentarily on our consciousness. Such a reader should be conscious of the rhyming of *herd* and *beard* in sonnet 12, but, unless he is engaged in the grammar school rite of ticking off the rhyme scheme, he is not likely to notice.[10] Instead, a modern ear hears a crude accidental harmony between *bier* and the modern sound of *beard.* The reader's easy adjustment to a sound pattern other than the formal pattern of the rhymes is made possible here by the multiple independent phonetic

9. Helge Kökeritz vouches for no standard pronunciation of *beard,* but notes that it is sometimes spelled *berd* and that Shakespeare rhymed it with *heard* as well as *herd.* See Kökeritz, *Shakespeare's Pronunciation* (New Haven, 1953), pp. 207, 409, 448.

10. Discussions of Shakespeare's rhyme scheme or pronunciation take note of the (now) false rhyme *herd-beard,* but I know of no commentary on the poem per se that mentions the rhyme.

organizations present throughout the poem. At the end of line 6 the sound of *herd* strikes the ear not only as a sound requiring the fulfillment of an echo two lines later, but as itself a partial echo of elements in *erst* and *heat*. Moreover, the requirement of a rhyme for *herd* is partially satisfied before the end of line 8, the point of formal necessity, by *girded* in the middle of line 7. Similarly, the modern pronunciation of *beard* does not sound wrong but harmonizes so well with *beare* and the vowel sound of *leaves* and *sheaves,* the alternate rhyme-pair of the quatrain, as to seem excessively rich.

The excess perceptible to Keats and other modern readers is the product of a historical accident by which one sound pattern has become dominant. In its presumed original pronunciation sonnet 12 is like the rest of Shakespeare's sonnets in that none of its several phonetic organizations dominates the others.

The third quatrain is typical of third quatrains of the sonnets in that patterning of sound is less dense in it than in the first eight lines:

> Then of thy beauty do I question make
> That thou among the wastes of time must goe,
> Since sweets and beauties do them-selves forsake,
> And die as fast as they see others grow

The syntactical expansiveness already noted is matched by a corresponding loss in this quatrain of stress on the line as a phonetic unit. There is a running pattern in the quatrain of various combinations of *s* and *t* in *question, wastes, must, sweets, beauties,* and *fast,* but the individual lines do not have the intricate internal phonetic tensions of the lines of the octave. In lines 9 and 10 there is no single pause that can be called the caesura, but rather several small pauses that mark the logical step from *when* to *then* with a change in rhythm. The new looser rhythm is not based on the simultaneous unity and division of two half lines; and that looser rhythm, in combination with looser sound patterning and a larger syntactical unit, makes the third quatrain sound less complicated than the octave and leads into the general simplification of the couplet:

> And nothing gainst Times sieth can make defence
> Save breed to brave him, when he takes thee hence.

The optimistic conclusion that *breed to brave him* gives the poem does not grow out of this sonnet and is appropriate not to this particular context but to the general context of this part of the sequence. The *sounds* of the couplet, however, do grow from the lines that precede it and give an extra-logical sound of truth, sense of propriety, inevitability, and completeness to the sonnet. The *s-t* pattern in quatrain 3 continues in *gainst,* and the *f* and *v* sounds that run through the poem in *brave, violet, silver'd, lofty, leaves, sheaves, themselves, forsake,* and *fast* reappear in *defence, save* and *brave.* Most important, however, is the assertion of division in the formally unified couplet between the negative statement of line 13 and the positive one of line 14. The *br* sound of *breed* and *brave* was introduced in line 2 (where *brave* is an adjective). The dominant *br* sounds of line 8 close the octave. Now in the last line the *br* sound is again dominant in a line directly contradictory to the pessimistic substance of line 8, of line 13, and of the rest of the poem in general. Throughout the poem its different elements are pulled apart and together by simultaneous likeness and difference. In line 14 a new idea and a new spirit are set against the rest of the poem in a line that is set off phonetically by a heavy alliteration in *br* from line 13. Line 13 is phonetically linked to the third quatrain, which was sharply divided syntactically and phonetically from the heavy alliteration in *br* in the last line of the octave. Line 14 is phonetically linked with line 8 and, like line 8, it contains an image of being carried away. In line 14, however, the *br* pattern that sounded inevitable doom in line 8 appears in *breed to brave him,* the hopeful note on which line 14 separates itself from the rest of the poem. The couplet may serve as a simple summary example of simultaneous unity and division, sameness and difference, throughout the poem: on the one hand, the substance and, in the first five syllables, the sound of line 14 is sharply divided from that of line 13; on the other hand, in simultaneous compensation, the unifying couplet rhyme is not monosyllabic but trisyllabic—*make defence, takes thee hence.*

Patterns of Diction

Everything mentioned or suggested in sonnet 12 has, as a common denominator, a relevance to mutability; everything mentioned is thus appropriate to everything else and to the poem. At the same time, however, there is, appropriately enough in a demonstration of the universality of flux, considerable emphasis on the variety of the examples, on the difference between one example and another *(clock, violet* and *curls,* for example, seem at first to be much more unlike than like). The likeness and unlikeness of the objects in the poem are simultaneously evident. Moreover, the simple paradox in which all are alike and all different is complicated by several lesser systems of relationship among the various objects of the poem. These in turn tend also toward simultaneously unifying and dividing it.

In any system of classification the components of the group will obviously depend upon the classifier's choice of a determining factor. As the reader is openly invited to see the poem in one organization by the rhyme scheme and in another by the syntax and pattern in anaphora, so this poem presents several different ways in which relationship among images is perceptible. As a single word may function simultaneously in several different sound patterns, so a single word may pertain simultaneously to several imagistic motifs.

The discovery and mapping of image patterns has been a popular and respectable critical pastime for so long now that no reader will be surprised to find them considered here or demand that such a consideration be justified. Regrettably, however, such receptiveness makes it more necessary here than elsewhere to insist that I do not mean to suggest a reduction of the experience of the poem to a perception of the relationships of the images. All I wish to point out about the images is what I have pointed out about the sounds: words that have a common factor (in this case meanings of a particular denotative or connotative class) have an extralogical pertinence to each other that is perceptible in a sense of a relationship to each other and an appropriateness to their common context of the statements in which the related words appear.

In sonnet 12 the objects in the first quatrain pertain to each other as successively larger units for measuring time: *clock,* in hours; *day,* in days; *violet past prime,* in seasons; and *curls,* in human lifetimes.

Running through the whole octave is a chain of color words, starting with a suggestion in line 2 of the gold of day and the black of night, and followed by *violet, sable, silvered, white, green,* and *white* again.[11]

Curls in line 4 pertains to *beard* in line 8.

Day in line 2 pertains to *heat* in line 6.

Prime in line 3 means the violet's period of perfection; it also means the springtime; in this context, however, a logically irrelevant sense of *prime,* a particular period in early morning, provides an extralogical continuity between line 3 and the clock in line 1 and the passage of day into night in line 2.

The violet, trees, summer's green, sheaves, grow, and *scythe* are all appropriate to each other. Less obviously, a consciousness of "up" and "down" persists in the poem in *sunk, lofty,* the fall of the leaves, *canopy,* and the *sheaves,*

11. This "lovely colour group" is duly noted by Caroline Spurgeon in *Shakespeare's Imagery* (Cambridge, Eng., 1934), pp. 68–69.

girded up to be borne away prone on the bier. Similarly, the prevalence of the idea of seeing and of the word *see* itself gives line 12 *(And die as fast as they see others grow)* an appropriateness in the whole that, except as it reflects a commonplace of the preceding eleven sonnets, it does not have to the first eleven lines of this poem. Something of the sort is true also of line 11 *(Since sweets and beauties do themselves forsake);* the imprecision of the line is considerably lessened by its appearance in a poem where a concern for forsaking is imperceptibly but persistently suggested in the going of the day, the passing of the violet, the fall of the leaves, the bearing away of the sheaves, and, in the line immediately preceding, the going of the beloved.

The sharpness of the break in subject matter after line 8 is similarly softened by the shrouded presence from the beginning of the poem of the paradox of the last two lines and of the first seventeen sonnets: time passes, but the hands of the clock will return to twelve and start again; the day dies, but the sun will rise again in the morning; the violet withers, but it is a perennial; the leaves fall, but the tree will leaf again. The two exceptions to the pattern are the sable curls in line 4, which, once silvered o'er, will not be black again, and the grain in lines 7 and 8, which, once harvested, will not grow again until the field is reseeded. The likeness of the curls and the grain, and their difference from the other objects in the octave, would be of no importance whatever if their perception demanded that a casual reader make such a display of ingenuity and botanical know-how as I have just made, but the equation of the curls and the grain and their separation from the other objects in the octave is evoked in two other systems of classification. A surface similarity between line 4 and lines 7 and 8 is evoked in the reminder in *white and bristly beard* of the curls *silvered o'er with white.* Moreover and more importantly, the fourth line is the only one in the octave that is overtly concerned with the aging of a human being. In line 8, however, the analogy between the harvest home and a funeral is so emphatic as to make the line all but explicitly concerned with human mortality. Effectively, then, the final lines of the two first quatrains are linked one to another, and their substance differentiated from the other objects in the octave. The third quatrain and the couplet go on to take up human mortality and to make explicit for the previous exception, human beings, the optimism of cyclical death and regeneration that was inherent in the natures of most of the examples in the octave. The essential motif of the group of sonnets of which this one is a part is revivified in the pertinence to the botanical imagery, in which so much of this poem is cast, of the idea of new seed as a defense against time's scythe.

MULTIPLICITY

In the preceding pages I have exacted a remarkable number of patterns from the innocent body of sonnet 12. What I have said is, I am sure, true: the patterns I have found in the poem are there, and I hope that my reader will not, after bearing with so long a dissection, question their existence. He might, however, justifiably question whether anything whatever is achieved by an anatomization so painstaking as this—whether a demonstration of multiple pattern is critically useful in approaching sonnet 12, or, if sonnet 12 is taken, as I mean it to be, as representative of the sonnets in general, whether such a demonstration is useful in approaching all of the sonnets. What does it all prove?

First of all, the various patterns overlap. One cannot say that a particular word, image, line, sentence, or quatrain functions structurally in the poem as a component of a particular pattern of sound, syntax, imagery, or logic and of no other. Future critics who do not expect to find one pattern predominant over the others—to find *a* structure for a sonnet—are less likely than their predecessors have been to feel that they have failed as critics and that Shakespeare has failed as a poet if they cannot find in a sonnet one pattern to which all others must be argued into auxiliary positions.

Secondly, I suggest that the demonstration of numerous coexistent schemes of organization in a single poem supports the thesis that a Shakespeare sonnet is "great and unobtrusive, a thing which enters into one's soul, and does not startle it or amaze it with itself but with its subject." Certainly, where no single rhetorical pattern dominates and any word or device participates simultaneously in several separate schemes of organization, no particular can distract the reader from the whole to the part, from the poem to the device. In short, the profusion of conflicting and overlapping schemes for division is so great as to make the experience of a part of the poem indivisible from the experience of the whole. I have culled the patterns one by one from sonnet 12 and described them as clearly as I could, but I cannot imagine any reader, even one fresh from this chapter, who could pick them all out as he read the poem. Each pattern is insistently defined in the poem, but, superimposed as they are one on another, the patterns obliterate each other from the reader's consciousness.

If it is granted that the patterns do not stand out from the poem and that even a meticulously gained awareness of their existence does not alter a reader's response, what, besides the negative value of being unobtrusive, do these patterns contribute to the poem? They all but destroy the possibility that anything can seem arbitrary. In sonnet 12, leaps in logic, changes of tone, subject matter, syntax, sentence length, rhythm, or sound pattern do not strike the reader as violent. Nothing that comes up in the sonnet is quite new; everything that is said is in one respect or another related to what came before. An awareness of the multiplicity of the designs to which a superficially new factor in a poem can be appropriate contributes one source for an explanation of the sense that the best of Shakespeare's sonnets give of rightness, inevitability, and incontrovertible truth.

At the beginning of this essay I said that a single poem was likely to suggest a relationship by diction or imagery or subject matter or physical proximity in the 1609 order to as many different other poems as it has elements. I said then too that it is not our sense of the disorder of the 1609 quarto that bewilders us but our sense of their order. I suggested that the uneasiness which the multiplicity of kinds of relationships among the sonnets brings to a reader of the sequence as a whole is mirrored within the individual sonnets by the similar multiplicity of kinds of relationships that I have now demonstrated in sonnet 12. The recurrence in the sequence of themes, situations, ideas, and images reinforces the sense inherent in the physical makeup of the 1609 quarto that the book, *Shakespeare's Sonnets,* is not an anthology but a single work of art. The sense that the sonnets belong together is very strong, but there are at least as many possible factors for demonstrating their interrelationship as there have been editors to rearrange them. At almost any given point in the sequence one senses the predominance of one of the different elements that appear and reappear in the sequence, and at that moment the sequence seems to cohere in the particular element that is then in sharp focus. A few lines or a few poems later, however, one experiences the same spurious sense of grasp but in the terms of an entirely other "key" to the whole. Such a vacillation is disquieting.

In the individual sonnets the multiplicity of patterns similarly gives a sense that the poem is an inevitable unity. However, as one reads through a Shakespeare sonnet, the different patterning factors come into focus and out of it constantly, rapidly, and almost imperceptibly, "each changing place with that which goes before." The mind of the reader is kept in constant motion; it is kept uneasy as it is made constantly aware of relationships among parts of the poem that are clear and firm but in an equally constant state of flux. The bulk of the remainder of this essay will be concerned with examining the causes and effects of fluidity of relationship within the Shakespeare sonnet. First, however, I will devote a chapter to a related phenomenon whose persistence in the sonnets has already been evident in this essay: the many manifestations of simultaneous unity and division.

Chapter 4

Unity and Division, Likeness and Difference

In the preface to *Lyrical Ballads* Wordsworth says that his limits will not permit him to enter upon "the various causes upon which the pleasure received from metrical language depends," but in passing he states very well a principle that most critics before and after him have stated or assumed:

> Among the chief of these causes is to be reckoned a principle which must be well known to those who have made any of the Arts the object of accurate reflection; namely, the pleasure which the mind derives from the perception of similitude in dissimilitude. This principle is the great spring of the activity of our minds, and their chief feeder. From this principle the direction of the sexual appetite, and all the passions connected with it, take their origin: it is the life of our ordinary conversation; and upon the accuracy with which similitude in dissimilitude, and dissimilitude in similitude are perceived, depend our taste and our moral feelings.

I suggest that simultaneous similitude and dissimilitude is akin in its effect to the simultaneous unification and division of which I have already noticed so many examples in Shakespeare's sonnets. Things that are alike belong together; things that are different belong apart.

In this chapter I propose to investigate the devices from

which these related effects are achieved in the sonnets. I mean ultimately to demonstrate that the suggestion of pulsation which is inherent in simultaneous unity and division, likeness and difference, is characteristic of Shakespeare's sonnets and manifests itself at every level of investigation, from the smallest phonetic detail to the situations described in the poems.

Most of the effects I will describe are not, of course, unique to Shakespeare's sonnets. For example, I have already said that the sonnet is at once a short, unified statement on a single theme and a form that can be differentiated from any fourteen-line rhymed poem only by the several kinds of formal division within the fourteen-line unit. That is as true of all sonnets as it is of Shakespeare's. What is unique is the number of different ways in which Shakespeare presents or suggests contrary but coexistent actions and states. What is unique is not that the sonnets contain paradoxes of substance and of style, but that the particular paradox of unification and division, likeness and difference, so permeates the sonnets as to be of their essence.

Phonetic Unity and Division

The smallest scale in which the sonnets exhibit the principle of simultaneous likeness and difference, unity and division, is phonetic. In talking about sonnet 12 I have already noticed some examples of pulsating alliteration: *i, o,* and *l* first separated, then together, in *I behold the violet; g* and *r* first together, and then separated, in *green all girded; b* and *r* in *bristly beard.* This particular phonetic construction is everywhere in the sonnets. Time after time in the sonnets a pair of sounds will come together and then pull apart. Of course, such constructions are common in everyday speech: "*f*ree *f*or all," "gi*lt* le*tt*ers," "*bl*ack *b*al*l*," "*d*i*r*t *r*oa*d*," "*s*ing-*s*ong," "*f*or you *f*rom. . . ." They go unnoticed in everyday speech, and they go unnoticed in the sonnets; but in the sonnets they appear in great quantity and in a context of numerous other rhetorical suggestions of contraction and expansion.

Although the persistent splitting apart and coming together of pairs of sounds provides an auxiliary undercurrent to the general uneasiness about relationship in the sonnets, it is not, obviously, a matter of prime importance. I therefore see no useful purpose in attempting a statistical analysis of the frequency with which the phenomenon occurs. Moreover, I doubt that the patience of either the writer or the reader could survive it. I also doubt that without a computer such an analysis could be anywhere near accurate. All I really want to indicate is that pulsating alliteration is very common in the sonnets and to that end I offer the token demonstration that follows.[1]

Sonnet 33 is a good example of contraction and expansion of phonetic particles operating in conjunction with other manifestations of unity and division. When I talked about octaves, I pointed out as an example of simultaneous unity and division the potential syntactical completeness of the first quatrain of sonnet 33 and the subsequent unification of the first eight lines by means of the additional verb *permit* in line 5. The first eight lines, containing the analogy, are at once separated from and joined with the application of the analogy in quatrain 3. There is again both unity and division between the first twelve lines and the summary moral statement of the couplet:

> Full many a glorious morning have I seen
> Flatter the mountain tops with sovereign eye,
> Kissing with golden face the meadows green,
> Gilding pale streams with heavenly alchemy;
> Anon permit the basest clouds to ride
> With ugly rack on his celestial face,
> And from the forlorn world his visage hide,

1. For some others, see Note 5 of the Appendix, pp. 199–206.

Stealing unseen to west with this disgrace:
Even so my sun one early morn did shine
With all-triumphant splendor on my brow;
But, out alack, he was but one hour mine,
The region cloud hath masked him from me now.
  Yet him for this my love no whit disdaineth;
  Suns of the world may stain when heaven's sun staineth.

A further sensation of things pulling apart and coming together is evoked in *f* and *l* sounds, first separated in *full* (line 1), then together in *flatter* (line 2). Hard *g* and *l* are first together in *glorious* (line 1), then separated by a long vowel sound in *golden* (line 3), then less widely separated by a shorter vowel sound in *gilding* (line 4). The pattern continues in *clouds* (line 5), where the sound of hard *c* and *l* resembles the *gl* sound of *glorious,* and where the *ld* sound of *golden* and *gilding* is split apart by the long vowel sound *ou.* The *gl* sound is again split in the syllabification of *ugly* (line 6); the combination of *l* plus dental is further split in *celestial* (line 6) and reunited in *world* (line 7). There are two other patterns in the phrase *from the forlorn world* in line 7: the *fr* sound of *from* is split apart in *forlorn,* and the sounds of *r* and *l,* syllabically split in *forlorn,* are united in *world.*

The sonnet as a whole is full of *n* sounds; *n* is a function of three of the rhyme-pairs.[2] The *n* sound also figures in a pattern of pulsating alliteration more subtle and more complicated than those in *fl, gl, ld,* and *fr.* Beginning in line 1 with *many,* where the two consonants are separated only by a short vowel, the sounds of *m* and *n* pull apart and come together throughout the sonnet. They pull apart in *morning*

2. Kökeritz *(Shakespeare's Pronunciation,* pp. 313–14) presents evidence that final *ing* in *Kissing* (line 3), *gilding* (line 4), and *Stealing* (line 8), would have been pronounced to rhyme with the final syllable of *mountain* (line 2). The concentration of *n* sounds would then have been even greater than is now perceptible. Kökeritz also provides a complete phonetic transcription of this sonnet (p. 347).

(line 1) and *mountain* (line 2), and farther apart in *meadows green* (line 3). The pattern appears chiasmically in the next few lines, where the two sounds are not only in reverse order but so widely separated as to make it more than usually difficult to be sure that it is not foolish to suggest that the continuation of the pattern in *m* and *n* could be perceptible to the ear: *gilding* [pronounced "gilden"] *pale streams* (line 4), *heavenly alchemy* (line 4), *Anon permit* (line 5), *and*[3] *from* (line 7). In the third quatrain and the couplet the *m* and *n* sounds continue, first coming closer together again in lines 9 through 11, then pulling apart at the beginning of line 12 and coming closer together in the last words of the quatrain. In the couplet *m* and *n* appear in combinations where they are at a mean distance from each other, neither far apart nor close together. The third quatrain and couplet of sonnet 33 follow; I have indicated the *m* and *n* sounds in italics:

> Eve*n* so *m*y su*n* o*n*e early *m*or*n* did shi*n*e
> With all-triu*m*pha*n*t sple*n*dor o*n* *m*y brow;
> But, out alack, he was but o*n*e hour *m*i*n*e,
> The regio*n* cloud hath *m*asked hi*m* fro*m* *m*e *n*ow.
> Yet hi*m* for this *m*y love *n*o whit disdai*n*eth;
> Su*n*s of the world *m*ay stai*n* whe*n* heave*n*'s su*n*
> stai*n*eth.[4]

ANTANACLASIS

There are countless other examples of pulsating alliteration in the sonnets, but to spend longer on it would be to risk exaggerating its importance. I will have occasion to point out other instances of pulsating alliteration incidentally as I go

3. Probably pronounced without the final *d*, and sometimes spelled that way. See Kökeritz, p. 271.

4. Although the pulsation of *m* and *n* sounds runs through the whole poem, it is the only one of those I have described that does. As I have noted before, stylistic and substantial density and complication usually diminish after the second quatrain of a sonnet.

on to examine the next of the related phenomena that I have grouped in this chapter: simultaneous parallelism and non-parallelism. For example, sonnet 89 presents both a striking example of pulsating alliteration *(forsake . . . for some,* line 1) and a good introduction to the persistent minor device of simultaneously emphasized parallelism and nonparallelism:

> Say that thou didst forsake me for some fault,
> And I will comment upon that offense;
> Speak of my lameness, and I straight will halt,
> Against thy reasons making no defense.
> Thou canst not, love, disgrace me half so ill,
> To set a form upon desirèd change,
> As I'll myself disgrace; knowing thy will,
> I will acquaintance strangle and look strange,
> Be absent from thy walks, and in my tongue
> Thy sweet belovèd name no more shall dwell,
> Lest I, too much profane, should do it wrong
> And haply of our old acquaintance tell.
> For thee, against myself I'll vow debate,
> For I must ne'er love him whom thou dost hate.

The verb *will* appears five times (twice in contracted form) in this sonnet. At the end of line 7, following and immediately followed by uses of *will* as a verb, is *will* the noun. The figure, antanaclasis (in which a repeated word shifts from one to another of its meanings), is a common one: *To England will I steal, and there I'll steal (Henry V,* V.1.92). Its use in the sonnets is remarkable only because Shakespeare uses it both constantly and with minimal effect. Antanaclasis is ordinarily an ostentatious figure for making blatantly mechanical puns. Puttenham exemplifies antanaclasis or "the Rebound, alluding to the tennis ball which being smitten with the racket rebounds back again," like this:

> Or as we once sported upon a country fellow who came to runne for the best game, and was by his occupation a

dyer and had very bigge swelling legges.

He is but course to runne a course,
Whose shanks are bigger than his thye:
Yet is his lucke a little worse,
That often dyes before he dye.[5]

Sister Miriam Joseph gives numerous examples from the plays of Shakespeare's similarly crude use of the crude figure.[6]

In sonnets 135 and 136, the "will" sonnets, Shakespeare uses antanaclasis with all the ostentation that the figure invites; he plays there in rapid succession on the verb *will,* the abstract noun *will,* and the proper noun *Will.* Elsewhere in the sonnets, however, his use of the figure is similar to the play on *will* in sonnet 89, where it has, as far as I know, quite reasonably gone without critical comment. The antanaclasis in *As I'll myself disgrace; knowing thy will,/I will acquaintance strangle* . . . is not likely to impinge at all on the reader's consciousness. Puttenham recommends antanaclasis among the other figures of repetition because "your figure that worketh by iteration or repetition of one word or clause doth much to alter and affect the eare and also the mynde of the hearer" (p. 198). I assume from his examples that by "affect the mynde" Puttenham means to say that the figure sustains the sense, points up the argument, and "maketh your information no lesse plausible to the minde than to the eare" (p. 197). Certainly an antanaclasis that is not consciously heard does not affect the mind in Puttenham's sense. On the other hand, the play on *will* in 89 could not be described as Puttenham describes useless repetitions:

> These repetitions be not figurative but phantastical, for a figure is ever used to a purpose, either of beautie or

5. Puttenham, *The Arte of English Poesie . . .* , ed. Gladys Doidge Willcock and Alice Walker (Cambridge, Eng., 1936), p. 207.

6. Sister Miriam Joseph, C.S.C., *Shakespeare's Use of the Arts of Language* (New York, 1947), pp. 165–66.

> of efficacie: and these last recited be to no purpose, for neither can ye say that it urges affection, nor that it beautifieth or enforceth the sense, nor hath any other subtilitie in it, and therefore is a very foolish impertinency of speech and not a figure. (p. 202)

There *is* a "subtilitie" in the play on *will* in sonnet 89. The simultaneous likeness and difference of antanaclasis goes unnoticed. The play on *will* is of no substantial importance; the difference between the verb and the noun does not enforce the sense. But the device is, I think, effective. On its minute scale insignificant antanaclasis, like pulsating alliteration, evokes a sense of insecurity, of flux, of motion. The incidental play on *will* demands an incidental and presumably unconscious adjustment by the reader. It tickles the reader's mind, without diverting his attention.

The same is true of the equally impertinent play on *for* in the couplet of the same sonnet:

> For thee, against myself I'll vow debate,
> For I must ne'er love him whom thou dost hate.

Here the insignificant play on unimportant words is accentuated by anaphora. Both the likeness and the difference between the prepositional and conjunctive uses of *for* are emphasized, but the words and the construction are so common and the syntax is so simple that no editor or commentator has thought the device worth mentioning. After all, this kind of antanaclasis happens every day in conversation: "go to town to shop," "went with . . . to fight with." Still, in the sonnets there is so much of this inconsequential play on little words that denote relationship that, even though this sentence contains a play on *that* that no sane critic could consider worthy of notice, the effect of equally insignificant byplay on a series of poems concerned with unsteady relationships is worth some consideration.

The word *for* appears more than once in forty-eight of the sonnets. Nine of these are sonnets in which one meaning of *for* is consistent throughout (11, 32, 42, 44, 70, 85, 106, 113, 152); in four of these the substantial relevance of the repetition is underscored by anaphora in *for* (44.3, 7; 70.2, 7; 113.5, 9; 152.7, 9, 13). The rest of the time that Shakespeare repeats the word *for* in a sonnet, he does not repeat it in its preceding sense. Most such instances of incidental antanaclasis must be discounted, even in this context, because the repetitions are widely separated in the sonnet and cannot be thought to function even on the unconscious of the reader.[7] In an even half of the sonnets where *for* is repeated, however, the irrelevant antanaclasis demands that the reader make a slight adjustment from the syntactical pattern he expects.[8] Here, for example, are four other instances of antanaclasis in *for* in which, as in the couplet of 89, simultaneous parallelism and nonparallelism are stressed by anaphora:

> For shame, deny that thou bear'st love to any
> Who for thyself art so unprovident:
> Grant, if thou wilt, thou art beloved of many,
> But that thou none lov'st is most evident;
> For thou art so possessed with murd'rous hate (10.1–5)

7. For example, *for* appears in the second and thirteenth lines of sonnets 104, 133, and 147. In 104 it is a conjunction introducing a reason in line 2 and a preposition meaning "on account of" in line 13. In 133.2 it is the preposition, and in 133.13 it it the conjunction. In 147.2 it means "with a desire of," and in 147.13 it means "because." Although I am making extraordinary claims for powers of minor fluctuations of sound and meaning, a reader would have to have an ear as good as, and probably better than, Shakespeare's to be affected by a play on insubstantial monosyllables that are not pointed up by anaphora and are separated from each other by ten full lines.

8. Sonnets 6.7,8; 10.1,2,5; 20.9,13; 24.5,9; 25.4,8,9,12; 27.2,5; 38.4,7; 40.5,6; 48.14; 54.4,9; 61.12,13; 62.3,7,13; 72.4,6,10,13; 87.5,6; 88.10,14; 89.13,14; 92.2,4; 99.4,6; 109.12,13; 111.1,3; 120.2,5; 134.6,7; 136.11,14; 154.12,13. Note also similarly unostentatious word plays like 23.5 *for fear . . . forget),* 89.1 *(forsake . . . for some),* and 124.2 *(for Fortune's).*

. . . too excellent
For every vulgar paper to rehearse?
O, give thyself the thanks if aught in me
Worthy perusal stand against thy sight,
For who's so dumb that cannot write to thee (38.3–7)

And for this sin there is no remedy,
It is so grounded inward in my heart.
Methinks no face so gracious is as mine,
No shape so true, no truth of such account,
And for myself mine own worth do define (62.3–7)[9]

But do thy worst to steal thyself away,
For term of life thou art assurèd mine,
And life no longer than thy love will stay,
For it depends upon that love of thine. (92.1–4)

The commonest play on *for* is an alternation between its prepositional and conjunctional usages. Besides those already quoted, there are fourteen such alternations, of which the following are good examples:

For truth proves thievish for a prize so dear. (48.14)

To leave for nothing all thy sum of good;
For nothing this wide universe I call (109.12–13)[10]

In addition to those cited among the examples of anaphora and antanaclasis in combination, there are six poems in

9. In line 3 the preposition *for* indicates appropriation *(OED,* A.13.c). In line 7 it seems to indicate advantage *(OED,* A.16). There have been a lot of fruitless and needless efforts to emend *for* in line 7 (See Rollins, *Variorum, 1,* 165–66). The line makes good sense as it stands, and, in view of the word play effected by the repetition of *for myself* in line thirteen (where *for* indicates substitution: *OED,* A.5), I see no grounds for emendation.

10. The other examples are 24.5,9; 25.4,8,9,12, where three different prepositional uses of *for* coexist with the conjunction in line 9; 27.2,5; 40.5,6; 54.4,9; 72.4,6,10,13; 87.5,6; 88.10,14; 92.2,4; 120.2,5; 134.6,7; 136.11, 14.

which antanaclasis is evoked in differing prepositional uses of *for;* for example, here are lines 7 and 8 of sonnet 6:

> That's for thyself to breed another thee,
> Or ten times happier be it ten for one.[11]

If this inconsequential word play were peculiar to the word *for,* it would not be even the minor factor it is in the total effect of the sonnets. In fact, however, the same sort of simultaneous likeness and difference is evoked in all the other common prepositions and conjunctions.[12]

The next chapter will deal with matters closely related to antanaclasis in prepositions and conjunctions. For now, I will move on from these minutiae to demonstrate the broader aspects of simultaneous unity and division, likeness and difference, parallelism and nonparallelism in the sonnets. As I have suggested previously, most of the phenomena I have discussed function to accentuate both unity and division in a sonnet. I propose, therefore, to examine one sonnet in all of its aspects.

Paradoxical Style

Sonnet 53 is one of the poems listed in Chapter 2 as having no perceptible octave. That is to say, the reader does not sense, as he finishes line 8 and begins line 9, that he is moving from a unified and clearly defined logical or rhetorical stage in the poem to another. In sonnet 53 there is a pattern of syntactical units that goes 2, 2, 2, 2, 4, 2. Expressed numerically as it is here, the break between the four two-line units and the syntactically unified third quatrain suggests that a distinction between the first two quatrains and the third might be

11. The other five examples are 20.9,13; 61.12,13; 99.4,6; 111.1,3; and 154.12,13.

12. Shakespeare's play on *with* and *but* in the sonnets is described in Note 6 of the Appendix, which also gives some examples of his uses of *of, to, so,* and *in* (pp. 204–07).

perceptible as the poem is read. A reading of the poem belies the suggestion:

> What is your substance, whereof are you made,
> That millions of strange shadows on you tend?
> Since every one hath, every one, one shade,
> And you, but one, can every shadow lend.
> Describe Adonis, and the counterfeit
> Is poorly imitated after you.
> On Helen's cheek all art of beauty set,
> And you in Grecian tires are painted new.
> Speak of the spring and foison of the year:
> The one doth shadow of your beauty show,
> The other as your bounty doth appear,
> And you in every blessèd shape we know.
> In all external grace you have some part,
> But you like none, none you, for constant heart.

The reader has no sense of the first two quatrains as a self-contained unit and, for simple mechanical reasons, can have none. For one thing, there is nothing until he is well into quatrain 3 to show the reader that the pattern of two-line units will not continue. On the contrary, the grammatical parallel between *Speak of the spring and foison*—the imperative with which line 9 begins—and the two imperatives in line 5 and 7 is an apparent signal that, as the spring and foison of the year are in substantial apposition to Adonis and Helen, the syntactical pattern of examples in two-line units will be continued along with the giving of the examples themselves.

The numerical pattern 2, 2, 2, 2, 4, 2 does, however, function in the effect of the poem. The rhythm of the syntactical pattern gives rhetorical conviction to the logical pattern, which, for the first eight lines, is this: a two-line sentence stating the problem in a question (lines 1–2), a two-line sentence justifying puzzlement (lines 3–4), a two-line sentence exemplifying the puzzling nature of the beloved (lines 5–6), another two-line sentence with another example of the same thing (lines 7–8). Lines 9 through 12 are a single sentence. Like the previous two sentences, it provides exemplification of the problem, and, like them, it is a command. Unlike the preceding pair of sentences, the imperative in this sentence has two objects: *the spring and foison*—lumped together in line 9, given a line each in the next two lines, and forgotten in the broad generalization *And you in every blessèd shape we know* (line 12). The progress of the three quatrains is from one element in the initial paradox to the other, from *your substance* to *millions of strange shadows*—from the individual to the universal. Adonis and Helen, the first two examples, are particular individuals other than the beloved. The next example is larger not only in that *spring* and *foison* are seasons and thus big, general, and vague, but also in that the simple mechanics of expression are also larger: *spring* and *foison,* taken together in line 9, are grammatically double the size of *Adonis* in line 5 and of *Helen* in line 7. At the same time, the expansion of the syntactical unit from two lines in the first two quatrains to four in the third sustains the growing expansiveness of the examples by which in line 12 the reader is brought to accept the syntactical appendage *And you in every blessèd shape we know* as a demonstrated fact, capable of being further summarized and commented on in the couplet.

The 2, 2, 2, 2, 4, 2 pattern is all but unnoticeable. It does its job, but it is completely unobtrusive. This is not, I think, simply because a reader is unlikely to take conscious notice of sentence lengths, but because the syntactical pattern is only one of several that, like those I have demonstrated in sonnet 12, emerge and vanish as the reader moves through the poem. One of the commonest is an effective sense of the separate identity of the first two lines, by which, in Lewis' terms, a 2, 12 or 2, 10, 2 pattern is superimposed on the 4, 4, 4, 2 pattern of the formal structure and on whatever other patterns are also in the poem. As the examples in Note 4 of the Appendix demonstrate, the separate unity of the first two lines may be logical, rhythmic, phonetic, or metaphoric; it may also result from a combination of those factors. In sonnet 53 the first two lines are a question to which the next ten lines are not an answer but a demonstration of the validity of the lover's puzzlement. The couplet, formally separated by its rhymes from the body of the poem, accepts the demonstrated situation and goes on to an additional statement. As the couplet is cut off by rhyme and antimetabole in *you like none, none you* from the poem at the end, so the first two lines are less firmly and by subtler means cut off at the beginning:

> What is your substance, whereof are you made,
> That millions of strange shadows on you tend?

These lines do not, of course, rhyme, but they are given a separable identity both by the traditional pairing of *shadows* and *substance* and by assonance. The fifth syllable of line 2, *strange,* is a mutation with additions of the sounds of *stance,* the fifth syllable of line 1. The last unaccented syllable of each line is the same word, *you,* giving a rhymelike unity to the rhythmically identical *whereof are you made* and *shadows on you tend.*

If the separate identity of the first two lines were a unique characteristic of sonnet 53, the trouble I take about it here would hardly be justified outside of an elaborate dissection of this particular sonnet. The phenomenon, however, is common in the sonnets and, more important, it is, like everything else I have talked about, a manifestation of the particular kind of stylistic effect for which I am making a general case. The pattern of the rhyme scheme, by which the first two lines of an English sonnet are pulled apart, is countered by unifying phonetic parallels in the first two lines of 53. That conflict is a small and unimportant manifestation of the simultaneous unification and division that is inherent in the sonnet form itself and in the simultaneous existence in many of Shakespeare's sonnets of an octave and the three-quatrain pattern. Moreover, the separate identity of lines 1 and 2 is like the phenomena already discussed in that it is a temporary identity and demands that the reader see the lines first as a unit, then as half of the first quatrain, and ultimately as an element of the unified and undivided whole that the summary effect of the couplet makes of the first twelve lines. Thus the temporary identity of the first two lines makes one more demand for redefinition of the units of the poem; it is one more demand for intellectual commitment from the reader; it is one more strange shadow to keep the reader's mind in motion.

There are many poems that have phonetically unified, final-sounding opening lines; they are described in Note 4 of the Appendix. Although the phonetic patterns there demonstrated are not found exclusively in the first two lines, they are more common in the first two lines than elsewhere. They are also more important there than elsewhere because they provide a phonetic unit before the formal poetic unit, the quatrain, is established. This "pre-rhyme" effect gives one more kind of pattern, one more fleeting structural unit, to poems that, as has been and will be demonstrated, are peculiarly crowded with conflicting patterns otherwise.

In addition to the 4, 4, 4, 2 pattern of the rhyme scheme, the 2, 2, 2, 2, 4, 2 pattern of syntactical units, and the 2, 10, 2 pattern suggested by the phonetic unity of the first two lines, there is also a 4, 8, 2 pattern in sonnet 53. The second and third quatrains are three imperative sentences, and in their grammatical likeness they come together into a unit which, as one reads through the poem, sets the first quatrain and the couplet apart from them. The three imperatives evoke a sense of what could be called an internal octave in much the same way that in 22, 23, 24, and 27 the first two quatrains are set apart from the third by a change in line 9 from declarative to imperative.[13]

All of these patterns coexist with the formal pattern 4, 4, 4, 2. My description might suggest that the identity of the quatrains is obliterated by the other patterns. Obviously it is not. A rhyme scheme is a powerful thing, particularly in a poem like this, where syntactical units do not cross the lines of formal division. In this case, moreover, the quatrain pattern is reinforced by anaphora in *And you,* the phrase with which the fourth line of each quatrain begins. The second line of the couplet continues the pattern in a modified form: *But you like none, none you, for constant heart.* Where the pattern of repeated words emphasizes the formal pattern in the quatrains, the echo of that pattern in the couplet tends to diminish the reader's sense of the overall formal pattern by suggesting equality between the couplet and each of the three quatrains. Wherever one looks in this sonnet, unifying elements balance dividing elements: likenesses and differences coexist.

The four lines that begin in a conjunction plus *you* are to that extent similar one to another, but Shakespeare makes no effort to heighten that similarity syntactically. Throughout the sonnets Shakespeare regularly avoids opportunities to add syntactical parallelism to lines or phrases that are similar in some other respect.[14] Sonnet 53 is not unusually conspicuous among the sonnets for the numerousness of its partially parallel constructions, but its second quatrain is particularly well suited as a basis for a discussion of the effective signifi-

13. The 4, 8, 2 pattern is generally established by the same sort of elements that establish the octave in the 8, 4, 2 pattern discussed in Chapter 2. See Note 7 of the Appendix, pp. 207–09, for additional examples of sonnets in which quatrains 2 and 3 are in one or more respects a distinct eight-line entity.

14. Partial parallelism is so common in the sonnets that its detailed exemplification is impractical and probably unnecessary. I will point out examples incidentally as I go along.

cance of the phenomenon and of its relation to a style that is a vehicle for paradoxes:

Describe Adonis, and the counterfeit
Is poorly imitated after you.
On Helen's cheek all art of beauty set,
And you in Grecian tires are painted new.

An easy explanation for the nonparallel construction of *Describe Adonis, and the counterfeit* and *On Helen's cheek all art of beauty set* is that the change in construction puts *set* at the end of the line, where it will satisfy the poet's need of a rhyme for *counterfeit*. That explanation appeals strongly to common sense and I see no need to reject it. I am not, after all, attempting to say that Shakespeare purposefully set out to counter the parallel elements in his poems with nonparallel elements. I mean only to point out the presence of such simultaneously parallel and nonparallel verses as these and to comment on their contribution to the overall effect of the finished product. Although it would be preposterous to suggest that Shakespeare set out to undercut parallelism in the sonnets, he went to no trouble to perfect it. In the present lines, even if we say that Shakespeare lacked sufficient ingenuity to find another rhyme for *counterfeit*, that he had to put his second imperative verb at the end of the sentence, and that he was thus prevented by the nature of the verb *set* from making *Helen* the direct object of the second imperative as *Adonis* is of the first, we must still admit that, had Shakespeare cared at all for the easy rhetorical value of syntactical parallelism, he had no need to introduce *Helen's cheek*. He could, if he had valued parallelism, have written some such line as "On Helen all the art of beauty set," and salvaged some grammatical parallelism between *Adonis* and *Helen* by making *Helen* the object, although indirect, of *set*.

Whatever the reason that this quatrain is as it is, there is an aesthetic value in the lines as they are that is superior to whatever surface glitter might have been had from either a simple or a chiasmic balancing of the two sentences. As they are, these lines draw the reader's attention not to themselves but to their substance. The two lines on Helen are in substantial apposition to the two lines on Adonis; Helen and Adonis are two examples of the same thing. The lines on Helen, however, cannot be read blandly through as more of the same. One cannot read these lines as, for example, one reads classical or medieval lists of trees, listening to the sounds, admiring the pictures, casually picking up the substance, but with as little intellectual commitment as one might make in walking across a real orchard. The unostentatious and regular absence of easy parallelism throughout the sonnets prevents a reader from being lulled or from relaxing. The change in the Helen lines of every grammatical construction in the Adonis lines gives some small part of the urgency of the first quatrain to the second, which might otherwise have relaxed into the simple hyperbole of courtly compliment. The small complication that a change of grammatical construction provides brings with it from the first quatrain genuine bewilderment at the miraculous nature of the beloved. That small complication also makes a demand on the reader. Like the demand that the reader make small but constant redefinitions of the nature of the units of the poems, the lack of grammatical parallelism in the Adonis-Helen quatrain is an unnoticeable, unimportant, but definite demand for the commitment of the reader's intellect to the substance of the poem before him.

One point more, and that the most obvious, is still to be made about the simultaneous parallelism and nonparallelism of this quatrain. The likeness between Adonis and Helen is immediately apparent. They are both figures of perfect beauty and, in a sequence where mythological references are notably rare, they are both from classical mythology. The difference between them is equally obvious: Adonis is male and Helen is female. Here, in a moderated form and incidental to the substance of the poem as a whole, is the essence of the master-mistress paradox from which the bawdy fun of sonnet 20 is contrived. The likeness between the open, self-conscious paradox central to sonnet 20 and the subdued, barely noticeable paradox in the equation of Adonis and Helen provides sorely needed assistance in making a point that probably cannot be made with scientific clarity and is hard to make at all: that, as the substance of the sonnets is paradox, so the style is paradoxical[15]—a thesis which everything I have so far said about the style of the sonnets and everything I will say goes to support.

Clearly, what I mean by a paradoxical style is central to this essay, but it is difficult to make that meaning clear without either overstating it and thus distorting the essay into an explanation of its author's ingenuity, or understating it and having "paradoxical style" give no more to the essay than the dubious ornament of a vaguely pleasing but generally hollow catch phrase. Clarification of the phrase depends, I think, upon the distinction between a paradox and the situation that evoked it. There is the same difference between the paradox of sonnet 20 and the experience of reading the Adonis-Helen quatrain. A paradox is comforting. It is the *statement* of a condition opposed to common sense; it is that condition codified, given form, brought back into the grasp of common sense, where it delights us not just because of its oddness and contrariness but also because, in the act of stating it, its oddness and contrariness is absorbed, albeit as an alien, into the world of common sense. A paradox is a miniature dilemma labeled and caged in a zoo. Recognizing a paradoxical condition alleviates the dismay we feel when things do not correspond to the patterns we assume for them or to the names we have for them, but before the paradox is stated

15. On the whole subject of Renaissance paradox, see Rosalie L. Colie, *Paradoxia Epidemica* (Princeton, 1966), a splendid book.

our dilemma is real. The dilemma can be of any size, from that of Oedipus to that of a person working his way to the realization that the English horn is a French woodwind. A paradoxical situation makes us uneasy about our competence to deal with matters in which we expect no difficulties. It puts us off balance.

I take the time to labor the distinction between our response to a paradox and our response to a paradoxical situation, because I think it is the essential distinction between Shakespeare's sonnets and other poems of similar substance. If I were to say that sonnet 53 is a tissue of paradoxes, I doubt that any reader of the poem would object. Even granting that an audience conditioned to modern criticism is likely to assent blandly to any statement with the phrase *tissue of* in it, it is strange that the truth of this statement should be so easy to accept and so hard to demonstrate. Except for the second sentence *(Since every one hath, every one, one shade, / And you, but one, can every shadow lend),* there is no paradox in the poem that can be satisfactorily restated in prose, and even that exception is doubtful.

As a paraphrase of the second sentence, the following statement is more satisfying than it should be: "one person can have only one shadow; you have many shadows." The paraphrase is a paradox, a paradoxical situation described, pinned down, understood as inexplicable. My paraphrase, like most paradoxes, gives solidity to the situation it describes by means of extralogical form: the verb *have* is repeated in the contrasting clauses; *one,* repeated in the first clause, is set against *many* in the second; *shadows,* the last word of the second clause, balances *shadow,* the last word of the first, and, paired as they are, the singular form and the plural form of the same word capsule the paradoxical situation so that it is an acceptably defined exception within the pale of human logic.

The lines themselves, on the other hand, haven't the simplicity of form or the simplicity of meaning of the paraphrase.

To take meaning first, here is an explication of lines 2 through 4 given in 1918 by C. K. Pooler in his Arden edition of the sonnets: the lines, he says, are

> based on a pun: shadow (shade l.3) is (1) the silhouette formed by a body that intercepts the sun's rays; (2) a picture, reflection, or symbol. 'Tend' means Attend, follow as a servant, and is strictly appropriate to 'shadow' only in the first sense, though shadow is here used in the second. . . . All men have one shadow each, in the first sense; you being only one can yet cast many shadows, in the second sense; for everything good and beautiful is either a representation of you or a symbol of your merits.

Pooler achieves the comfort of mastery over these lines not by composing their substance into a paradox but by analyzing them into submission to human understanding. He, too, oversimplifies: a third meaning of *shade* and *shadow* also functions in the first quatrain. Where the substance of a being is in doubt, there is a strong probability that that being is supernatural. The very idea of millions of strange shadows sounds supernatural, and the idea that these shadows tend, "follow as a servant," the being whose nature is under consideration brings with it suggestions of occult practices in which spirits dance attendance on a witch or magician. Line 3, of course, puts to rest any such suggestions by implying that *shadows* in line 2 meant not spirits but "silhouettes formed by a body that intercepts the sun's rays." However, the word *shadow* is replaced by the word *shade,* the most sinister of its synonyms and the one best calculated to reinforce the occult suggestions that the rest of the line has suppressed. Pooler's paraphrase is a satisfying critical performance, but once add my suggestions about ghosts to it and the paraphrase becomes so complicated that it defeats its own purpose. One is again in doubt what it is that these lines say and how it is that that is said.

Pooler's explication is formally reinforced by the carefully numbered meanings of *shadow*. My statement of lines 3 and 4 as a paradox (which, by the way, is valid even though Pooler's equally valid paraphrase explains it away) has a similar formal substance from its repetition of key words and its parallel clause structure. Both Pooler's analysis and my paradox have a formal solidity that makes them mentally graspable. They are defined, static; their internal dynamics are fixed; they are like physical things. What about the lines themselves?

> What is your substance, whereof are you made,
> That millions of strange shadows on you tend?
> Since every one hath, every one, one shade,
> And you, but one, can every shadow lend.

Obviously, the quatrain has formal integrity in its completed rhyme pattern, but there is something else about the quatrain that gives it the firmness of a paradox or an analysis. The words *one* and *every* are repeated much as *shadow* is in my paradox, but, although they present a complication and define it, that complication is gratuitous. The lines as they are sound like a paradox; the play on *every* and *one* gives a paradox-like solidity of form to "everybody, each person, hath one shade and you, a single individual, can every shadow lend." But the machinery of formal paradox is not applied to the paradoxical condition. The lines sound like a paradox, a petrified dilemma, but they are not. The dilemma is still active. There are three meanings of *shadow* in the quatrain, and as the reader moves from word to word, his mind jumps from one pattern of understanding to another; the jumps are small ones, but there are many of them. The reader's mind is in the state of constant motion appropriate not to paradoxes or poems but to the actual experience of a paradoxical situation.

Look at the syntactical structure of the quatrain: two two-line sentences. The first is a question, the second a statement. The word *since* indicates a logical relationship between them;

but what is that relationship, and how many mental steps are required to complete it? It takes a fraction of a second to see that the logical function of *since* is to introduce a justification for asking the question, but all the work of filling in the gap is done by the reader. When he comes to *shade* at the end of line 3, the reader, presented with the rhyme word—emotionally incontrovertible evidence of appropriateness—has to cast off the suggestions of ghosts and spirits and select for himself the one meaning for *shade* that line 3 can admit.

At the end of line 4, *lend* certainly sounds meaningful; it completes the sentence and the rhyme pattern, but what does it mean? No reader who isn't under an obligation to produce an explication is likely to stop and wonder what *lend* means; its meaning is clear enough, but what is it? Schmidt's *Shakespeare-Lexicon* defines the present use of *lend* as a variation on "to afford, to grant, to admit to use for another's benefit," and says, "*Peculiarly* = to cast: *the mild glance that sly Ulysses lent,* Lucr. 1399. *you, but one, can every shadow lend.* Sonn. 53, 4 (forming the rhyme in both passages)." Schmidt is perfectly right. The only thing one can reasonably expect the possessor of a shadow to do with it is to cast it. His implied further argument is also valid enough as far as it goes. Because *lend* is the rhyme word, two different schemes of organization sustain its appropriateness: the meaning, "cast," is put upon it by the reader's expectation that the missing verb in the syntactical pattern "you . . . a shadow" will be "cast"; the sound, "lend," is appropriate to the formal phonetic pattern of the quatrain. In combination, the two organizations make the word *lend* into a synonym for "cast" that rhymes with *tend.*

If Schmidt was right in 1875, why in his edition of 1881 should Dowden have glossed line 4 thus: "You, although but one person, can give off all manner of shadowy images?" Dowden's "give off" does not completely contradict Schmidt's "cast," but the Dowden paraphrase does omit the suggested description of the physical relationship between the "body that intercepts the sun's rays" and the silhouette that it forms. Dowden's "shadowy images" carry occult suggestions appropriate to the preceding lines, and "images" makes line 4 a fitting antecedent to the quatrain on portrait drawing that follows, but since it denies the pertinence of the simple process of casting a shadow, it does not properly describe what line 4 says to a reader immediately after he reads line 3 and before he reads line 5.

The same kind of objection applies to a new and eminently reasonable reading of *And you, but one, can every shadow lend,* offered in a gloss by Alfred Harbage in The Pelican Shakespeare edition of the sonnets: "each 'shadow' can reflect but one of your excellences (with 'you' the object of 'lend')." The substitution in this gloss of *reflect* for *lend* makes line 4 a logically fitting antecedent to the next eight lines, in which it is the shadows who are the actors. The difficulty in taking the syntax of line 4 as inverted is that a reading that makes *shadow* the lender also inverts the reader's probable view of the relationship in the first three lines between an object and its shadow. There are two reasonable ways of thinking about the relationship of an object and its shadow: either one thinks of the object as the doer and its action as casting the shadow, or else one thinks of the shadow as the doer and its action as imitating the shape of the object. Lines 5 through 12 are concerned with the nature and potential of shadows, but lines 1 through 3 are concerned with the nature and potential of the object upon which the strange shadows tend. It is hard to deny the validity of the impression common to earlier editors that, as he reads the first three lines, a reader thinks of the person to whom the poem speaks as a man with a great many shadows—that is, of a great many silhouettes formed by a single body that intercepts the sun's rays. A reader who does not know what the second quatrain will say cannot, I think, be expected to take *you* at the beginning of line 4 as the object of the verb that is still to come. Only when he reaches *lend* does he know that the syntactical pattern suitable to the equally appropriate "you can shadows cast" does not make clear sense when the verb is *lend*. By glossing line 4 as he does, Harbage, who in addition glosses *strange shadows* as "foreign shades (Venus, Adonis, etc.)," restricts the sense of the first quatrain to the terms of the last two.

Actually, all the glosses I have cited are right. What happens as the reader moves through the poem is that the lines that follow quatrain 1 change its terms. A given word in the sonnet is likely to be sharply separated from one scheme of coherence and integral to another: *lend,* for example, breaks from the scheme in which the reader expected "cast," is integral to the rhyme scheme, and comes to cohere with the terms of the following quatrains. In the next chapter I will take up fluid frames of reference in detail. For my purposes here, it suffices to say that words that are simultaneously appropriate to one frame of reference and inappropriate to another provide additional manifestations of simultaneous unity and division in the sonnets.

Unity and Division as a Theme

The largest scale in which simultaneous unity and division, likeness and difference, are present in the sonnets is thematic. The subject is most obviously treated in sonnet 20: men are like men, and, to put it as crudely as Shakespeare does, they don't fit together; men are unlike women, and they do fit together. The idea of simultaneous unity and division and ideas related to it are almost as pervasive in the substance of the sonnets as in their style.

The substance of sonnet 53 is an inquiry to determine whether the nature of the beloved is single and unified or multiple and divisible.

The first seventeen sonnets play constantly on singleness and on the possibility of true possession of one's self by giving up oneself to marital union.[16]

16. See particularly sonnet 8, whose metaphor is harmony in music, *being many, seeming one.*

Sonnets 27 *(Weary with toil, I haste me to my bed)* and 28 *(How can I then return in happy plight)* are concerned with a physical journey, carrying the lover away from the beloved, and a mental journey, carrying him back.

Sonnet 35 *(No more be grieved at that which thou hast done)* concerns itself with civil war within the lover, and 139 *(O, call me not to justify the wrong)* demonstrates it.

Sonnets 44 *(If the dull substance of my flesh were thought)* and 45 *(The other two, slight air and purging fire)* play on the unity and division of the four elements in a human body and personality; 46 *(Mine eye and heart are at a mortal war)* and 47 *(Betwixt mine eye and heart a league is took)* present parts of the body as distinct entities capable of conflict among themselves.[17]

Sonnet 36 begins with a direct statement of one variation on the paradox of simultaneous unity and division and ends with another:

> Let me confess that we two must be twain
> Although our undivided loves are one:
> So shall those blots that do with me remain,
> Without thy help by me be borne alone.
> In our two loves there is but one respect,
> Though in our lives a separable spite,
> Which though it alter not love's sole effect,
> Yet doth it steal sweet hours from love's delight.
> I may not evermore acknowledge thee,
> Lest my bewailèd guilt should do thee shame;
> Nor thou with public kindness honor me
> Unless thou take that honor from thy name:
>   But do not so; I love thee in such sort
>   As, thou being mine, mine is thy good report.

This sonnet rests on the Neoplatonic commonplaces that the lover and the beloved are one and that the lover becomes the

17. See also sonnets 24 and 113.

beloved. The stylistically complicated investigation of the literal and the metaphoric validity of that unity begun in this sonnet continues in the sonnet that follows in the 1609 sequence. The discussion of the likeness and difference, unity and division, of the lover and the beloved is mirrored in the poem's construction, which presents a mind-boggling array of unifications of unlike things and divisions of similar ones:

As a decrepit father takes delight
To see his active child do deeds of youth,
So I, made lame by Fortune's dearest spite,
Take all my comfort of thy worth and truth. (37.1–4)

In line 1 the incompatibility of the states suggested by *decrepit* and *delight* is countered by the unification implied by the identity of their first syllables. Roughly the same is true of *To see* and *do deeds* in line 2. *Truth* at the end of line 4 completes the rhyme pattern and ends a sentence. It thus makes a clear division between this and the following quatrain. At the same time, however, *truth* functions in the phonetic unit *worth and truth,* which links itself by echo to the various *th* sounds in the first line of quatrain 2: *For whether beauty, birth, or wealth, or wit.* Additionally, *worth* rhymes with *birth,* a part of the unit *beauty, birth* evoked by alliteration. That unit is balanced by *or* against the similarly evoked *wealth or wit.* The balance of the two phrases is perfect rhythmically, but the second *or* in *beauty, birth, or wealth, or wit* denies the logical likeness of the two phrases. However, *wealth or wit* is also established as a unit by its likeness of sound, rhythm, construction, and position to the indisputably unified *worth and truth* at the end of the preceding line.

This maze of overlapping systems coexists with another pattern that also ties the two quatrains together: the *for* sounds in *Fortune*'s and *comfort* in the first quatrain are echoed in *For,* the first word of line 5. *Or,* the first word of line 6, rhymes with *For*. The word *or* appears five times in the first two lines of quatrain 2. Its significance and effect make a good emblem of the substance, spirit, and style of the poem:

> For whether beauty, birth, or wealth, or wit,
> Or any of these all, or all, or more,
> Intitled in thy par*ts* do crownè*d sit,*
> I make my love ingrafted to this *st*ore.
> *S*o then I am no*t* lame, poor, nor *despised*
> Whil*st* that thi*s* sha*d*ow *d*oth *s*uch *s*ub*st*ance give
> That I in thy abun*dance* am *s*uffi*ced*
> And by a part of all thy glory live.
> Look wha*t* *is* be*st,* that be*st* I wish in thee.
> Thi*s* wish I have; then *t*en *t*ime*s* happy me! (37.5–14)

The italics in the lines above indicate a contracting and expanding pattern in *s* plus dental that not only demonstrates unification and division in its own right but runs across, and thus counters, the division between quatrains 2 and 3. The pattern here also links these lines with the first three, where a pulsating pattern in *s* and *t/d* also appears: *As a decrepit, takes delight, To see, his active, deeds, So I made, Fortune's dearest spite.*

There is a play in sonnet 37 on *parts* (line 7), meaning "endowments," and *part* (line 12), meaning "portion of the whole."[18] An investigation that tests the literal truth of the unity between lovers is bound to discover that the evil endowments, qualities, fortune, and deeds of one lover are unfairly annexed to the other, and, conversely, that what is praiseworthy in one is usurped to the other. Sonnet 36 wrestles with the implications of the first, and sonnet 39 with those of the second:[19]

18. See also sonnet 69.

19. See also 62, and note the likeness and difference of *And for* in line 3 and *And for* in line 7.

O, how thy worth with manners may I sing
When thou art all the better part of me?
What can mine own praise to mine own self bring,
And what is't but mine own when I praise thee?
Even for this let us divided live
And our dear love lose name of single one,
That by this separation I may give
That due to thee which thou deserv'st alone.
O absence, what a torment wouldst thou prove
Were it not thy sour leisure gave sweet leave
To entertain the time with thoughts of love,
Which time and thoughts so sweetly doth deceive,
  And that thou teachest how to make one twain
  By praising him here who doth hence remain![20]

The difficulty of accepting as real in one frame of reference (here, the physical) a unity that exists in another (here, the spiritual) reaches its height in sonnet 42:

That thou hast her, it is not all my grief,
And yet it may be said I loved her dearly;
That she hath thee is of my wailing chief,
A loss in love that touches me more nearly.
Loving offenders, thus I will excuse ye:
Thou dost love her because thou know'st I love her,
And for my sake even so doth she abuse me,
Suff'ring my friend for my sake to approve her.
If I lose thee, my loss is my love's gain,
And losing her, my friend hath found that loss:
Both find each other, and I lose both twain,
And both for my sake lay on me this cross.
  But here's the joy: my friend and I are one;
  Sweet flattery! then she loves but me alone.[21]

20. Note the simultaneous likeness and difference of *That* in line 7 and *That* in line 8.

21. See also 40, 41, 133, and 134.

That the stylistic phenomena to which I have devoted the bulk of this chapter reflect one of the substantial concerns of the collection is probably sufficiently demonstrated not to require the many more examples I could give. Harmony of substance and style is a critical requirement of any work of art. What is remarkable here is that the style re-creates the experience of paradox, of coping with things in more than one frame of reference, not *for* but *in* the reader.

Chapter 5

Motion of the Mind

Child psychologists use a species of test in which a subject is given a pile of blocks and asked to divide it into smaller piles by type. In such a test there might be two dozen blocks: six cubes, six spheres, six cones, and six pyramids. Each of the six blocks in each of the four shapes would be a different color: one red cube, one blue, one yellow, one green, one orange, one purple; one red sphere, one blue, and so on. The red cube, the yellow, and the blue would each have a hole through it; the green, orange, and purple spheres would have holes, and so the yellow, purple, and green cubes, and the red, orange, and blue pyramids. The child can divide the blocks into two piles, those that have holes and those that don't, or he can set cubes and pyramids, which have angular corners, against spheres and cones, which have round, or he can divide cones and pyramids, which come to a point, from spheres and cubes, which don't. The child can divide the blocks into four groups by shape or six groups by color. The twenty-four blocks present several obvious qualities, each of which insistently suggests itself as a basis for classification, but none of which is preferable to any other. No system for grouping can be perfectly satisfying because the choice of a classifying factor demands that equally valid classifying factors be ignored.

As I suggested in an earlier chapter, the problem of a critic, when he senses that the 154 sonnets fall into groups, is similar to the problem of the child with the blocks. Although even a casual reading of the 1609 sequence will suggest a confusing number of different factors in which relationships among the sonnets are perceptible, no one of them dominates. The analogy of the blocks pertains also to the overlapping patterns that I have been exhibiting within the individual sonnets. Like the child taking the test, the reader of one of Shakespeare's sonnets is presented with a great many different ordering systems, none of which can reasonably be subordinated to any other. Both the blocks and a sonnet promise to display an ordering principle; both are troublesome because they overpay the promise.

I don't know which system of classification psychologists hope a child will choose, nor do I know whether any psychologist could in charity use a test so diabolically unsatisfying as mine, but I assume that children who are to be certified healthy in tests like this pick some one of the possible ways to divide the blocks and adhere to it until all the blocks are sorted. I also assume that a psychologist would fear for a child who started with a red cube, put a red pyramid next to it, put a blue pyramid with a hole in it next to that, then added a red cube with a hole in it next to that, then a green cone with a hole in it, then a yellow pyramid without a hole, and so on. I suggest that, in the process of reading a Shakespeare sonnet, the reader is very like the child so much in need of psychiatric care. As the child's mind moves into and out of different systems for perceiving relationships, so does the mind of Shakespeare's reader.

As I describe the sonnets, one would expect a reader to react to them in a way analogous to the reaction to the blocks of a possible third kind of child. Some children would probably give up trying to sort the blocks and just sit and cry with frustration. Looking analytically at the whole of a sonnet at once, a critic who does not follow the lead of the healthy child and choose one of the ordering principles of the sonnet, and deny the validity of the rest, will in his frustration probably reject the test as faulty: witness John Crowe Ransom. On the other hand, a casual reader whose first duty is not to analysis will ordinarily submit himself without complaint to the multiple systems of a Shakespeare sonnet: witness all the people who read Shakespeare's sonnets in hammocks in the summertime. The obvious fact that readers do not ordinarily react to the sonnets as they would to my pile of blocks casts doubt on the validity of the analogy and on the value of everything I have said in this essay. If multiplicity of patterns is as essential to the experience of a Shakespeare sonnet as I say it is, how does it happen that its reader is not driven mad? I will use this chapter and the chapter that follows to try to answer the question.

Time's Continual Haste—Sonnet 73

Is it because the minde is like the eye,
Through which it gathers by degrees—
Whose rayes reflect not, but spread outwardly:
Not seeing it self when other things it sees?
(John Davies, *Nosce Teipsum,* stanza 27)

The first step in answering my question is to face up to a truism that, understandably enough, is often forgotten in criticism: a poem is an experience in time. As the sonnets themselves insist, things look different at different times, *made more or less by* time's *continual haste.*

Of critics who have written about the sonnets, Arthur Mizener has come closest to describing the effects of a sonnet as it is read.[1] The occasion of Mizener's article is Ransom's "Shakespeare at Sonnets." By way of exemplifying the "curious results" of Ransom's arbitrarily narrow standards for verse, he says:

1. Mizener, *The Southern Review,* 5 (Spring 1940), 730–47.

For instance, Mr. Ransom says of the opening quatrain of sonnet LXXIII ("That time of year thou may'st in me behold") that the metaphor here is compounded and that "the two images cannot, in logical rigor, co-exist." It is true that *choirs* can be looked on as a metaphorical extension of *boughs,* but it is only by a pun that this extension can be maintained in the phrase "sweet birds" and Mr. Ransom cannot allow puns. Not even a pun, moreover, will bring "shake against the cold" within the limits of the figure, since by no stretch of the imagination can ruined cathedrals be thought of as shaking against the cold.

But it is plain before one reaches the end of this analysis that the success of Shakespeare's compound metaphor does not depend on the strict logic of its vehicle. His purpose is apparently to relate to his time of life, by some other means than the strictly logical elaboration of vehicle, both the boughs which shake against the cold and the bare ruined choirs. The age of Shakespeare's love, which is his life, is like the autumnal decline of nature, and thus natural, inevitable and, perhaps, only the prelude to a winter sleep rather than death; it is at the same time like the destruction of an artificial and man-made thing by man's wilful violence, and thus not inevitable, save as evil is inevitable, but regrettable as is the destruction of a building beautiful not only in itself but as a symbol. The fusion of these two meanings brought about by the compound metaphor is richer and finer than the sum of them which would be all the poem could offer if the two metaphors did not coexist. The fact that this fusion gives the vehicle, not logic, but an ingeniously devised air of being logical really deceives no one (least of all, I suspect, Mr. Ransom) into supposing that Shakespeare's lines depend for their power on the rigorous logic of the metaphor's vehicle. (pp. 731–32)

To the preceding paragraph Mizener offers the following note; it is the note that evokes my particular admiration for his article:

> The fusion is brought about by Shakespeare's slurring up from *boughs* to *choir*s and then down again. He gets up to choirs with the adjectival sequence "bare ruin'd"; "bare" modifies, primarily, *boughs,* and it is only through the diplomatic mediation of "ruin'd," primarily the modifier of *choirs,* that "bare" becomes intimate with *choirs.* He gets down again to *boughs* with the pun on "sweet birds"; in the phrase's secondary, euphemistic sense these are the choristers, but in its primary sense they are the quondam occupants of the now shivering boughs. (p. 732, n. 4)

This small paragraph, with its improbable critical vocabulary, describes better than anything I have read what actually happens in a Shakespeare sonnet and in the mind of its reader while he reads it. Mizener's description indirectly suggests a valuable insight into a defining peculiarity of Shakespeare's sonnets: as the line in which it appears is read, any given word is likely to slide imperceptibly from one system of relationship into another. The shifting of the contexts in which the reader takes the meaning of a given word is like the sonnet characteristics I have already discussed in that, in making the shifts from one context to another, the reader's mind is required constantly to act. The shifts from one pattern to another come in all sizes, from the major one that Mizener describes in sonnet 73 to the shift from one sound pattern to another within the first line of the same poem, where a pattern in *m (time of, mayst in me)* fuses into another kind of minor sound pattern when *me* rhymes with the first syllable of *behold.*[2] As in most of the other sonnets the shift-

2. Kökeritz confirms the rhyme. See his phonetic transcriptions of *me* and *behold* in *Coriolanus* V.3.167,173 *(Shakespeare's Pronunciation,* p. 362).

ing contexts of sonnet 73 function at the same time as all the other substantially gratuitous demands on the reader's intellectual energy. The following attempt at tracing a reader's mind through sonnet 73 will illustrate the shifting of contexts and the several other qualities whose effects are analogous to it.

Line 1 introduces and relates four elements: a season, the speaker, the opportunity to behold, and a beholder—*That time of year thou mayst in me behold.* The first two of these elements provide the substance of line 2, which straightforwardly identifies the season whose likeness is visible in the speaker: *When yellow leaves, or none, or few, do hang.* The reader is the beholder as he goes through the poem, and this line is calculated to be looked at quickly and passed over. It shows the reader what the demonstrative, *that,* in line 1 was pointing to, and, since it answers a question left over from line 1, it leads the reader on toward another kind of answer in line 3—this one the completion of the syntactical unit left urgently wanting at the end of line 2. By pointing in line 1 to something unspecified until line 2, Shakespeare lets his reader participate in the certainty that the speaker is the image of autumn. The reader is given the desire to see what season *that* season is. This much Shakespeare can literally show him. Logically, the proposition, "I personate Autumn," is a conceit; but grammatically, because of the placement of the demonstrative adjective, the lines are a demonstration. Rhetorically, the effect of the lines results from a combination of their logical and grammatical natures. I think the grammatical dominates; after all, what a reader beholds is not the speaker of the poem but the poem itself.

The quick movement from answer (the time of year is autumn) to question (do hang on what?) in line 2 evokes a sense in the reader of looking, seeing, knowing—a sense of an active journey into demonstrable truth. The reader's progress into line 3 is not slowed by anything in line 2. However, even though words in series, like all lists, ask to be read quickly, and even though the reader's inclination to slide over a list is enhanced in this case by the near rhyme *(few-do)*[3] by which the series of subjects fuses into the verb, the reader's progress through line 2 is not passive. The order of *yellow leaves, none,* and *few* is not at all what might be expected. To begin with, the sequence does not follow the sequence of nature: in nature there are yellow leaves first, then few, then none. As it is, this list does not flow into the reader's mind as it would if it came to him neatly generalized in almanac order. At a given moment in autumn an actual beholder of trees shifts his eyes, turns his head, looks around, and sees some trees with full yellowed foliage, some bare, and some with a few leaves; the same variation is likely among the various branches of a single tree. Reading this line is like looking at nature unmethodized. I am not saying that the action of reading the line suggests to its reader the action of looking at a tree or any other such anamorphous claptrap. I do say that reading this line *is* an action, that the reader is active. The reading of the line demands that the reader perform the intellectual action of looking, seeing, and grasping what he perceives. The perception of the line is like the perception of physical things only in that, in both cases, the mind of the beholder is presented with related but not yet strictly ordered objects—objects that have not yet undergone the process of being sorted and organized into an experience, something shaped into usefulness so that it can be carried as a conscious memory and reported.

This seems a curious thing to say about a poem that is generally considered a masterpiece. A work of art is almost by definition a sorting and organizing of experience. Randomness is the last thing for which it can be legitimately praised. Besides, Shakespeare's sonnets are, from the nature of the sonnet form if nothing else, strictly artificial. The relation-

3. See Kökeritz, pp. 209–10 and "Appendix 3: An Index of Shakespeare's Rhymes," s.v. *do* and *you*.

ships of thing to thing in the sonnets don't seem random; on the contrary, the unpredictable sequence of *yellow leaves, none,* and *few* in the present line has seemed sufficiently right and natural to have escaped critical comment.[4] Surely no reader of a line that is read as quickly as this one must be

4. Most interest in this line has centered on its punctuation (Rollins, *Variorum, 1,* 189–90). The 1609 text reads *When yellow leaves, or none, or few do hange.* Most modern editors add a third comma after *few.* I don't see that it makes any difference in a reader's experience of the line. In his edition of 1924 T. G. Tucker turned his full attention to the punctuation of the line. He took out both the modern editors' comma after *few* and the comma after *none* in the 1609 text. He then says that *or none* and *or few* with no comma between them mean " 'either none or few' ('only few, if any'). . . . The comma usually placed after 'none' produces the inferior 'there hang leaves which are yellow, or (there hang) none at all, or (in any case) few.' " The distinction Tucker thought was determined by punctuation is between a pair of possible alternatives to *leaves* (as punctuated in 1609) and a descriptive phrase (as punctuated by Tucker). Tucker, I think, greatly exaggerates the extent to which punctuation can counteract a reader's syntactical expectation. The use of "or . . . or" where we would use "either . . . or" is common enough in the seventeenth century, but so was the "or . . . or" construction used as we now use it: *A or B or C or D . . . ,* in which *A* appears before "or" and each succeeding member is a possible alternative to *A.* Rollins seems to give some credence to Tucker's theory: after he quotes Tucker in the *Variorum,* he notes that "or . . . or" is used in 37 and 81 to mean "either . . . or." I find no examples, however, either inside or outside the sonnets where a word that, like *leaves,* could be the first member of a series is followed by "or" meaning "either." There is no reason to think that the absence or presence of a comma would make a seventeenth-century reader break the syntactical habit of a lifetime any more than it would a modern reader, who, when he sees *or* after *leaves,* assumes that *few* and *none* are alternatives to it.

Since I object to Tucker's ingenuity, I ought to protect myself from the charge that I exercise as much or more ingenuity by making a great fuss about the word order of a line in which the word order is easily accountable to Shakespeare's desire for the assonance of *few-do.* I don't deny that possible motive, but I am concerned with the effects upon a reader of what Shakespeare did, not with his particular motives for doing it.

would pause to juggle *yellow leaves, none,* and *few* into the order demanded by his knowledge of the abstract laws of botany. Still, even though the chronologically random sequence of these words does not call enough attention to itself to obtrude upon the reader's consciousness, that randomness does require more intellectual energy than is usually required of a casual reader of a straightforward line in a straightforward poem.

This same line requires the same sort of attention and imperceptible energy in another way: the three members of the sequence are parallel grammatically, but they are not precisely parallel. The first alternative to *yellow leaves,* an adjective and a noun, is not the strictly parallel "no leaves" but the pronoun *none;* the second alternative, *few,* functions like a pronoun but is actually an ellipsis for "few leaves." Any two members taken as a pair are closer parallels than the three are together: *yellow leaves* is an adjective-noun combination, and *few* is an elliptical form of the same thing; *none* is a pronoun, and *few* functions as one; *none* replaces *leaves.* The reader experiences neither difficulty nor surprise in reading the series, but his mind does act upon it, going through the instantaneous process of adjusting itself to receive adjective-noun combination, pronoun, and adjective-noun combination in elliptical form.

The mind of a reader of line 2 of sonnet 73 is in motion. His mind does not puzzle as it does when it tries to understand an obscure line, but neither does it receive the stimuli of the poem passively. The sonnets are not what we ordinarily call hard poems, nor are they easy ones. They are uneasy: the relationships within the poems are in flux and the reader's mind is too. People are always saying that the sonnets are unique. They are. While it may be that the paragraphs immediately preceding this one treat ephemeral matters at such length and in such detail as to be more irritating than illuminating, I have risked my reader's patience because I think that the kind of mental commitment demanded by line 2 is like that which Mizener has shown to be demanded by the next two lines and that which is demanded in all the elements of the sonnet by manifestations of the kinds of multiple patterning I have discussed in previous chapters.

To demonstrate, I will return in somewhat less detail to sonnet 73:

That time of year thou mayst in me behold
When yellow leaves, or none, or few, do hang
Upon those boughs which shake against the cold,
Bare ruined choirs where late the sweet birds sang.
In me thou seest the twilight of such day
As after sunset fadeth in the west,
Which by and by black night doth take away,
Death's second self that seals up all in rest.
In me thou seest the glowing of such fire
That on the ashes of his youth doth lie,
As the deathbed whereon it must expire,
Consumed with that which it was nourished by.
  This thou perceiv'st, which makes thy love more strong,
  To love that well which thou must leave ere long.

The artificial order of this sonnet is particularly insistent: there are three quatrains, one each for the tree, twilight, and fire; each quatrain is a single sentence; and the couplet is a fourth and summary sentence. The formal identity of the three quatrains is reinforced substantially and syntactically: the three quatrains compare the speaker to a tree, twilight, and fire respectively; each quatrain is a single sentence; and the first lines of the second and the third quatrains echo line 1.

Moreover, there are several coexistent progressions in the quatrains. Time is measured in progressively smaller units: a season of a year, a part of a day, and the last moments of the hour or so that a fire burns. Color grows increasingly intense:

yellow leaves, twilight after sunset, fire. Light grows dimmer: daylight (presumably) in quatrain one, twilight, night; space constricts from the cold windy first quatrain to the hot suffocating grave of ashes in the third. In a progression concurrent with all these the metaphors give up an increasingly larger percentage of each succeeding quatrain to the abstract subject of the sonnet, human mortality. In the first quatrain the reader's need to see the likeness between autumn and the speaker is not urgent; line 1 makes the connection but, except for suggestions—first of aged human limbs in the *boughs which shake against the cold* and then of the universality of mutability in the fusion of substances that follows—the first quatrain focuses its reader's attention on the autumn scene rather than on the speaker. The progression toward the dominance of the tenor begins in quatrain 2, where *twilight* is a step closer than *boughs* had been to being personified.[5] The suggestion of physical abduction latent in the phrasing of *black night doth take away* asserts itself in the apposition of *Death's second self* to *black night;* because death and its traditional second self, sleep, pertain only to animate objects, human mortality is much more evidently inherent in the metaphor of quatrain 2 than it was in that of quatrain 1. By the end of the third quatrain the metaphor is all but dwarfed by its tenor: after the introduction of the *fire* and its ashes comes explicit personification in *his youth*[6] and *deathbed.* The tenor so completely emerges from the metaphor that,

5. Boughs are like human arms, and both boughs and arms can shake. Shaking *against* the cold suggests that the shaker feels cold and thus goes some way toward presenting the reader with a solid equation between a leafless tree and an aging man, but the image of a tree never crystallizes in the poem, and the boughs are immediately equated with the also inanimate *ruined choirs.*

6. *Youth* is much stronger evidence of a specifically human reference than *his,* which was still used in sixteenth-century English as a possessive form of the neuter pronoun *it.* It was, however, already usual to use *its* and *his* just as they are used in later English.

although the shift in *form* between the third quatrain and the couplet is, as usual, pronounced, the reader accepts the unadorned statement of the couplet with no sense that the *mode* of the poem has shifted from exemplum to moral.

All of these orderly progressions go to reinforce the formal order of the three-quatrain pattern. However, as the formal break between the third quatrain and the couplet is countered by the gentleness of the modulation between the three exempla and the moral, so in the poem as a whole the three-quatrain pattern and the progressions that support it are so offset by other factors that the poem provides the artistic security and stability of predictable pattern without allowing its reader the intellectual repose that predictability can entail. A principal factor in offsetting the potential liabilities of regularity is the numerousness of the different progressions within the pattern of quatrains. The progressions are consistent with one another and with the nature of the three metaphors, but they are not mechanically parallel and do not lump together in the mind: the time units get smaller; the speaker looms larger; the color gets brighter; the light gets dimmer; the temperature gets hotter.

Moreover, the intellectual gymnastics that Mizener has described for the reader of quatrain 1 are required in less spectacular form throughout the rest of the poem. In the first lines of quatrain 2, the precise meaning of *twilight of such day* shifts as the lines are read. Meeting *twilight of* a reader expects *day* because the possessive is ordinarily pertinent only to *day;* he therefore takes something like the meaning "twilight of such *a* day" from *twilight of such day.* The next line begins with the word *as,* which, in the usual pattern of the language, is a sign to the reader that the clause it introduces will tell him about the departed day whose twilight is under discussion. Such a clause can be reasonably expected to be in the past tense. The clause actually introduced by *As* is not in the past tense and is not the expected parenthetical identification of the day in question: *As after sunset fadeth in the west.* The modifying clause acts upon both *day* and *twilight* and effectively makes the reader understand *twilight of such day* as "what little is left of the day." Although it is unfulfilled, the syntactical promise in *As* of defining detail to follow is sufficient in itself to give the reader a sense that the metaphor has been precisely established. Weighing against that sense of sureness is the action of the line that actually follows *As.* It pushes forward in the present tense and makes the reader participate in little in a mutability in the lines themselves that seems so powerful it cannot be stopped even for the moment it would take to establish a definition.

In the next lines the reader's mind is again in motion. *Night,* in the context of *twilight,* is expected, but here *night* is called *Death's second self.* Since *black night* suggests a ghostly figure capable of abducting the twilight, the equation with death is easy to accept. However, *Death's second self* suggests the traditional epithet for sleep, "the younger brother of Death." The suggestion of sleep inherent in the epithet is then confirmed by the rest of the line: *that seals up all in rest.* Night and sleep are closely related concepts, and there is nothing startling about the mention of one leading to the mention of the other. Here, however, the reader's mind must act upon the lines, adjusting its understanding as the idea of night fuses into, and at last is almost lost in, the idea of sleep, which, in *lie* and *deathbed,* is still dimly present in the next quatrain.

Another kind of demand for mental activity is put upon the reader by the parallelism between the second and third quatrains. Except for the replacement in line 9 of *glowing* and *fire* for *twilight* and *day* in line 5, the first lines of the two quatrains are identical. The reader is prepared to see line 10 continue the parallelism. The explanation demanded by *such* in *of such day* is introduced by *as;* the reader, set firmly in a repeating pattern, expects line 10 to begin as line 6 had. Instead of "*As* on the ashes of his youth doth lie," the line is

"*That* on the ashes of his youth doth lie."[7] Then, reconciled to the miniscule disappointment of the broken pattern, the reader meets *As,* the word expected at the beginning of line 10, in the same position but with a different syntactical function in line 11: *As the deathbed whereon it must expire.* As he reads quatrain 3 a reader's mind recognizes a repeating pattern, adjusts to a break in it, and then must accept a factor in the original pattern used randomly.

Something of the same sort happens in the couplet where the verb *leave* is a substantially irrelevant, almost purely phonetic, echo of the *leaves* at the beginning of the poem:

> This thou perceiv'st, which makes thy love more strong,
> To love that well which thou must leave ere long.

The couplet requires further adjustment of the pattern in which the reader conceives relationship in the poem. The couplet is in perfect accord with the substance of the poem. Moreover, it begins *(This thou perceiv'st)* like the three previous formal units, each of which introduces its metaphor with a statement that what follows is to be seen in the speaker. The construction of the final clause of the poem, however, contradicts the pattern for syntactically secondary action in the poem. The person to whom the poem is addressed has been the actor in the main clause of each sentence, but the bulk of each of the quatrains is devoted to metaphoric statements of the impending departure of the speaker. Here, in *which thou must leave ere long,* the action is stated in reverse. The beholder is the actor; now the beholder must leave the speaker. The reader has no difficulty in understanding the

7. Edwin Abbott demonstrates that Shakespeare uses *such as* when *which* follows and *such that* when *as* follows *(A Shakespearian Grammar* [London, 1870], pp. 190–91). The availability of a reasonable grammatical explanation for the break in parallelism does not, I think, affect the validity of my description of a reader's reaction to it. As Abbott explains it, the necessity for using *that* where *as* was used before is only signaled to the reader by *as* in line 11. By then, the reaction I describe is already past.

line. He simply understands *leave* as "give up" or "lose."[8] Even so, the reversal of the previous action is effective. It brings the threat of mortality closer to the beholder, completing the reader's sense that mutability is universal. More importantly, the change itself and the reader's need to follow it provide one more demand for the reader's activity, commitment, and participation in the process of the poem.

The Comfort of the Couplet—Sonnet 60

No, doubtless; for the mind can backward cast
Upon herself her understanding light
(John Davies, *Nosce Teipsum,* stanza 28)

Most of the sonnets become decreasingly complex as they proceed. The effect of the couplet usually is to sum up the poem or draw a moral. Essentially, it offers the reader a sound, simple reason why the poem was written and an oversimplified suggestion of what it was about. The couplet is often gnomic; it is almost always so in tone. It sounds simple and it is usually easily grasped.[9] The couplet ordinarily presents a coincidence of formal, syntactical, and logical structure, and it ordinarily gives the impression that the experience of the preceding twelve lines has been a good deal simpler than in fact it has been. Even in the case of sonnet 73, where the reader's mind is still required in the couplet to make some adjustments in its patterns of understanding, the couplet is intellectually much more comfortable than the early lines and suggests that the miniature dilemma that has been evoked

8. Gerald Massey actually printed "lose" for *leave* in 1866, and in 1899 Samuel Butler suggested that *leave* is an error for "leese." See Rollins, *Variorum, 1,* 189.

9. As there are to anything else that can be said about the sonnets at large, there are exceptions to this rule. See 69 (which has a triple pun on *common* in line 14), 106 (where *for* appears in line 11 and, in a different sense, in line 13), 108 (where the last six lines of the poem are generally more complex than the beginning), 115, 139, and, above all, 124 (where, although the couplet is difficult to understand, it sounds very simple).

in the reader by the multiple systems in which the body of the poem is organized has not really existed at all. The couplet of 73 begins: *This thou perceiv'st;* the presence of the pronoun not only implies that everything else in the poem is capable of summation in *This,* but also inclines the reader to sort out as pertinent only those reactions to the quatrains which could be said to make *love more strong,/To love that well which thou must leave ere long.*[10] The couplet concludes the poem, and it is reasonable but not accurate for a reader to assume that *all* that goes before it is directed toward that conclusion and is summed up in it. Thus an effect of the couplet of sonnet 73 is to tell the reader that the poem he has just finished has been calculated simply to arouse greater affection in the beloved, and that his own experience of universal mutability has been illusory.

By means of the analyses that follow, I hope to suggest that the couplets, even those as apparently debilitating as the grandly hollow couplet of 116, serve a purpose similar to the speeches of political reestablishment at the ends of *Hamlet* and *Macbeth.* The tragedies put their audiences' minds through a turmoil of conflicting systems of value. Fortinbras and Malcolm return order to the stage; they do not resolve the conflicts in the mind of the onlooker, but they do reestablish order in one of the threatened systems. The completion of the story, the completion of the artistic whole, and the resolution of the *particular* conflict of the play puts a frame to the audience's experience of intellectual turmoil and makes it bearable. Similarly, I think, in the miniature scale of the sonnet the couplet ties off one set of loose ends, brings the reader's mind back to conceiving of experience in a single system, and keeps him from worrying about or even bringing to consciousness the intellectual upheaval in which he has just participated.

10. *This, which,* and similarly summary pronouns are used this way in many couplets. For example, *this* functions as it does here in the couplets of 33, 45, 64, 95, 116, 123, 124, and 129.

The ease with which a reader's mind moves from one system of relationship to another and the effect of the intellectual relaxation usual[11] at the end of the poem are well illustrated by sonnet 60. Its last three lines are a prosaic and simpleminded reversion to a commonplace of the sequence:

> And nothing stands but for his scythe to mow:
>   And yet to times in hope my verse shall stand,
>   Praising thy worth, despite his cruel hand.

Like the last lines of sonnet 73, these lines are only comparatively undemanding of the reader's energies: the phrase *to times in hope* requires an adjustment of the reader's understanding of the word *time,* which has been the personified subject of the whole third quatrain, and is the antecedent for *his* in *his scythe* and *his cruel hand.* Nonetheless, these last lines bring the reader to the comfort of an intellectual rest, partly because the paradox of the couplet is so easy *(nothing stands—my verse shall stand),* and partly because, whatever complexity the couplet may have, it does away with all the complexities that precede it. Those complexities are so many that the reader earns and needs the comfort of the couplet:

> Like as the waves make towards the pebbled shore,
> So do our minutes hasten to their end;
> Each changing place with that which goes before,
> In sequent toil all forwards do contend.
> Nativity, once in the main of light,

11. It is a gross but valid generalization that the sonnets become less dense and generally simpler as they near the couplet and are at their simplest in the couplet itself. I can find no methodical way to demonstrate the generalization short of going through all the poems and explaining just why the last lines of the majority seem less complex to me than the first. As a token demonstration of the diminished intellectual challenge of the last lines, I offer the following. Sonnet 60 is one of seven poems in which the stock figure of time or death as an old man with a scythe appears; in only one of the seven does it appear before line 10, and the exception, 126, is not technically a sonnet. Father Time appears in the couplets of sonnets 12, 100, and 123, in 60.12, 74.11, and 116.10.

Crawls to maturity, wherewith being crowned,
Crooked eclipses 'gainst his glory fight,
And Time that gave doth now his gift confound.
Time doth transfix the flourish set on youth
And delves the parallels in beauty's brow,
Feeds on the rarities of nature's truth,
And nothing stands but for his scythe to mow:
  And yet to times in hope my verse shall stand,
  Praising thy worth, despite his cruel hand.

The simile with which the poem opens and which is continued metaphorically through the first five lines is easy enough to understand but keeps the mind in constant action. Without regard to the logic of the sentence, the reader selects from the connotations of *waves* and *pebbled* those appropriate to *minutes,* a word logically apposite to *waves* but physically adjacent to *pebbled*. Minutes, like the rhythm of line 1 and like the waves of which it speaks, pass with inexorable power. On the other hand, minutes, unlike waves, are minute and insignificant, like pebbles.

The syntactical relationship of line 3 to its neighboring clauses is not fixed; nor does the line make literal sense. Both deficiencies are such as to keep the reader's mind moving. As the reader comes from line 2, the participial phrase modifies *waves* and *minutes* in the preceding clauses;[12] as the reader leaves line 3 and reads line 4, the participial phrase becomes an adjunct of line 4, similar to *In sequent toil* in its syn-

12. The 1609 quarto prints a comma at the end of line 2. The modern text in which I cite the poem puts a semicolon. I don't see that the change of punctuation makes any real difference in the way a reader actually reads the poem. A student assigned to write about the poem may go back and check the punctuation in order to get a probably misleadingly firm indication of what it is that he has read or was supposed to have read, but I think that the existence of a probable need to seek clarification from the punctuation is the best proof there is that punctuation is not a factor in the first reading of the quatrain.

tactical action upon *all forwards do contend.* At the same time that his mind is shifting with the syntax, the reader is taking the meaning demanded by the nature of waves rather than the literal meaning of the line from *Each changing place with that which goes before.* Various critics have pointed out an echo in this quatrain of the following lines from Ovid; I quote Golding's translation:

> As every wave dryves other foorth, and that that commes behynd
> Bothe thrusteth and is thrust itself: Even so the tymes by kynd
> Doo fly and follow bothe at once.[13]

Ovid accurately describes the physics of the progress of waves toward the shore. Shakespeare does not; waves don't exchange places with each other.

No critic or editor of the sonnets has felt it necessary to dispel from a reader's mind a possible image of pairs of waves trading places with each other. Presumably no such image has ever formed; why? Most importantly, of course, because the reader's knowledge of the ways of waves is fully as strong as his understanding of the statement before him. Line 3 is sufficiently imprecise to allow him to understand from it what it must say rather than what it does say. Even so, why is the possibility that a reader will be conscious of something wrong with line 3 so slight that even those editors whose desire to gloss is more than usually intense have let the line pass unmolested? Because in effect line 4 is itself a gloss: *In sequent toil all forwards do contend.* I will return to the subject of explanations and clarifications of one line offered by the line that follows. For the moment I mean only to point out that line 4 offers the reader a moment of sureness in the midst of flux which is just sufficient to send him on into further un-

13. W. H. D. Rouse, ed., *Shakespeare's Ovid Being Arthur Golding's Translation of the Metamorphoses* (London, 1904), p. 299 (Bk. xv, lines 201–03). See *Variorum 1,* 160.

stable relationships without letting him become conscious of the complexity through which he is moving.

The ideas, words, and sounds of the lines that follow slip into and out of focus in several different patterning schemes as the reader goes through them. His progress through the lines is sustained by the steady logic of their syntax, but he is simultaneously perceiving several other kinds of coherence in the lines. He is not conscious of all the fleeting connections his mind makes, but his mind presumably makes them all the same. The nature of the substance before him is never fixed until the last lines, and the energy expended by the reader in moving from one pattern to another transmits urgency to the poem itself.

In the second quatrain the reader's mind is immediately reengaged in the process of the poem by *Nativity,* the abstract noun that begins a new quatrain and presents a new topic. It also presents the probable grammatical subject of the new sentence. The phrase that follows, *once in,* confirms the probability that *Nativity* will be the syntactical actor in the sentence; *once in* also makes *Nativity* liable to definition in time and space and thereby personifies it. The only person that *Nativity* could logically describe is a baby, and so a baby emerges as the probable actor in the following action.

The next words, *the main,* seem foreign to *Nativity. Main,* however, does pertain to the waves, a metaphor from which the new quatrain seemed to have broken completely. On the other hand, the completed phrase *main of light* pertains to the new subject of the new quatrain, *Nativity.* As *of light* changes the signification of *main* from literal to metaphoric, so it imposes a still very dim suggestion of "a Nativity," a horoscope, upon *Nativity.* Principally, however, *the main of light* introduces still another concrete identity for the syntactical actor indicated by *Nativity:* the sun, whose nativity is the sunrise and whose progress makes it the literal inhabitant of *the main of light.*

The line presents a fusion of ideas, each of which is separately perceptible but of which none is fully developed. Mr.

Mizener, who describes and discusses suggested but undeveloped themes within individual sonnets, would say that line 5 is in soft focus.[14] Although the phrase is a good one, I quibble with the overtones of *soft;* the word is likely to make the very critics Mizener is cautioning, those who assume that Shakespeare's sonnets are metaphysical poems *manqués,* forget the word *focus. Soft* focus suggests that Shakespeare's reader gets the same impression of pseudoethereal haziness one gets from a carefully unfocused "artistic" photograph or the worst of Swinburne's poems. Actually, in a line like this one, the focus is soft only in that it is capable of constant change; the change is from one clear impression to another. The ideas fuse into one another, but they should not confuse the reader or seem confused. Unfortunately, an analysis like this one or Mizener's similar analysis of 106 seems, because it is demonstrating a multiplicity, to be demonstrating a confusion. A reader who is convinced by my analysis of line 5 may in unreasonable humility assume that only some obtuseness of his own has previously prevented him from being confused by the line dissected on the page before him.

The experience of line 5 is not confusing, and no amount of commentary will make it so: *Nativity, once in the main of light.* The first word presents the reader with the abstract idea of birth; *once in* personifies the abstraction as a baby; *the main* connects this line, the new quatrain, and its subjects with the preceding lines; when it is completed, the phrase *the main of light* introduces still another actor, the sun, the actor appropriate to the now established scene of the succeeding action. Because the last phrase introduces the idea of planetary movement, it also introduces astrology, a frame of reference appropriate to the syntactical subject, *Nativity,* and to the baby and the sun, the two concrete identities that have emerged for *Nativity.* As a whole, the line thus comes to present the reader with a human being about to live out his

14. *Southern Review, 5* (Spring 1940), 733.

destiny; the sun, whose daily journey mirrors the lifetime of a human being; the motion of the spheres, from which the particular destiny of a particular person can be predicted; and a nativity, the chart in which a particular destiny is mapped. The line as a whole contains all these, but it presents them one at a time and in a sequence of words in which each new subject seems not only appropriate to something that precedes it but a reasonable development from the preceding words. The ideas are fused in the line, but they do not become confused in the reader's mind. The reader's mind is constantly moving, constantly working, but he makes all the connections that have taken me pages to describe in the few seconds it takes to read seven words. The reader is not confused; he is simply proceeding toward a verb, an action. In the next line he finds it: *Crawls*. He then continues the process of jumping easily and quickly from one system of relationship to another.

Crawls to maturity pertains to *Nativity* both because the idea of birth carries the idea of continued growth toward maturity and because babies crawl; the phrase also continues the idea of forward motion from *make towards, hasten to,* and *forwards do contend* in quatrain 1. In the next phrase, *wherewith being crowned,* the primary meaning of *wherewith* is "with which," but the word carries with it suggestions both of "at which place," which is inherent in the first part of the compound, and of "whereupon."[15] The two suggestions offer the reader an impression that the multiply conceived event in progress is sufficiently concrete to be fixed in place and time; the event seems as precisely defined as one that can be visualized.

A critic analyzing the poem will probably find *being crowned* less pertinent to the diction that precedes it than a casual reader would. The idea of royalty is new, but *crowned* functions in a pronounced alliterative pattern whose mem-

15. *OED,* s.v. *wherewith,* 4.b.

bers constitute an abstract of the substance of the quatrain: *Crawls, crowned, Crooked.* Moreover, because a crown suggests both the top of the body and the peak of achievement, *crowned* pertains both to the idea of the crawling baby who must stand *up,* grow *up,* and achieve his ambition, and to the sun climbing in the sky.[16] A crown is also sunlike in that it glitters and shines.

Crooked at the beginning of line 7 suggests old age and, by completing the cycle *Crawls, crowned, Crooked,* anticipates the logic of the poem, which will not overtly take up old age until quatrain 3. As the reader comes upon *Crooked,* it pertains to the birth and development of a human being, but *Crooked* modifies *eclipses,* and, as the reader moves on from *Crooked,* it pertains to the sun.

Most editors gloss *Crooked* as "malignant," and in the company of *eclipses* it does indeed solidify the earlier astrological suggestions. However, the hazard of the gloss and many others like it is that it seems to tell a modern reader that part of his experience of the poem is invalid. A modern reader is not likely to be sufficiently familiar with astrology and astrological terminology to understand *Crooked eclipses* as a seventeenth-century reader would have understood it. An editor has no choice but to gloss *Crooked,* but by putting his authority behind the meaning *Crooked* has when it modifies *eclipses,* he seems to say to his reader, "Read *Malignant* for *Crooked;* the idea of crooked old age that crossed your mind as you read *Crooked* was only a product of the ignorance I am here to correct." A modern reader needs the help of a modern editor, but both should remember that one cannot often say accurately what a word means in a Shakespeare sonnet; one can only say what it means at a given instant during the reading of the sonnet. Indeed, in this line the astrological meaning of *Crooked eclipses* fully emerges only in the second half of the

16. Quatrain 1 describes lateral motion. In this quatrain the action is vertical and upward. In quatrain 3 the verbs *transfix, delves, feeds,* and *mow* either describe or suggest downward vertical motion.

line: *'gainst his glory fight.* Moreover, while that phrase completes the idea of adversely active astrological influence, *his glory* reasserts the physical presence of both "the glorious sun" and the young man, *crowned* in the preceding line and now under treasonous attack.

The next line is rhythmically and logically summary of the quatrain it concludes: *And Time that gave doth now his gift confound.* The line doesn't evoke the mental activity required by those that precede it. Even more than the last line of the first quatrain, line 8 offers the reader a plateau upon which to rest and be sure of his bearings. *Time,* the subject of the clause, has been the common denominator of the poem from the beginning: the first quatrain is about minutes in the likeness of waves; in the second the diurnal course of the sun, the lifetime of a man, and the two together in a horoscope all pertain to time.[17]

The noteworthy word in line 8 is *confound.* In a line that suggests Job's resigned "The Lord giveth, and the Lord taketh away" in the burial service,[18] *confound* is curiously violent. The poem has been concerned throughout with inevitable and presumably irresistible motion, but that motion is never unresisted. A sense of conflicting force was also introduced by the diction at the end of quatrain 1, *toil* and *contend* suggest that the grand and inevitable progress of the waves and time is a constant struggle. *Nativity crawls* laboriously,

17. Line 8 is also tied to the preceding line by an overriding phonetic pattern in *s* and hard *g: eclipses 'gainst his glory, his gift.*

18. *Liturgies . . . Set Forth in the Reign of Queen Elizabeth,* ed. William Keatinge Clay, Parker Society (Cambridge, Eng., 1847), p. 233. Another passage from Job (14:1–2) follows this one in the burial service. Its concern with birth, the passing shadow, the flower, and vertical and lateral motion make it similar to this sonnet: "Man that is born of a woman hath but a short time to live, and is full of misery: he cometh up, and is cut down like a flower; he flieth as it were a shadow, and never continueth in one stay." Here again the likeness between the service and the sonnet is outweighed by the violence and conflict absent from the service and ever present in the sonnet.

but it is not eclipsed without a *fight*. The tone of the opening lines of the poem is one of contented resignation, but from line 4 onward the reader is denied an intellectual comfort latent in the subject matter, the comfort of resigned contemplation of the order of God's universe. Here *confound* suggests violent, chaotic demolition, and self-contradiction in the order of things.

Confound at the end of line 8 is phonetically similar to *contend* at the end of line 4. The likeness of the two words makes the reader briefly aware of a unity in the two quatrains that overrides the obvious formal and substantial break between them. This shadow of an 8, 4, 2 pattern coexists with a 4, 8, 2 pattern that is triply defined: the third quatrain is tied to the second by the repetition of *And,* the first word in lines 8, 10, and 12.[19] *Time,* the subject of the last clause of quatrain 2, is the subject of the first clause of the new quatrain; the second and third quatrains are the complementary halves of a single action, rising in quatrain 2 and falling in quatrain 3. At the same time, each of the formal units is a distinct substantial unit; the basic 4, 4, 4, 2 pattern is never obscured.

Although no one has ever had any trouble understanding what the first line of the third quatrain means, there has been considerable doubt about what it says: *Time doth transfix the flourish set on youth.* The difficulty has been with *transfix* and *flourish.*[20] The third stanza sets out to give the specifics of the destruction indicated in the preceding

19. *And* is also the first word of the couplet and thus provides a slight extralogical link between the couplet and the body of the poem.

20. Rollins (*Variorum, I,* 161) gives the following account of the controversy, to which I know of no additions since 1940:

> *transfixe:* Schmidt (1875): Transplace, remove. ——Onions (1911) also gives "remove," citing this line, though *N.E.D.* (1914) does not recognize such a meaning. The ordinary meaning, "pierce through" (="destroy"), makes good sense for Time's dart. But G. G. Loane (Philological Society *Transactions* 1925–30, 1931, p. 192) inquires, "Can it mean unfix?"

line; *Time doth transfix* echoes *Time . . . doth . . . confound.* The reader should reasonably take something like the meaning of *confound* from *transfix.* Even so, although the apparent apposition of *transfix* to *confound* is sufficient to govern the reader's understanding of the line, "pierce through," the usual meaning of *transfix,* is also present. Even more literally, *transfix* means "fix across," and since *transfix* comes immediately after a quatrain about eclipses in the passage of a heavenly body across the heavens, I think it has a propriety in this poem that makes a gloss unnecessary for a reader meeting it in the course of an uninterrupted reading of the poem.

The direct object of *transfix* is *flourish.* It is hard to conceive of running a spike through a spray of blossoms. The metaphoric meanings of *flourish,* however, are pertinent to the themes of the preceding quatrain; both as "a waving of a weapon" and as "the highest degree of prosperity," "perfection," "prime" *(OED,* s.v. *flourish,* sb. 2b), *flourish* is appropriate to *crowned* and *glory.* The most usual gloss for flourish is "ostentatious embellishment." The *OED* gives an example from 1653 of *flourish* used in that sense as a technical term in penmanship, and Nashe talked about a "florish with a Text-penne" in 1593.[21] A reader is not likely to imagine Time transfixing an ostentatious embellishment; but the drawing of a line through a scribal flourish is easily imagined and, I think, appropriate to what has gone before. In the context of crooked eclipses *transfix the flourish* suggests intersecting planetary lines in a highly embellished astrological map.

---

florish: Malone (ed. 1780): External decoration. ——Schmidt (1874): Ostentatious embellishment. [So *N.E.D.* (1897), citing this line.] ——Alden (ed. 1913): Outer adornment of youth. ——Pooler (ed. 1918): Painting, *i.e.* bloom.

21. The quoted phrase is from the dedicatory epistle for *Christ's Teares Over Jerusalem* as given in *The Works of Thomas Nashe, 2,* ed. Ronald B. McKerrow (Oxford, 1904), 9.

If the botanical connotations of *flourish* are dormant in *transfix the flourish,* they begin to emerge in *flourish set on youth,* where the juxtaposition of *flourish* and *set* suggests the gardening contexts of both. As a result, the next line seems more to be a continuation of a theme than the introduction of a new one: *And delves the parallels in beauty's brow.* The downward thrust of *delves* recalls the similar action of *transfix. Delves* is appropriate to planting, but *parallels* are military trenches,[22] and *delves the parallels* is more likely to reestablish the warfare of *'gainst his glory fight* in the mind of the reader than it is to suggest ploughing. *Parallels* also is a reminder of the waves in quatrain 1, but these parallels are *in beauty's brow,* and, by the end of the line, Time is only putting wrinkles in a once young face.

Beauty's brow marks a change in the reader's relationship to the poem. From this point on the reader can stand back from the words before him:

> And delves the parallels in beauty's brow,
> Feeds on the rarities of nature's truth,
> And nothing stands but for his scythe to mow:
>   And yet to times in hope my verse shall stand,
>   Praising thy worth, despite his cruel hand.

The lines still have the rhythmic force of inevitable power. *Feeds on* suggests bestial ravening, and the very vagueness of *the rarities of nature's truth* vouches for the delicacy it asserts. Even the cliché figure of Father Time is effective in the despairing trail of monosyllables on which the quatrain ends. These lines make a reader react to the situation described in the poem, but as compared with the lines that precede them, they make small demand upon the reader's mind to act in and on the lines as he reads them. These last

22. *OED,* s.v. *parallel,* B.3. The meaning was first pointed out by Pooler in his edition of 1918.

lines release him from intellectual involvement in the fabric of the poem. His mind is no longer scrambling. The end of the sonnet assures him that, after all, he has only been reading a poem.

Chapter 6

All Forwards Do Contend

The Thrust of the Sonnets

I set out in the last chapter not only to demonstrate the amazing number of shifts and connections that a reader must make as he reads a Shakespeare sonnet but also to give some reasons why the reader ordinarily doesn't fear for his sanity. I have already suggested two reasons: the ease with which the shifts and connections are made, and the usually diminished thematic complexity of the final lines. A third reason is a combination of the two: the easy fusion of ideas in the body of the poem keeps the reader moving steadily forward toward the uncomplicated last lines. An example of this forward thrust less complicated than 73 or 60 is sonnet 130.

The first quatrain of 130 *(My mistress' eyes are nothing like the sun)* has color as a common denominator. The second talks about roses *red and white* and then slips easily from roses, which are as much noted for their scent as for their color, into *perfumes* and *the breath that from my mistress reeks*. The step from breath in line 8 to speech in line 9 is equally easy, and is further eased by a near-rhyme between *reeks* and *speak* and by the similarity of the opening of line 9 to that of line 5. The pattern established by *I have* and *I love* is continued in line 11 by *I grant,* where it carries the reader from the sounds of speech and music in lines 9 and 10 to the respective gaits of a goddess and the mistress in lines 11 and 12. The surprise of the speaker's final reversal of attitude is diminished by the expletive *by heaven,* because one sense of *heaven* is thematically akin to *goddess* in line 11, and another is the directional opposite of *ground* in line 12. *Heaven* also pertains to *the sun* in line 1 and brings the reader full circle, without leaving any opportunity for a pause along the way:

> My mistress' eyes are nothing like the sun;
> Coral is far more red than her lips' red;
> If snow be white, why then her breasts are dun;
> If hairs be wires, black wires grow on her head.
> I have seen roses damasked, red and white,
> But no such roses see I in her cheeks;
> And in some perfumes is there more delight
> Than in the breath that from my mistress reeks.
> I love to hear her speak; yet well I know
> That music hath a far more pleasing sound:
> I grant I never saw a goddess go;
> My mistress, when she walks, treads on the ground.
> And yet, by heaven, I think my love as rare
> As any she belied with false compare.

When I talked about sonnet 60 I pointed out the gloss-like function of line 4 and the simplification in line 8 of the complexity that precedes it. Such lines offer the reader a fleeting moment of mental rest similar to that provided by the simple summary sound of the couplet. By seeming to deny the relevance of a complex maze of connotations in the preceding lines, such lines prevent the reader from pausing in his progress toward the couplet.

For example, the first quatrain of sonnet 85 is full of conflicting and yet related impressions:

> My tongue-tied Muse in manners holds her still
> While comments of your praise, richly compiled,
> Reserve their character with golden quill
> And precious phrase by all the Muses filed.

The quatrain has no fixed place or substance. Oral silence

is compared with written speech. The *tongue-tied Muse* is set against not an articulate counterpart but the products, *comments,* of a busier muse.[1] The relationships of *Reserve* to the rest of the quatrain are so doubtful, so many, and so mutually contradictory that editors since Gildon have been trying to argue the word away and replace it.[2] In a sequence where the preservation of the time-threatened beloved is a recurring theme, the meaning "preserve" for *Reserve* is certainly appropriate. What is reserved is *character.* Throughout the sequence the speaker assumes that the function of a poet is to preserve the character, the nature, of the beloved for posterity. The statement the reader expects to hear from this source on this subject is part of his experience of what he actually does hear: witness the numerous emendors who have changed *Reserve their character* to one or another variation on "Reserve your character." On the other hand, any reading that goes so far in endorsing the reader's expectations about the poet's function contradicts the spirit of the poem by giving too favorable an estimate of the efficacy of the rival poet's work. As the phrase stands, *Reserve their character* introduces an impression reinforced in subsequent lines of cold, mechanically ornate, virtuoso pieces that brashly show off their author's attainments rather than their subject's virtues. In the context of *richly, golden,* and *precious* the banking and hoarding connotations of *Reserve* emerge and reflect adversely on the rival poet, whose comments are storehouses of bejeweled handwriting *(character).*

The reader is next faced with the further intellectual effort of reading *golden quill* and *precious phrase* as if the two nouns as well as the two adjectives presented parallel ideas. Once he has accepted the real relationship between *quill* and *phrase* in place of the logical parallelism he ex-

1. The careful fusion of the identities of the rival poet, the rival muse, and the rival poems becomes overt in the pun on *hymn* in lines 6 and 7: *cry 'Amen' / To every hymn that able spirit affords.*

2. See Rollins, *Variorum, I,* 214–15.

pected, the reader comes on *filed*. *Filed* pertains literally to a *quill* (which has to be sharpened) and is only metaphorically and alliteratively appropriate to *phrase*, the word it actually modifies; it thus suggests that the two words really are logically parallel. Lastly, although the idea of a filed phrase had been a cliché for 1,500 years when Shakespeare used it, the metaphoric relevance of *filed* to *phrase* has been difficult for some readers to recognize.[3] The root of the difficulty is apparently in the rhyme scheme *(still, compiled, quill, filed)*, which seems to have led many readers to hear the half-rhyme "quill-filled" instead of the "b" rhyme required by the quatrain form. Every important eighteenth-century editor before Malone accepted a reading first given by Gildon: they printed *by all the Muses filled*.[4]

All in all, the quatrain is a maze and might be expected to upset a casual reader as much as it has the editors and commentators. However, I doubt that it does. A reader has no chance to stop and puzzle. The first line of the next quatrain gives *a* meaning (which is easily assumed to be *the* meaning) for quatrain 1: *I think good thoughts whilst other write good words*. The first line of the third quatrain performs much the same function for the second, whose last two lines return the reader to multiple and doubtful relationships like those in quatrain 1. Ultimately the reader is delivered safe and sound at a simple summary in the couplet:

3. Schmidt *(Shakespeare-Lexicon)* glosses *filed* as "polished," "refined," and so do most modern editors. In the 1609 text the word is spelled *fil'd*. The 1609 text gives line 13 of 86 (which is on the same subject as 85) as, *But when your countenance fild up his line*. Schmidt glosses *fild* in 86 just as he does *fil'd* in 85. The same sort of unfounded assumption of consistency may partially account for the eighteenth-century reading of *fill'd* in both cases.

4. I am not inclined to discount this reading as a mystery of eighteenth-century taste. I first became interested in this sonnet when, without knowing its editorial history, I noticed that I had just read and presumably had always read *filled* where any edition I was likely to use had *fil'd* or *filed*.

I think good thoughts whilst other write good words,
And, like unlettered clerk, still cry 'Amen'
To every hymn that able spirit affords
In polished form of well-refinèd pen.
Hearing you praised, I say, "'Tis so, 'tis true,'
And to the most of praise add something more;
But that is in my thought, whose love to you,
Though words come hindmost, holds his rank before.
  Then others for the breath of words respect;
  Me for my dumb thoughts, speaking in effect.

The determination with which the sonnets drive toward their conclusions also partly accounts for the impression they give—even when they contradict each other and are internally inconsistent—of incontrovertible truth. Sonnet 129, whose subject is unstoppable energy, is itself unstoppable:

Th' expense of spirit in a waste of shame
Is lust in action; and, till action, lust
Is perjured, murd'rous, bloody, full of blame,
Savage, extreme, rude, cruel, not to trust;
Enjoyed no sooner but despisèd straight;
Past reason hunted, and no sooner had,
Past reason hated as a swallowed bait
On purpose laid to make the taker mad:
Mad in pursuit, and in possession so;
Had, having, and in quest to have, extreme;
A bliss in proof, and proved, a very woe;
Before, a joy proposed; behind, a dream.
  All this the world well knows; yet none knows well
  To shun the heaven that leads men to this hell.[5]

The forward motion of sonnet 129 is partly achieved in its sound. In the first quatrain the convoluted and contorted

5. Lines 9 and 11 as given here are the almost universally accepted emendations of the 1609 readings: *Made In pursut and in possession so* and *A blisse in proofe and proud and very wo.*

relationships of the nouns to one another are vouched for by a succession of *s* sounds frustrated by stopped consonants; the lines spit. The pattern in *sp* and *st* sounds in *expense, spirit,* and *waste* in line 1 is picked up in *lust* in line 2. The equation made by the first clause between *Th' expense of spirit in a waste of shame* and *lust* is logically only an assertion, but phonetically it is proved.

The *sh* of *shame* in line 1 reappears in *action*[6] in line 2; *in* appears in both lines. The change in the middle of line 2 from *lust in action* to the time before action is bridged by *till action, lust,* the distorted mirror image of *lust in action. Is,* the first word in line 2, is also the first word in line 3, and the pattern in *s* plus consonant continues in *Is perjured* and *murd'rous, bloody.* A pattern in *rd* holds *perjured* and *murd'rous* together; the *d* reappears in *bloody,* which in turn begins a new yoking pattern in *b* and *l* in *bloody, full of blame.* Such interlinked sound patterns and repeated words and rhythms continue throughout the poem. They preclude any sense of pause, and their principal effect is to carry the reader forward with power similar in intensity to that described by the poem.

The headlong action of sonnet 129 is also largely accountable to the fact that the poem does not come to a satisfyingly complete rhythmic stop until it is over. The only full syntactical stop before line 12 comes in the middle of the second line on an unstressed syllable. The formal pause at the end of line 1 comes when the sentence still lacks a verb; the pause at the end of line 2 comes immediately after a new subject that waits for predication in the following line. The formal stop at the end of line 3 is potentially also a logical stop, but the still incomplete rhyme scheme leads the reader on into line 4 and a continuation of the sequence of epithets: *Savage, extreme, rude, cruel, not to trust.* Here the quatrain pattern

6. For the pronunciation of *action* as "akshun," see Kökeritz, *Shakespeare's Pronunciation,* p. 317.

is complete, and the syntactical pattern is again potentially complete. Had the reader not come immediately from the experience in line 3 of a sequence of epithets that paused at the end of the line only to continue in the next, or had Shakespeare written "Savage, extreme, rude, cruel, *and* not to trust,"[7] the reader might have a sense of finality at the end of line 4. As it is, however, he does not expect an end to the epithets and does not hear rhythmic finality in the line.

In the second quatrain the listing of the qualities of lust continues. The whole second quatrain, like the second two lines of the first, follows from *lust is*. At the end of the quatrain rhythmic, syntactic, and formal finality coincide in *On purpose laid to make the taker mad*. The stop is sufficiently strong to establish a fleeting identity for the octave, but the first word of line 9 is a repetition of the last word of line 8, *mad,* and since the third quatrain is a further appendage of the statement begun in line 2, the momentary sense of rest and completeness is denied.

The hectic forward motion of the sound and the syntax carries the reader across a wilderness of intellectual contortions: the first halves of lines 6 and 7 are pointedly parallel, and their second halves pointedly nonparallel; the first words of lines 2 and 3 are identical, but *Is* in line 2 follows a long subject and precedes a short object, while *Is* in line 3 follows a one-word subject identical with the object of the first clause, and precedes a list of objects that goes on for ten lines; the first words of lines 9 and 10 rhyme, but the lines that follow them are syntactically and rhythmically dissimilar.

The whole poem is perversely vigorous. As the reader

7. *Cruel* in line 4 is disyllabic, but the time span of the two syllables is very short. In sonnets 1 and 131, *cruel* appears at the end of lines in which it is difficult to say whether it is the tenth syllable or the tenth and eleventh. In any case, words like *cruel, jewel,* and *fuel* appear to have been pronounced much as they are now, as slurred disyllables or very long monosyllables. Unless they appear in meter, one is hard put to label them long monosyllables or short disyllables, and even in a case

rushes through it, he is put on a whirligig of time. At the beginning the poem is concerned with *lust in action.* In the middle of line 2 the point in the history of lust changes straightforwardly to the time before action. At the beginning of line 5 the moment of action is past and is made momentary by the past participle, *Enjoyed.* Line 5 is concerned with the time after action. In the next three lines the speaker first jumps back to the time before action *(Past reason hunted),* then, again with past participles, presents the moment of action as past while it is present *(and no sooner had,/ Past reason hated),* and then sums up reaction, the attitude after lust in action, in a simile *(as a swallowed bait)* that is defined in terms of time before action *(On purpose laid to make the taker mad).* The next four lines are a chronological maze in which time changes nine times in rapid and irrational sequence: before, action (line 9); after, action, before (line 10); action, after (line 11); before, after (line 12). The reader is hurried through a jumble of time in which the moment of lust in action is lost. He arrives at the summary in the couplet ready to agree with it on the basis of a miniature experience of its justice.

Of the sources of forward thrust in the sonnets, the last one I discussed—the lure of an unfinished syntactical unit—is the most important and the commonest. As long as the syntax marches along without interruption, a reader will follow it across mires of conflicting meanings and impressions toward the clarification that the incompleteness of a syntactical unit allows him to assume will follow. As long as the syntactical unit is incomplete, the reader's understanding can be incomplete or even uncertain without disturbing him. He assumes that the completion of one will complete the other. In the sonnets the completion of a syntactical unit will often neither disappoint the reader nor straighten out

---

like line 4 it would be wrong to think that a seventeenth-century reader would take as long to say *cruel* as he would to say *savage* or *extreme.*

the preceding conflicts. Probably the best example of this and of all the other phenomena I have described in this chapter is sonnet 94, which has lately acquired a formidable reputation as a hard poem.

The Progress of Sonnet 94

Sonnet 94 is a great and beautiful sonnet, and I mean it no disrespect when I suggest that its current vogue is partly accountable to the qualities in it that make it such a useful example here: it displays the stylistic particulars I have been describing throughout the essay, but it does so more obviously, more crudely, and to that extent less satisfactorily than the other poems I have discussed:

> They that have pow'r to hurt and will do none,
> That do not do the thing they most do show,
> Who, moving others, are themselves as stone,
> Unmovèd, cold, and to temptation slow;
> They rightly do inherit heaven's graces
> And husband nature's riches from expense;
> They are the lords and owners of their faces,
> Others but stewards of their excellence.
> The summer's flow'r is to the summer sweet,
> Though to itself it only live and die;
> But if that flow'r with base infection meet,
> The basest weed outbraves his dignity:
> For sweetest things turn sourest by their deeds;
> Lilies that fester smell far worse than weeds.

Recent interest in 94 got its start from a lengthy account of the sonnet by William Empson in 1933. All of Empson's comments on the poem are constricted by his assumption of not only the justice but the comprehensiveness of the following précis:

> The best people are indifferent to temptation and detached from the world; nor is this state selfish, because

> they do good by unconscious influence, like the flower. You must be like them; you are quite like them already. But even the best people must be continually on their guard, because they become the worst, just as the pure and detached lily smells worst, once they fall from their perfection.[8]

In 1938 John Crowe Ransom responded to Empson with his own equally just and equally incomplete abstract of sonnet 94. Like Empson, Ransom suppresses or subordinates most of the experience of the first eight lines in the interests of developing a coherent and consistent statement based on his reaction to the last six. Both abstracts make heavy use of conjunctions ("because" and "but" for Empson, "but" for Ransom), which furnish the subordination of idea to idea that Shakespeare pointedly omits to make:

> You have your own free will, to be unchaste or not, and your beauty exposes you to the temptation of women. But consider yourself as sole inheritor from heaven of this beauty, and expected to keep it to yourself; those who share their beauty in sex must regard themselves as but its stewards. There is no reproach upon the flower for being self-contained. But infected flowers smell to heaven.[9]

Both abstractors are trying to make the poem internally consistent in *one* of its own terms. Ransom has noticed that, although the poem Empson wants us to see may be internally consistent, it is inconsistent with its context in the 1609 sequence: whatever the offenses of the beloved may be, sonnets 92 and 93 suggest to the reader that the beloved is any-

8. William Empson, *Some Versions of Pastoral* (London, 1935), p. 89. Empson first published the substance of his discussion of 94 in Tokyo Imperial University *Studies in English Literature, 13* (1933).

9. John Crowe Ransom, "Mr. Empson's Muddles," *The Southern Review, 4* (Winter 1938), 329.

thing but cold, aloof, or "detached from the world." On the other hand, although Ransom makes 94 fit for the handmaid of 92, 93, 95, and 96, he ignores Shakespeare's probable awareness of a reader's antipathy to people who are cold as stone.

On no internal evidence whatever, both Empson and Ransom paraphrase the poem as a direct statement to and about the beloved. The assumption is unwarranted, but it is entirely understandable. As more naïve critics have needed to anchor their understanding in Elizabethan politics or society, so Empson and Ransom need to assume a fixed point of reference for the sonnet before they can attempt to line up its elements and make them march single-mindedly in one direction.

Under usual critical conditions, the critic can assume that, when he looks at a poem and likes it, the essential statement of the poem will be capable of reduction into prose. He is probably quicker than his readers to stress the implications of the word *reduction;* nevertheless, experience has taught him to assume that from a coherent poem he will be able to perceive and state a general and inclusive attitude evoked in the reader toward the subject matter of the poem. That is a hard assumption for men who are rational by profession to give up. Empson and Ransom hold on to it with as much difficulty as tenacity. Notice the urgency with which each of them fights down his lurking dislike of those who are *as stone*—Empson: "nor is this state selfish"; Ransom: "There is no reproach upon the flower."

In 1952 Hallett Smith quoted Empson's and Ransom's abstracts and commented on them:

> It might be possible to reconcile the differences between these two versions, and preserve what each of them has of truth, by examining first the structure of the sonnet. The first eight lines constitute a definition

of the true and false heirs of "heaven's graces" or "nature's riches"—perhaps not exactly true and false heirs, but heirs who are real owners, lords, and masters, as distinguished from mere stewards, managers, or tenants. The inheritance is clearly one of physical beauty, "their faces," and its value is clearly considered to be very great, since it is inherited from heaven. Physical beauty is, however, to be regarded as the wealth of nature, "nature's riches," and this gives rise to the figure of the beautiful as either owners of this wealth or mere stewards of it. Perhaps the class distinction here has something to do with the aristocracy of the supposed addressee of the sonnets, but in any case there is the feeling about the responsible lord, who "husbands" natural wealth from "expense." This last word reminds us of its use in the first line of sonnet 129. "Th' expense of spirit." Whether a beautiful person is a lord-owner or a mere steward depends upon whether he makes use of his powers or refrains from doing so. The cautious vagueness of the first few lines, especially the second, conveys a sense of shame about the wrong to be committed "That do not do the thing they most do show."

The octave of the sonnet, then (for the image structure here is Italian, though the rhyme scheme is English), seems to urge the hoarding or at least husbanding of this beauty: the doctrine is the exact opposite of the argument in the first seventeen sonnets of the cycle. [Empson had tried to reconcile 94 with 1–17.] It needs some justification. This justification is provided by the device of a metaphor: the summer's flower. The self-sufficiency of a flower was of course established or fortified by a sacred text, "Consider the lilies of the field, how they grow; they toil not, neither do they spin," and it may well have been the recollection of this verse which brought into Shakespeare's mind the line . . . which ends the sonnet: "Lilies that fester smell far worse than weeds."[10]

These are remarkable paragraphs, first for introducing the obvious relevance of the Sermon on the Mount into criticism of this sonnet,[11] and secondly for being incoherent. Like his immediate predecessors, Smith assumes an obligation to assign a single fixed meaning to any given word or phrase in the poem;[12] thus, although the repetition of *clearly* suggests some self-doubt, *their faces* in line 7 establishes the fact that back in line 5 the reader's only legitimate reaction to *heaven's graces* was to understand it to mean heaven-sent physical beauty. Most of the time, however, particularly in the first of these paragraphs, Smith sets out firmly to fix the sense of a word or line and then, with admirable honesty, modifies his position until it dwindles away into nothingness. This is not the sort of prose one expects from Hallett Smith, but it is the sort one expects to see evoked by this poem.

Edward Hubler says that " 'They that have power to hurt' is both a great poem and an imperfect one."[13] The bulk of his discussion of the sonnet is devoted to a solid and sober attempt to eke out its imperfections by recourse to the plays and other of the sonnets. When one is faced with an obscure

10. Hallett Smith, *Elizabethan Poetry* (Cambridge, Mass., 1952), p. 190.

11. Smith does not appear to hear an echo of the Sermon on the Mount before line 9. I hear an echo of the beatitudes in *They . . . inherit heaven's graces.* Here *inherit* has the common sixteenth- and seventeenth-century meaning, "possess," just as it does in Matt. 5:5 of Tyndale, of The Geneva Bible, and of the Authorized Version, where *Blessed are the meek: for they shall inherit the earth* derives from *Beati mites, quoniam ipsi possidebunt terram.*

12. Some of the glossarial notes for this sonnet contributed by Alfred Harbage to the Pelican Shakespeare are an excellent recent instance of the hazards of benevolent clarification. Here are three of his notes. They are perfectly reasonable, but they stamp out as much meaning as they give: "1 *and . . . none* i.e. without actively trying to hurt"; "5 *rightly* as a right, veritably"; "8 *stewards* dispensers."

13. Hubler, *The Sense of Shakespeare's Sonnets,* p. 104.

line, one can do no better than go to a writer's other work to see what he is likely to have meant. However, where a line or, as in this case, a whole poem makes sense, one needs to remember that any such search for clarity is posited on the assumption that the writer lacked the skill both to achieve the effect he wanted and to see that he had failed. For Hubler the source of the imperfection he finds in the poem seems to be Shakespeare's inability to articulate a clear-cut attack on those who, like Rosencrantz, Guildenstern, and Northumberland, are lords and owners of their faces (p. 106). As his predecessors tried to ignore the bad qualities of the people described in the octave, Hubler exaggerates them at the expense of the good qualities. He protests too much:

> On first reading the sonnet, we shall, of course, notice the irony of the first eight lines; and everything that we find in the other works will confirm it. It is preposterous on the face of things to proclaim as the inheritors of heaven's graces those who are "as stone." It can be other than ironical only to the cynic, for even the hardhearted man thinks of himself as generous and cherishes an abstract admiration for warmth. In addition, it will be noticed that what Shakespeare says here contradicts everything that he has said elsewhere on the subject. The irony of the octave is Swiftian in both method and force. In specious terms the poet states as true that which he is well known to consider false: those men whose appearance does not square with reality, whose deeds do not fulfill their promise, who move others while remaining cold, are proclaimed the heirs to heaven's graces. They are the owners of themselves, whereas throughout Shakespeare's works self-possession in the sense of living without regard for others is intolerable. (p. 104)

The most extensive commentary on 94 is by Hilton

Landry.[14] Although he attempts to harden the meanings of some words and phrases that resist his efforts, and although he is inclined to overstress a reader's negative reactions to the unmoved movers, his line-by-line analysis of the poem is generally sensible and I am grateful for it. He prefaces his concluding chapter with the following quotation from Coleridge's *Table Talk,* and in his practical criticism demonstrates an awareness of its justice:

> In Shakespeare one sentence begets the next naturally; the meaning is all inwoven. He goes on kindling like a meteor through the dark atmosphere. . . .
>
> Shakespeare's intellectual action is wholly unlike that of Ben Jonson or Beaumont and Fletcher. The latter see the totality of a sentence or passage, and then project it entire. Shakespeare goes on creating, and evolving B. out of A., and C. out of B., and so on, just as a serpent moves, which makes a fulcrum of its own body, and seems forever twisting and untwisting its own strength.

I do, however, quibble with some of Landry's general principles and statements. He says that "interpretation consists of rejecting some contexts and readings while accepting others, of deciding what a poem does not mean as well as what it does" (p. 11). That sounds truer than it is. A major duty of a critic of any noncontemporary literature must be to acquaint his reader with the background against which a work was written, and conversely, to remove historically irrelevant notions from a modern reader's mind. In sonnet 127, for example, one cannot have twentieth-century memories of a children's book about a horse impinging on *black beauty's successive heir.* Neither, however, can one legitimately bar some historically probable contexts and set up others as what Landry calls controlling contexts. At one point, after quoting some earlier critics of sonnet 94, Landry

14. Landry, *Interpretations in Shakespeare's Sonnets,* pp. 7–27.

says, "What the critical labors of these literalists illustrate is that how one reads this Sonnet is largely a matter of what contexts are brought to bear on it" (p. 15). No. How one reads this sonnet or any other work depends on what contexts it invades: within what systems of relationships does it demand consideration from any reader historically equipped to recognize the demands?

Landry's governing contexts for sonnet 94 are sonnets 87–93 and 95–96, on the one hand, and sonnet 4 and the parable of the talents,[15] on the other. Surely for a reader following the 1609 sequence, any echoes of a sonnet immediately preceding 94 will make that sonnet a relevant context for this one. Moreover, a clear reminder of a sonnet as far from this one as sonnet 4 could bring the reader's experience of the distant poem to bear here. But on what basis can Landry limit relevance to the two contexts to whose terms he would subordinate all others? After objecting to an oversimplification by J. Q. Adams, Landry says, "It is ironic that Mr. Adams should be aware of the relevance of the Parable of the Talents to Sonnet 4 and utterly fail to perceive its bearing on this poem" (p. 11). I don't perfectly see that irony, but if it is there it is surely no greater than that in which Landry sees the parable of the talents and ignores the Sermon on the Mount.

All in all, I don't see how any effort to dismiss or subordinate any historically valid reaction evoked by sonnet 94 or any of the other sonnets can be useful or (considering the ability of the sonnets to spring back into shape after undergoing definitive criticism) possible. The essence of this sonnet will not fit into any neat package except the one it is in. I offer the following loose package in evidence.

They that have pow'r to hurt should not endear themselves to a reader first coming upon them, but *They that*

15. The relevance of the parable to 94 was first suggested by Empson, *Some Versions of Pastoral*, p. 94.

have pow'r to hurt and will do none sound like the stuff of heroes.[16] Having the power to hurt makes them sound bad, or at least dangerous; not using it sounds good. This first line describes a dichotomy in the nature of its subjects. The only two qualities it presents for "them" are irrevocably connected and also antipathetic. The line also begins a process of creating a state of mind in the reader in which contrary but inseparable reactions uneasily coexist. The key word in line 1 is *and,* which connects the mutually contradictory impressions in the line as if the second were a straightforward extension of the first. The use of *but* would have presented the reader with a formally structured antithesis that he could have taken in whole. As it is, the reader's attitude toward the subjects of the line is in active flux as he reads it.[17]

In line 1, *that* appears in a perfectly usual relative construction, but in the parallel construction in line 2, *That* is physically so far separated from the grammatical subject as to accentuate the impersonality implied by Shakespeare's use of "that" rather than "who."[18] The word *That* reintroduces the disapprobation dispelled in the previous line by *and will do none.* The reader's coldness toward "them" increases as their own impersonality becomes more evident: *do not do the thing they most do show. Thing* is ominously mechanical, and *show* adds a suggestion of theatrical distance and detachment which intensifies the threat inherent in the

16. Hallett Smith suggests Prince Hal in particular *(Elizabethan Poetry,* p. 189).

17. While the reader's opinion is shifting, he is simultaneously engaged in following Shakespeare's abstraction of the pronoun *none* from the verb *to hurt.*

18. Schmidt *(Shakespeare-Lexicon,* s.v. *That,* relat. pron.) says that Shakespeare often alternates *that* with *who* "without any perceptible difference." Schmidt gives a long list of examples in which he does not note that in constructions like this the use of *that* for *who* in the plays is ordinarily reserved for application to people whom the speaker is deriding.

fact that *the thing they most do show* is *the pow'r to hurt.* On the other hand, the substance of this line is a restatement of another fact: they do no hurt. The double response of the reader is comparable and appropriate to the conflict between the internal and external natures of the subjects of the lines.

At the beginning of the next line *Who,* introducing the third relative clause of the quatrain, simultaneously presents change and continuity; it breaks the pattern established by the preceding *that* clauses, but its vowel sound participates in a phonetic pattern established in the repetitions of *do* in the preceding lines and echoed in *moving.*[19] The hint of comparative humanity in *Who* is also present in *moving others,* which suggests some positive relationship between "them" and other people; in the contexts of the sonnet convention in general, this collection, and the particular poem that precedes this one in the 1609 sequence, *moving others* is likely to suggest that "they" move others by their physical beauty. The reader may be expected at this point to be swaying toward the admiration he felt at the end of line 1, but the completed line brings him back more strongly than ever to the antipathy he felt for "them" at the end of line 2: *Who, moving others, are themselves as stone.*

The next line maintains the reader's antipathy in *Unmovèd, cold.* Between *stone* and *cold, Unmovèd* can only confirm the impression made by those two words, but *to temptation slow* is linked—by another casual *and*—to the series that began with *as stone, Unmovèd,* and *cold.* To be slow to temptation is an admirable quality in any context and one that here suggests another way of evaluating *Unmovèd.* At the same time, however, *to temptation slow* also

19. See Kökeritz' transcription of *remove* in sonnet 116.4, of *do* in sonnet 18.3, and of *who* in *Hamlet* III.1.70 *(Shakespeare's Pronunciation,* pp. 348, 345, 365).

reflects the idea of enticement back upon *moving others* in line 3. None of the qualities listed in the first quatrain is inconsistent with any other, but the reader's reactions are inconsistent with one another. Unmoved people who are cold as stone are unfeeling and unadmirable. Unmoved people who are slow to temptation are steadfast and admirable.[20] Shakespeare is not describing the vacillation of a lover, but re-creating a lover's state of mind in the reader by putting him through a miniature but real experience of an attempt to think coherently about people who are both worthy and unworthy objects of admiration.

The syntactical unit begun in line 1 is still incomplete at the end of the first quatrain; the promise of completion is sufficient to push the reader on without pause into quatrain 2. The new quatrain makes a new start on the same statement, repeating the subject and immediately predicating it: *They rightly do inherit heaven's graces.* After evoking such a range of reaction to the subject, the repetition of *They* in line 5 has a forward-thrusting effect comparable to that of the unfinished syntactical unit; in effect, the capability for concrete identification in a pronoun of the people to whom the reader's attitude has been so fluid and unsure gives him a sense of solid grasp on his experience of the poem and gives him the sureness to go on without puzzlement.

It is quite reasonable in this context to expect the reader to hear faint overtones of "as a right" or "as if by right" in *rightly*. Since "they" are so self-controlled, the same is true of the meaning "decorously." Still, the most obvious significance of *rightly do* must be "have a right to," because the usual practice of the language makes a reader expect *rightly* to indicate the speaker's judgment rather than describe the subjects' behavior. Moreover, the reader's understanding of

20. Hubler says that "it is preposterous . . . to proclaim as the inheritors of heaven's graces those who are 'as stone.' " It is not preposterous to proclaim the same of those who are *to temptation slow*.

rightly as indicative of the speaker's approval is heightened by its position in a line that echoes the beatitudes. Still, the assertion that it is right that "they" prosper carries with it the open admission of possible doubt in the matter, and thus confirms the reader's experience of conflicting evidence in quatrain 1. An effect of *rightly* is thus to do what *but* would have done and *and* did not do in lines 1 and 4: it gives rationally graspable form and substance to the contradictions in quatrain 1. The reader gets that comfort, however, after the fact of the experience of the contradictions.

The echo of the beatitudes in *inherit heaven's graces* is appropriate to *will do none* and *to temptation slow,* but the first quatrain gives no suggestion that "they" are meek or poor in spirit. The strongly religious context created by the juxtaposition of *heaven's* and *graces* suggests grace, unearned and from heaven, but *grace* here is plural, and *graces* has only secular meaning. By Shakespeare's time the metaphoric nature of "grace" in love sonnets was so nearly forgotten that, even juxtaposed to "heaven," its sense is secular. Moreover, the reader is prepared to take *heaven's graces* as an atrophied courtly-love metaphor by the fact that *moving others . . . themselves as stone,/ Unmovèd, cold, and to temptation slow* is an excellent description of courtly "daunger."

The reader's sense of the secular nature of the blessedness described here is increased by the next line: *And husband nature's riches from expense.*[21] Although *heaven's graces*

21. Empson and Landry insist that the sonnet demands that its readers recall the parable of the talents. The moral of that parable is relevant to the sonnet, but I am not sure that Shakespeare could reasonably have relied on these lines to bring it to mind. A reader so sensitive to references to parables could sooner be expected to remember the parable of the wasteful steward (Luke 16:1–13), the conclusion of which also appears in the Sermon on the Mount (Matt. 6:24). Such a Bible-conscious reader would probably also bear in mind the relevance of Matthew 5:15–16: "Neither do men light a candle and put it under a bushel."

and *nature's riches* are sharply distinguished in theology, a reader is likely here to take the second as a gloss for the first, because the phrases are parallel, and because it is natural to assume that what is *h*usbanded will be identical with what is in*h*erited. When the reader first comes upon it in the preceding line, *inherit* gives the general sense of "possess." Here, as the theme of estate management begins to develop, it brings with it the particular sense which has become the only modern meaning of *inherit*. The idea of the succession of physical property from one mortal generation to another emerges to weigh against the suggestions of stonelike immutability in quatrain 1 at just the moment when they are about to be made explicit: *They are the lords and owners of their faces,/ Others but stewards of their excellence.*

As he was in the first quatrain, the reader is here actively engaged in the experience of contradiction. In the lines quoted above, the contradiction is between the response to *stewards* and *owners* that the poem seems to require and the reader's everyday knowledge of the activities of real stewards and owners. In the poem "They" are definable as *lords and owners* because they *husband nature's riches*. Therefore it follows that *Others* are but stewards because they do not exercise like thrift. One of a steward's duties is likely to be dispensing funds, but the usual connotations of "steward" suggest the conservation and thrifty husbandry he is hired to provide. In the ordinary course of things the verb *husband* goes with *stewards,* not with *lords* and *owners*. The sense these lines demand depends on the distinction between owners who possess the land and stewards who do not. The distinction, however, is presented in two related but not interchangeable systems at once: in terms of ownership it makes sense, and in terms of thrift it does not.

Another kind of contradiction is present in *Others but stewards of their excellence*. In the estate metaphor *their* most reasonably refers to the lords and owners. On the other hand, because of the parallelism of *owners of their faces* and *stewards of their excellence, excellence* presents itself to the reader as a synonym for *faces. Faces* is foreign to the metaphor, and one is either lord or steward of one's *own* face. In addition, Landry points out that " 'faces' is both a reminder of the deceitful looks and face of sonnet 93 and, as the equivalent of physical beauty, a representative of *all* their excellences" (p. 23). In quatrain 1 the reader's attitude vacillated. Here contrary reactions are evoked simultaneously. The reader now cannot really have an opinion of "them." The tone of this quatrain demands that he consider it a virtue to be *lords and owners of their faces,* but the proximity of sonnet 93 suggests that the virtue may be a talent for hypocrisy; the proximity of *heaven's graces* and *nature's riches* suggests that outright possession of one's body is a mortal impossibility; and the presence in this collection of sonnets 1–17 suggests that such hoarding is selfish and unnatural.

One cannot, I think, give a reading, in the usual sense, of the first eight lines. I have given a description of the experiences of reading them. I cannot validly generalize from the description further than to say that the lines exercise the reader's mind within the boundaries of their several artistic patterns. That exercise is possible because, although Shakespeare is constantly and overtly informing the reader of "their" nature, "their" qualities do not all admit of evaluation within a single system of values. Shakespeare invites the reader to judge "them," but the implied standards for judgment change from phrase to phrase and from word to word. The reader's essential experience of the lines is the experience of his own mind in flux.

Line 9 both sharply divides and firmly unites the octave and the last six lines:

> The summer's flow'r is to the summer sweet,
> Though to itself it only live and die;
> But if that flow'r with base infection meet,

> The basest weed outbraves his dignity:
>   For sweetest things turn sourest by their deeds;
>   Lilies that fester smell far worse than weeds.

The new subject of the new sentence is very different from "them." The subject of the first eight lines was animate and plural; *flow'r* is inanimate and singular. "They" are powerful and steadfast; a flower is a traditional emblem of transitory frailty *(no stronger than a flower,* 65.4). "They" are cold, and this is *summer's flow'r.* On the other hand, the flower and "they" have their beauty in common. Moreover, the rhyme between the fourth syllable of line 1 and the fourth syllable of line 9 phonetically makes the equation of "them" and the flower that most readers have taken for granted: *They that have pow'r/ The summer's flow'r.*[22] The flower is also a reasonable extension of *nature's riches* in the estate metaphor that precedes it.

Lines 9 and 10 limit the significance of the first eight lines by providing an incomplete but satisfying gloss for them. In effect, these lines say that the octave has made the simple statement that its subjects keep themselves to themselves. The apparent restatement of the octave invites the reader's approbation. One cannot reasonably think of blaming a flower for lack of gregariousness, and so the reader gives "them" the moral benefit both of the limitations imposed on a flower by its physical nature and of his fondness for flowers.

Just when the reader has come to see "them" as flower-like, the next lines present him with another contradiction of common sense. The first overt statement of the danger of corruption and the responsibility of the potentially corrupt being for maintaining his purity is made not about those *that have pow'r to hurt* but about the frail and inanimate flower. *Meet* in line 11 comes closer to describing physical

22. The rhyme reappears in *sourest,* a vital word in the first line of the couplet.

motion than any previous verb; *outbraves* in line 12 suggests glorious array and chivalric vigor more appropriate to the subjects of the octave than to flowers and weeds. Finally, in the couplet, where the reversion to a plural subject fully equates "them" and the flower, Shakespeare presents his reader with *their deeds;* "they" in the octave who are capable of deeds do none; it is *sweetest things* that are made likely to act.

Throughout the poem the reader has to cope with conflicting reactions, impressions, and systems of coherence.[23] Still, the reassuring presence of conjunctions in the third quatrain and couplet make them much easier to think about than the octave. The third quatrain offers a clean antithesis hinged on *But;* the couplet begins with *For* and formally presents itself as a neat, simple, explanation in a proverb of the essence of the poem:

> For sweetest things turn sourest by their deeds;
> Lilies that fester smell far worse than weeds.

The couplet talks with the directness and simplicity of a medieval tragedy about the total power of change, about the ease with which the best *things turn* into bad. However, the reader of the firm and rational couplet comes to the direct statement from an actual experience of mutability, in which anything is likely to turn into anything else at any moment.

The experience of reading through a Shakespeare sonnet is like a dream where one accepts improbable transformations without hesitation and where one slips imperceptibly from one frame of reference to another. The couplet is like an awakening in which one knows and still does not know that the experience of the dream was unreal. Intellectually

23. Consider, as an extreme example, the gratuitous complication for a reader of the 1609 sequence of meeting an echo of the noun *husband,* the key word in 93, in the form of the verb *husband,* in the otherwise perfectly foreign context of 94.6.

and in miniature, the awakening of the couplet is like the awakening Clarence describes in *Richard III:*

> I trembling waked, and for a season after
> Could not believe but that I was in hell,
> Such terrible impression made the dream. (I.4.61–63)

Chapter 7

Recapitulation and Conclusion

Shakespeare and the Essence of Verse

An artist usually presents a given object or idea in one relationship to other objects and ideas; if he opens his reader's consciousness to more than one frame of reference, he focuses on the object in one of its relationships and subordinates all other relationships to it. The essential action of the artist in creating the experience of an audience is the one that in grammar is made by indicators of relationship like "although," "but," "after," "because," "however." In literature such indicators of relationship tell the reader that he is not in the borderless world outside art where he himself has always to work upon what he perceives, to arrange it around a focal point chosen and maintained by himself. Syntactic organization tells the reader that he is dealing with what we are likely to label "truth," experience sorted, classed, and rated, rather than with "what is true," the still to be sorted data of "real" experience.[1]

1. It might be argued that, strictly speaking, no experience is completely unorganized, since, by definition, experience implies a perceiver who in various ways shapes the raw materials, whatever they are, which provide the ingredients of any perception. But even if, philosophically speaking, the disjunction between organized and unorganized experience is false, it nevertheless remains valid to speak of degrees of organization and to distinguish as sharply as I have done between the highly organized world of art and the comparatively shapeless world of everyday existence. Whether or not this difference is one of degree, it is so great as to warrant speaking of it for critical purposes as if it were a difference in kind.

The great distinction between the experience of life and of art is that art, by fixing one or more sets of relationships, gives its audience an experience in which objects *are* as they must be to be thought about, in which the audience can see what I have called "truth" without having to hunt it out and pull it out, in which "what is true" and "truth" can be the same. Art presents the mind with an experience in which it is at home rather than one in which it must make itself at home by focusing, stressing, and subordinating. All works of literary art, from the simplest sentence of the simplest mind to *King Lear,* are alike in that they are fixed orderings that place their audiences in an experience ready fitted to the experiencer's manner and means of experiencing.

Such orderings incline to be self-defeating. What we ask of art is that it allow the mind to comprehend—know, grasp, embrace—more of experience than the mind can comprehend. In that case, art must fail because the impossibility of its task is one of its defining factors. To state it simplemindedly, we demand that the impossible be done and still remain an impossibility. When an artist focuses his audience's mind and distorts what is true into a recognizable, graspable shape to fit that mind, he not only does what his audience asks but what cannot long satisfy audience or artist just because the desired distortion *is* a distortion. Art must distort; if it is to justify its existence, it must be other than the reality whose difficulty necessitates artistic mediation. It must seem as little a distortion as possible, because its audience wants comprehension of incomprehensible reality itself. We do not want so much to live in *a* world organized on human principles as to live in *the* world so organized. Art must seem to reveal a humanly ordered reality rather than replace a random one. Our traditional values in art exhibit its self-contradictory nature; all the following adjectives, for example, regularly say that the works of art to which they are applied are good: "unified," "sublime," "clear," "subtle," "coherent," "natural." In a style we are likely to value both simplicity and complexity; we ask that a character be both consistent and complex. Above all, what we want of art is the chance to believe that the orderliness of art is not artificial but of the essence of the substance described, that things are as they look when they have a circle around them. We don't want to feel that art is orderly. We want to feel that things are orderly. We want to feel that art does not make order but shows it.

There are as many ways of trying for the contradictory effects of art as there are artists. All of them aim at replacing the complexities of reality with controlled complexities that will make the experience of the orderly work of art sufficiently similar to the experience of random nature, so that the comfort of artistic coherence will not be immediately dismissed as irrelevant to the intellectual discomfort of the human condition. No work of art has ever been perfectly satisfactory. That is obvious. No work of art has ever satisfied the human need to hold human existence whole in the mind. If a work of art ever succeeded perfectly, it would presumably be the last of its kind; it would do what the artist as theologian describes as showing the face of God. All works have failed because the experience they are asked for and give is unlike nonartistic experience. Neither reality nor anything less than reality will satisfy the ambitions of the human mind.

Of all literary artists, Shakespeare has been most admired. The reason may be that he comes closest to success in giving us the sense both that we know what cannot be known and that what we know is the unknowable thing we want to know and not something else. I have tried to demonstrate that in the sonnets Shakespeare copes with the problem of the conflicting obligations of a work of art by multiplying the number of ordering principles, systems of organization, and frames of reference in the individual sonnets. I have argued that the result of that increase in artificiality is pleasing because the reader's sense of coherences rather than coherence gives him both the simple comfort of order and the comfort that results from the likeness of his ordered experience of the sonnet to the experience of disorderly natural phenomena. In nonartistic experience the mind is constantly shifting its frames of reference. In the experience of the sonnet it makes similar shifts, but from one to another of overlapping frames of reference that are firmly ordered and fixed. The kind and quantity of mental action necessary in nonartistic experience is demanded by the sonnet, but that approximation of real experience is made to occur within mind-formed limits of logic, or subject matter, or form, or sound.

Shakespeare's multiplication of ordering systems is typically Shakespearean in being unusual not in itself but in its degree. The principle of multiple orders is a defining principle of verse in general. Although "verse" and "prose" are not really precise terms, verse is ordinarily distinguishable from prose in that it presents its materials organized in at least two self-assertive systems at once: at least one of meaning and at least one of sound. Here, as an almost random example, are the first lines of Surrey's translation of the *Aeneid,* Book II:

> They whisted all, with fixed face attent,
> When prince Aeneas from the royal seat
> Thus gan to speak: "O Quene! it is thy will
> I should renew a woe cannot be told,
> How that the Grekes did spoile and ouerthrow
> The Phrygian wealth and wailful realm of Troy.[2]

As the principle of multiple ordering is common to poems at large, so its usual operation is different only in degree from its operation in a Shakespeare sonnet. Where one system tends to pull things together, another tends to separate. In the sample above, the syntax tends to unify and the form to divide. Similarly, in all literature any single system of organization is likely both to unify and to divide. Since not only verse but any literature, any sentence, is a putting together, the very nature of the undertaking evokes an awareness both

2. Padelford, ed., *Poems of Henry Howard Earl of Surrey,* p. 115.

of unity and of the division that necessitates the unifying. Thus, at the risk of belaboring the evident, the statement *They whisted all, with fixed face attent* is a clear unit of meaning made up of clearly articulated parts. The larger whole of the Surrey passage is similarly a unit made of distinct clauses and phrases. Formal organizations work the same way. The second line looks like the first and rhythmically is pointedly similar, but they are not identical either in appearance or sound. They look and sound as different from one another as they look and sound alike. Inside a line the same unifying and dividing exists. What is on one side of the pause, *They whisted all,* is roughly the same length as *with fixed face attent,* which balances it. Moreover, the fact that they make up a single line is just as active as the fact that they are divided by the pause.

The addition of rhyme to syntactic and metrical organization is the addition of one more independent system of organization. This is Dryden's version of the opening of the *Aeneid,* II:

> All were attentive to the godlike man,
> When from his lofty couch he thus began:
> "Great queen, what you command me to relate
> Renews the sad remembrance of our fate:
> An empire from its old foundations rent,
> And every woe the Trojans underwent[3]

Rhyme also adds another manifestation of the principle of unification and division. Aside from puns, rhyme presents the best possible epitome of the principle. Two rhyming words are pointedly like and unlike in sound, and they pull apart and together with equal force.

Any verse is capable of this kind of analysis. Since what it

3. *The Poetical Works of John Dryden,* ed. George R. Noyes (Boston, 1908), p. 536.

demonstrates is obvious, there is no need to prolong it. Still, if such analysis is unnecessary in most verse, what it reveals is nonetheless true: verse in general is multiply organized.

Shakespeare and the Sonnet Form—Sonnet 15

Although Wordsworth's "Scorn not the Sonnet" is not a good advertisement for the justice of its plea, the fact that Wordsworth himself wrote sonnets, that he wrote them when nobody else was writing sonnets, that Milton wrote them when almost nobody else was writing sonnets, and that Shakespeare wrote his well after the Elizabethan sonnet rogue had passed suggests that there may be something about the sonnet form that makes it not to be scorned. In an earlier chapter I said that the sonnet form in any of its varieties is simultaneously unifying and divisive. Those contradictory coactions result from its unusually high number of systems of organization. In the limited terms of my thesis that multiplicity of structures is an essence of verse, the sonnet is an especially poetic form. The first line of an English sonnet participates in a metrical pattern (fourteen iambic pentameter lines), a rhyme pattern *(abab)*, a trio of quatrains (alike in being quatrains, different in using different rhymes), and an overall pattern contrasting two different kinds of rhyme scheme (three quatrains set against one couplet). I suggest that the concentration of different organizing systems active in the form before any particulars of substance or syntax are added is such as to attract the kind of mind that is particularly happy in the multiple organizations of verse: witness Shakespeare, Milton, and Wordsworth. The different patterns inside the sonnet form pull together and pull apart just as the different patterns do in verse forms less crowded with coherences. The sonnet does what all verse does; it just does more of it.

As the sonnet form extends the basic verse principle of multiple organization, so Shakespeare's sonnets reflect and magnify the tendencies of the form itself. In superimposing many more patterns upon the several organizations inherent in the form, Shakespeare marshals the sonnet the way that it was going. Having talked at length about the kind, quantity, and operation of the patterns in which Shakespeare organizes his sonnets, I propose to pull together what I have said and summarize it, but to do so in the abstract would not, I think, be meaningful. Instead, I will take one sonnet, number 15, and use it to make a summary demonstration of the kinds and interactions of patterns in Shakespeare's sonnets generally:

When I consider everything that grows
Holds in perfection but a little moment,
That this huge stage presenteth nought but shows
Whereon the stars in secret influence comment;
When I perceive that men as plants increase,
Cheerèd and checked even by the selfsame sky,
Vaunt in their youthful sap, at height decrease,
And wear their brave state out of memory:
Then the conceit of this inconstant stay
Sets you most rich in youth before my sight,
Where wasteful Time debateth with Decay
To change your day of youth to sullied night;
And, all in war with Time for love of you,
As he takes from you, I ingraft you new.

On top of the formal pattern (4, 4, 4, 2) is a logical pattern (8, 6) established in the syntactical construction *when/then.* In the first eight lines, which are formally two quatrains and logically an octave, a 2, 2, 4 pattern arises from the three object clauses: [*that*] *everything* . . . (two lines), *that this huge stage* . . . (two lines), *that men as plants* . . . (four lines).

In addition to these three major structures and structuring principles, the nonformal phonetic patterns that operate in the poem are probably literally innumerable. They tend to interact with the other patterning systems in much the same way that the other systems interact with each other: an informal sound pattern will link elements that are divided, or divide elements that are linked, by the formal or logical or syntactical or rhythmic patterns.

Considering the great many words it takes to talk about sounds, it would not be profitable to talk about them here. Even a token description of sound patterns threatens to imbalance the discussion that contains it. I have therefore relegated a description of the liveliest of the sound patterns in sonnet 15 to the Appendix.[4] It should suffice here to say that informal sound patterns do what I have said the multiple patterns of the sonnets do generally. The mere fact of their presence adds to the reader's sense that he is engaged in an ordered, coherent, nonrandom, humanly geared experience. They help the poem give a sense of the intense and universal relevance of all things to all other things. The companion fact of their great number helps maintain in the reader an accompanying sense that, for all the artistic order of his reading experience, it is not a limited one. No one of the sound patterns dominates the others over the whole length of the poem; similarly, no one pattern of any kind dominates the whole poem. From moment to moment incidental sound patterns keep the reader aware of the orderliness, the rationality, of the experience, but the principal patterning factor does not stay the same from moment to moment. The multiplication of sound patterns, like the multiplication of structures generally, increases the reader's sense of order, while at the same time it diminishes the sense of limitation that a dominant pattern can add to the limitation inherent in the focusing of the reader's attention on particular subjects in particular relationships. In short, by fixing so many phonetic relationships and by putting a single word in so many of those relationships, Shakespeare overcomes the limitation that order entails. The reader is engaged in so many organizations that the experience of the poem is one both of comprehending (for which order, limit, pattern, and reason are necessary)

4. See Note 8, pp. 209–14.

and of having comprehended what remains incomprehensible because it does not seem to have been limited. Nothing in the poem strikes the reader as seen only "in terms of." Everything is presented in multiple terms—more as it is than as it is understood.

Shakespeare and the Sonnet Tradition—Sonnet 15

I have said that the peculiarly Shakespearean effect of these sonnets arises in part from a bold extension of a principle basic to verse generally and to the sonnet form particularly. The same can be said about an extension of the basic principle of courtly love in general and the sonnet convention in particular.

More than a writer in any other genre, a sonneteer depends for his effects on the conjunction or conflict of what he says with what the reader expects. Like the basic courtly love convention from which it grew, the sonnet convention is one of indecorum. Its essential device is the use of the vocabulary appropriate to one kind of experience to talk about another. The writer talked about his lady and his relation to her as if she were a feudal lord and he a vassal, or as if she were the Virgin Mary and he a supplicant to her. A witty emphasis on the paradoxically simultaneous pertinence and impertinence of the writer's language and stance to his subject matter is of the essence of the convention. The lady was not a deity or a baron, but she was virtuous, powerful, beautiful. In all stages of its development, the courtly love tradition relies upon a reader's sense of the frame of reference in which the writer operates and the writer's apparent deviation from that pattern in a rhetorical action that both fits and violates the expected pattern.

By the time the first Italian and French sonnets were written, the conventions of courtly love were traditional, and a decorum, albeit a decorum of indecorum, was firmly established for aristocratic secular love poetry. Followers of

Petrarch wrote to be judged on their success in introducing variations within a narrow and prescribed space, using set vocabulary and subject matter. To be appreciated, the sonneteer presupposed an audience whose presuppositions he could rely on. An audience for a sonnet had to be able to recognize a new surprise in a convention of long established paradoxes.

Perhaps the poems most typical of all the rhetorical actions of courtly love writers are those which exploit the apparently inexhaustible surprise of returning the language of religion to religious subject matter inside the courtly love and sonnet conventions. Dante did it in the thirteenth century; Donne did it in the seventeenth. A good example is this sonnet which George Herbert sent home to his mother from Cambridge:

My God, where is that ancient heat towards thee,
  Wherewith whole showls of *Martyrs* once did burn,
  Besides their other flames? Doth Poetry
Wear *Venus* Livery? only serve her turn?
Why are not *Sonnets* made of thee? and layes
  Upon thine Altar burnt? Cannot thy love
  Heighten a spirit to sound out thy praise
As well as any she? Cannot thy *Dove*
Out-strip their *Cupid* easily in flight?
  Or, since thy wayes are deep, and still the same,
  Will not a verse run smooth that bears thy name?
Why doth that fire, which by thy power and might
  Each breast does feel, no braver fuel choose
  Than that, which one day Worms may chance refuse?[5]

Exaggerated predictability and surprise, pertinence and impertinence, are in the nature of the convention; and all the devices I have talked about have a common denominator with the more grossly effective conjunction of frames of ref-

5. *The Works of George Herbert,* ed. F. E. Hutchinson (Oxford, 1941), p. 206.

erence in the earliest courtly love poetry, in Donne's *Holy Sonnets,* and in such collisions of value systems as that between the last line of this Sidney sonnet and the rest of the poem:

It is most true, that eyes are form'd to serve
The inward light: and that the heavenly part
Ought to be king, from whose rules who do swerve,
Rebels to Nature, strive for their owne smart.
  It is most true, what we call *Cupid's* dart,
An image is, which for our selves we carve;
And, fooles, adore in temple of our hart,
Till that good God make Church and Churchman starve.
  True, that true Beautie Vertue is indeed,
Whereof this Beautie can be but a shade,
Which elements with mortall mixture breed:
  True, that true Beautie Vertue is indeed,
  And should in soule up to our countrey move:
  True, and yet true that I must *Stella* love.[6]

Sometimes, as in the following sonnet from *Arcadia,* the whole effect of a poem will depend upon a reader's familiarity with the genre being so great that for an instant he will hear only the poet's manner and not his matter:

  What length of verse can serve brave *Mopsa's* good to show,
Whose vertues strange, and beuties such, as no man them may know?
Thus shrewdly burdned then, how can my Muse escape?
The gods must help, and pretious things must serve to shew her shape.
  Like great god *Saturn* faire, and like faire *Venus* chaste:
As smooth as *Pan,* as *Juno* milde, like goddesse *Isis* faste.

6. Ringler, ed., *The Poems of Sir Philip Sidney,* p. 167.

With *Cupid* she fore-sees, and goes god *Vulcan's* pace:
And for a tast of all these gifts, she borowes *Momus'* grace.
Her forhead jacinth like, her cheekes of opall hue,
Her twinkling eies bedeckt with pearle, her lips of Saphir blew:
Her haire pure Crapal-stone; her mouth O heavenly wyde;
Her skin like burnisht gold, her hands like silver ure untryde.
As for those parts unknowne, which hidden sure are best:
Happie be they which well beleeve, and never seeke the rest.[7]

Like his predecessors, Shakespeare plays openly on his reader's expectations about the sonnet convention in poems like sonnet 130 *(My mistress' eyes are nothing like the sun)* and in the bawdy conclusions of sonnets 20, 144, and 151. Shakespeare's dark lady is traditionally cited as contrary to the traditional beloved, but the very impropriety of a technically unattractive and morally vicious beloved is a consistent enlargement on the standard rhetorical principle of the convention; and, whatever other significance there may be, certainly addressing love sonnets to a man is an all but predictable extreme of courtly love technique. Shakespeare's surprises, like Dante's, Donne's, and George Herbert's, come from going farther in the direction natural to the convention.

Although Shakespeare exploits the reader's expectations in the largest elements of the sonnets, similar smaller plays on the reader's expectations about syntax and idiom are more numerous. Moreover, their effects are more typical of the general rhetoric of the sonnets. Where both the traditional clashes of contexts in courtly love poetry, and Sidney's sud-

7. Ringler, p. 12.

den shifts in clearly distinguished systems of value call attention to themselves, the comparable actions in the syntactical fabric of sonnets like number 15 do not fully impinge on the reader's consciousness, and so do not merely describe inconstancy but evoke a real sense of inconstancy from a real experience of it. In sonnet 15 the reader is presented with the subject, verb, and direct object of the potentially complete clause *When I consider everything that grows.* The next line continues the clause and requires an easy but total reconstitution of the reader's conception of the kind of sentence he is reading; he has to understand *When I consider* [*that*] *everything that grows/ Holds in perfection but a little moment.* The kind of demand on the reader made syntactically in the first two lines is made in lines 11 and 12 by a nonidiomatic use of the common construction "debate with":

> . . . wasteful Time debateth with Decay
> To change your day of youth to sullied night. . . .

Having newly learned to understand *with* as "in the company of," the reader is forced by the couplet to readjust his understanding when essentially the same idiom appears in a variation on its usual sense, "fight against":

> And, all in war with Time for love of you,
> As he takes from you, I ingraft you new.

Just as the reader's mind moves from one to another formal or logical or phonetic structure, it also moves back and forth among metaphoric frames of reference. The terms in which the speaker presents his meaning, the "things" of the poem, are from a variety of ideological frames of reference, and the reader's mind is in constant motion from one context to another. Like all the other stylistic qualities I have talked about, the variation and quick change in the metaphoric focus of the sonnets presents in little the basic quality of courtly love and sonnet convention.

The first active metaphor of the poem, *grows,* carries a

vaguely botanical reference over into line 2, whose substance lends itself to overtones of traditional floral expressions of the *carpe diem* theme. The overtones would have been particularly strong for a reader accustomed to *perfection* in its common Renaissance meaning, "ripeness":

> When I consider everything that grows
> Holds in perfection but a little moment

Line 3 begins a new object clause, logically and syntactically parallel with the first. That parallelism helps the reader accept the new theatrical metaphor as an alternative means of simply restating the substance of the first clause. Moreover, the theatrical metaphor continues and reinforces the *watcher-watched* relationship established first in line 1 for the speaker and what he considers, and fully mirrored when line 4 introduces a new metaphor, the secretly influential stars, which are to the world-stage roughly as the powerless speaker was to the mortal world in line 1:

> That this huge stage presenteth nought but shows
> Whereon the stars in secret influence comment

The tone of the quatrain is matter-of-fact as befits a declaration so simple and so obviously justified that it is a subordinate prologue to the statement proper. That the matter-of-fact tone withstands coexistence with three distinct metaphors would be remarkable if each new metaphor were not introduced into the reader's mind as if it were already there.

Parallel syntax and parallel relationships suggest equation between the two object clauses—an equation which gives the reader a sense that what is both new and separate from the first two lines is at the same time neither new nor separate. In short, the physics of the quatrain's substance are the same as those of its rhyme scheme. The three metaphors pull both apart and together. The stars in line 4 are both new to the poem and have been in it covertly from the start. Probably only a mind as pun-ready as Shakespeare's own could hear the echo of Latin *sidus, sider-,* "star," in *consider,* but for any reader the act of imagining *this huge stage* presupposes the vantage point of the stars; the reader is thinking from the heavens, and, when the stars themselves are mentioned, their propriety is immediately further established because the stars comment, like critics at a play.[8]

Just as such an incidental sound pattern as *cheerèd and checked* emerges (from *perceive* and *increase)* into dominance and then submerges again (in *sky* and *decrease)* into the music of the whole, so the substance of the poem slips into and out of metaphoric frames of reference, always in a frame of reference some of whose parts pertain incidentally to one of the other metaphors from which and into which it moves.

> When I perceive that men as plants increase,
> Cheerèd and checked even by the selfsame sky,
> Vaunt in their youthful sap, at height decrease,
> And wear their brave state out of memory

At the beginning of quatrain 2, *plants increase* returns the botanical metaphor to clear prominence. The next line, *Cheerèd and checked even by the selfsame sky,* pertains very well to a growing plant *(Cheerèd*—smiled upon—*and checked*—restrained, held back, by the vagaries of the weather), but the primary syntactical object here is *men,* and *Cheerèd and checked* suggests the theatrical metaphor, particularly in the second half of the line, when the encouragement and rebuke turn out to be given *by the selfsame sky* that has earlier been audience to the shows on the huge stage.[9] In

8. Moreover, in the pattern in *s* and *t* that runs across both lines, *stars,* the fourth syllable of line 4, alliterates with *stage* in the same metrical position in line 3.

9. "Cheer" has a specifically theatrical meaning for a modern reader that it did not have for Shakespeare, but, even though it did not yet refer to shouts of applause, "cheer" did have the general meaning "encourage," from which the later meaning presumably developed.

line 7, *Vaunt* confirms the metaphoric dominance of boastful, strutting actors, but in the phrase that follows, *youthful,* which pertains directly to men (actors), is coupled with *sap,* a word from the botanical frame of reference to which *youthful* applies only figuratively, and which itself is only metaphorically descriptive of the humors of men: *Vaunt in their youthful sap, at height decrease. At height* is metaphorically applicable to the careers of men and the performances of haughty actors, and it is literally descriptive of a plant at its full growth, but the context to which *height* more usually belongs is astronomy (its context in sonnet 116). The phrase *at height decrease* confirms an earlier suggestion of the sun's passage across the sky or of the waxing moon—a suggestion that does not conform logically to the other use of astronomical metaphor, but that does persist throughout the quatrain. At the end of line 5, *increase* pertained obviously to *plants.* Its noun-meaning "fruit of the harvest," appears prominently in sonnets 1 and 11 which precede this one in the 1609 sequence; here, however, astronomical senses of *increase* also pertain. The *OED* reports Renaissance uses of the noun form of *increase* to mean "the rising of the tide . . . the advance of daylight from sunrise to noon; the waxing of the moon," and cites Renaissance examples in which forms of *decrease* indicate the negative of all three astronomical senses of *increase.* In this context *at height decrease* suggests the waning of the moon (taking *at height* figuratively to mean "fullness"), the descent of the sun (taking *at height* literally, and *decrease* to mean the decline of daylight from noon to sunset), and a tidelike ebbing of once *youthful sap.*

The last line of the quatrain, *And wear their brave state out of memory,* brings back the actors strutting in their finery, but its juxtaposition with *at height decrease* and the vague, cosmic immensity of *out of memory* give the line a majestic fall more appropriate to the descent of the sun than the perseverance of a player king. The reader's experience of this line is a type of his experience of this sonnet and the sonnets in general. The line is easy to understand, but it would be hard to say just what it says or how it says it. *Wear* in combination with *their brave state* says something like "wear their fine clothes." Following on *at height decrease, and wear* has reference to movement in space *(OED,* s.v. *Wear,* v. 21), and so, still under the influence of *Vaunt,* the half line says: "continue to advance in their pomp and finery." Thus, when he comes upon *out of,* the reader is likely to take it spatially (as in "out of the country"). On the other hand, *out* is in the same line with *wear* and *brave state,* and so leads the reader's understanding into a context of wearing out clothes, a context that is an excellent metaphor for the larger idea of the decay in time of everything that grows. The syntax of the line presents *memory* as if it were a place, but its sense makes it capable of comprehension only in terms of time. In common idiom "out of memory" refers to the distant, unseen past; but in *wear their brave state out of memory* the reference must be to the unseeable future. The statement of the octave takes in everything that has grown, grows, or will grow, and the multiple reference made by the conflict between standard usage and the use of *out of memory* in this line allows the reader an approximation of actual comprehension of all time and space in one.

The last six lines of the sonnet are more abstract than the first eight, and the three metaphors become more separable from each other, from a new metaphor of warfare, and from the abstract statements that they figure forth. In line 10 the beloved is set before the speaker's sight in a refrain of the theatrical metaphor; in line 12 the astronomical metaphor appears overtly in a commonplace; in the last line *ingraft* brings the botanical metaphor into a final statement otherwise contained entirely in the metaphor of warfare:

> Then the conceit of this inconstant stay
> Sets you most rich in youth before my sight,
> Where wasteful Time debateth with Decay

To change your day of youth to sullied night;
  And, all in war with Time for love of you,
  As he takes from you, I ingraft you new.

After the experience of the octave, the experience of the sestet is a clear awareness of the simplicity hidden in a great —a lifelike—complexity of relationships. The couplet describes a facile and fanciful triumph over time. The reader's experience of it, however, is the justified culmination of a small but real intellectual triumph over the limits of his own understanding.

The Value of the Sonnets

A formulated idea—written down, ordered, settled, its elements fixed in permanent relationship to one another as parts of a whole—accentuates its reader's incapacity to cope fully with what is outside the description. Like a fort, any statement presupposes, and so emphasizes, the frailty of the people it serves. Wordsworth made the point more cheerfully and in specific praise of the sonnet:

Nuns fret not at their convent's narrow room;
And hermits are contented with their cells;
And students with their pensive citadels;
Maids at the wheel, the weaver at his loom,
Sit blithe and happy; bees that soar for bloom,
High as the highest Peak of Furness-fells,
Will murmur by the hour in foxglove bells:
In truth the prison, unto which we doom
Ourselves, no prison is: and hence for me,
In sundry moods, 'twas pastime to be bound
Within the Sonnet's scanty plot of ground;
Pleased if some Souls (for such there needs must be)
Who have felt the weight of too much liberty,
Should find brief solace there, as I have found.[10]

10. *The Poetical Works of Wordsworth*, ed. Thomas Hutchinson, rev. Ernest de Selincourt (Oxford, 1950), p. 199.

The many different patterns that exist in any sonnet by virtue of its form make it seem crowded or, if that word has irremediably derisive connotations, full. Shakespeare's enlargement of the number and kinds of patterns makes his sonnets seem full to bursting not only with the quantity of different actions but with the energy generated from their conflict. The reader has constantly to cope with the multitudinous organizations of a Shakespeare sonnet; he is engaged and active. Nonetheless, the sonnets are above all else artificial, humanly ordered; the reader is always capable of coping. He always has the comfort and security of a frame of reference, but the frames of reference are not constant, and their number seems limitless.

The solace to be found in a Shakespeare sonnet is brief indeed, but it is as great a solace as literature can give—the feeling that the weight of liberty is not too much. That is a remarkable achievement for a reader and for the writer who gives it to him. I think it is that achievement which readers acknowledge when they praise Shakespeare's sonnets.

An Appendix of Supplementary Notes

Note 1. A description of the establishment of the octave in the seven sonnets where, as in sonnet 32, quatrain 1 is an incomplete logical unit (see Chap. 2, n. 5):

In sonnet 47 a sentence begun in the first quatrain is incomplete and makes logical sense only after it has run on into the second quatrain. Logically, the two quatrains function as one, but the completion of the *when* clause and the resultant pause in the rhythm of the sentence coincide with the fulfillment of the rhyme pattern of the first quatrain. The reader is made aware of both the continuity of the whole and the identity of the parts:

> Betwixt mine eye and heart a league is took,
> And each doth good turns now unto the other:
> When that mine eye is famished for a look,
> Or heart in love with sighs himself doth smother,
> With my love's picture then my eye doth feast
> And to the painted banquet bids my heart;
> Another time mine eye is my heart's guest
> And in his thoughts of love doth share a part.

The eight lines are a unified description of the mutual advantages of cooperative action in anatomical economy. The ninth line plunges from whimsy into a relatively straightforward statement of the relevance of the preceding lines:

> So, either by thy picture or my love,
> Thyself away are present still with me;
> For thou not farther than my thoughts canst move,

And I am still with them, and they with thee;
Or, if they sleep, thy picture in my sight
Awakes my heart to heart's and eye's delight.

The break is sharp. *So* indicates a logical step and implies summation of the lines that precede it. Moreover, where in the octave the beloved had been referred to in the third person as *my love,* he is now addressed directly. All things conspire to emphasize the division at line 9. The same is true of sonnet 94. There, *They,* the subject of the main clause, is not predicated in quatrain 1, which otherwise consists of three subordinate clauses. Line 5 makes a new start on the original construction, repeating *They* and predicating it immediately. The third quatrain makes a new start formally, syntactically, and substantially.

The syntactical structure of 106 is similar to that of 32 and 47. The octave is one sentence; the first quatrain is a *when* clause; the second is a *then* clause. The third quatrain begins a new sentence and comments on the octave as a whole. In 23 and 118 the first quatrain is a simile, and the second applies it; the third quatrain is a new sentence which comments on the other two and thus unifies them. As in 32, 47, and 106, the first quatrain cannot stand alone but is syntactically and logically distinct, and, also as in 32, 47, and 106, the syntactical and logical structure of the octave simultaneously divides and unites the quatrains, while the syntactically separate third quatrain is connected only logically with what precedes it. The last of the sonnets in which the dependent clause of an octave in one sentence coincides with the first quatrain is 128. In its management of the octave this sonnet differs from 32, 47, and 106 only in that the division between quatrains is slightly softened by the internal rather than external subordination of the *when* clause to the main clause.

Sonnet 143 differs from the poems I have just described in that its first sentence does not become syntactically complete until the third quatrain. The poem begins *Lo, as a careful housewife;* the simile is potentially complete at the end of line 4, but the second quatrain expands it in a new clause: *Whilst her neglected child holds her in chase;* quatrain 3 applies the simile: *So runn'st thou after that which flies from thee.* The octave is defined by the coincidence with the start of the new quatrain of both a new clause and a major logical step.

Note 2. A description of octaves similar to that of sonnet 33, where a potentially complete statement in quatrain 1 is unexpectedly continued into quatrain 2 (see Chap. 2, n. 8):

The octaves similar to the octave of 33 differ from it in their particular means to achieve a common effect. In sonnet 20, where, as in sonnet 33, the second quatrain is unexpectedly yoked to the first, the connection is made by the continuation of a pattern already established in quatrain 1, where one subject and verb serve two objects; the second quatrain adds yet another object for the verb *hast.* Similarly, the second quatrain of 129 simply continues the list of qualities that follow from *Is* in line 3. In 68 anaphora is used for the same purpose; the reader's sense of delay is heightened by the exact repetition in line 5 of the construction used in line 3. There is a similar effect in the octave of 117, where the repetition is less mechanical and more complex, and where the repetition of the same construction is continued in each pair of lines through line 8.

The first four lines of 114 seem to be complete in themselves. The alternatives are set out in a pair of pointedly parallel constructions. This is the first quatrain of 114 as punctuated in the 1609 quarto:

> Or whether doth my mind being crowned with you,
> Drink up the monarch's plague this flattery?
> Or whether shall I say mine eye saith true,
> And that your love taught it this alchemy?

Most modern editors offer the reader the advantage of their foreknowledge of the text by putting a comma rather than a question mark after *alchemy.* Even so, the syntactical afterthought of the second quatrain makes an unexpected delay in the progress of the poem and enlists the reader's eagerness for a decision; when at last it comes in line 9, the reader's sense of delay combines with the rhythmic emphasis of the exclamatory *O, 'tis the first,* to make the division between quatrains 2 and 3 a major division in the poem:

> Or whether doth my mind, being crowned with you,
> Drink up the monarch's plague, this flattery?
> Or whether shall I say mine eye saith true,

And that your love taught it this alchemy,
To make of monsters and things indigest
Such cherubins as your sweet self resemble,
Creating every bad a perfect best
As fast as objects to his beams assemble?
O, 'tis the first; 'tis flatt'ry in my seeing,
And my great mind most kingly drinks it up:
Mine eye well knows what with his gust is 'greeing,
And to his palate doth prepare the cup.
  If it be poisoned, 'tis the lesser sin
  That mine eye loves it and doth first begin.

The octave of 72 is much the same in its effect as that of 114. The quarto punctuates the first quatrain likes this:

O lest the world should task you to recite,
What merit liv'd in me that you should love
After my death (dear love) forget me quite,
For you in me can nothing worthy prove.

A semicolon, which modern editors put after *prove,* is not sufficient to prepare the reader for the syntactical patchwork by which the second quatrain is tacked to the first:

Unless you would devise some virtuous lie,
To do more for me than mine own desert
And hang more praise upon deceasèd I
Than niggard truth would willingly impart.

In 153 the second quatrain is a syntactically unexpected relative clause. In 26 it is an unexpected gloss of the word *duty* in the first quatrain. In 21 and 29 the second quatrain begins with a present participle which trails off from the first. The fifth line of 21 accidentally defines its own action; the octaves of these eleven sonnets are achieved by *making a couplement:*

So is it not with me as with that Muse
Stirred by a painted beauty to his verse,
Who heaven itself for ornament doth use
And every fair with his fair doth rehearse;
Making a couplement of proud compare
With sun and moon, with earth and sea's rich gems,

With April's first-born flowers, and all things rare
That heaven's air in this huge rondure hems.

Note 3. On David Masson's "Free Phonetic Patterns in Shakespeare's Sonnets," *Neophilologus, 37* (October 1954), 277–89 (see Chap. 3, n. 3):

C. S. Lewis was altogether justified in his fear that "to some . . . such analysis will seem trifling." In fact, a mild persecution complex is all but indispensable to a stylistic critic attempting more than an anthology of impressionistic adjectives. Masson is a case in point of a critic too careless of the prejudices of his audience. His article is the last to be summarized in the following paragraph by Alexander Nejgebauer ("Twentieth-century Studies in Shakespeare's Songs, Sonnets and Poems: 2. The Sonnets," *Shakespeare Survey, 15* [Cambridge, Eng. 1962], 17). The paragraph purports to summarize everything written in the twentieth century about the phonetics of Shakespeare's sonnets. I quote it in its entirety:

> Alliteration in the sonnets has been examined statistically by R. T. Price *(Studies in Honor of Basil Gildersleeve,* 1902) who found it poetically significant, and by B. F. Skinner *(The Psychological Record,* III, 1939); the latter comes to the opposite conclusion that 'Shakespeare might as well have drawn words out of a hat.' A good reply, supported by an analysis and classification of uses of alliteration and assonance was provided by U. K. Goldsmith *(Journal of English and Germanic Philology,* XLIX, 1950); he shows that this element, mainly ornamental in function, was clearly both used and avoided by the poet for artistic reasons. Quite unlike this in treatment is D. J. Mason's study of 'free phonetic patterns' in the sonnets *(Neophilologus,* 1954): he employs a complicated descriptive terminology and then makes unrelated assessments, attempting to prove that these patterns express the finest shades of meaning. One wonders what sense he would extract from the repetition of patterns like '*m, i/y, n, d/t*' if unassisted by the text.

Granting that Nejgebauer had a lot to cover and that he had not sufficient time for Masson's article to get its author's name right, the easy gibe of his last sentence is inexcusable. On the other hand, although Nejgebauer might have had the charity to pay attention to Masson's statement that "the precise effect [of sound patterns] depends upon the details of the pattern and those of the significance of the words" (p. 281), it must be admitted that Masson does not insist either forcefully or often on the preeminence of substance in the lines he discusses. (He cannot, after all, be expected to insist upon the relative insignificance of the effects he is studying at the same time that he is attempting to show his readers that those effects exist and, although of less than primary importance, contribute to the experience of the sonnets.) Moreover, an audience of literary critics rather than linguistic scientists is so little prepared in outlook or vocabulary for phonetic criticism that reference to anything more complex than alliteration requires an expense of ugly mechanical terms or quasi-runic symbols. To point out the existence of a complex phonetic pattern in even a short phrase requires so much space on a page that a reader, who is perhaps already suspicious of the paraphernalia, is likely to think that the critic takes the demonstrated phonetic effect to be of importance commensurate with the number of words required for the demonstration. This is the paragraph that Nejgebauer singles out of Masson's article for particular scorn:

> Sonnet cxvi opens with the magnificent
>
> > Let me not to the marriage of true mindes
> > Admit impediments . . .
>
> The general effect of supra-logical argument is very strong. There are also specific connotations. Subpattern (a) in *m, n, t,* is perhaps an augmented 3-member figure, unknotted in 2 into two sections, "mindes" and "Admit". It is composed of two strands, (aa) a partly jointed switch in *t, m,* and (ab) a fully jointed 3-member sequence in *m, n.* In (aa) the switch at "true mindes/Admit" produces an impression of hesitation according with the sense; but (ab) ploughs steadily through this check, suggesting the poet's firm faith. Meanwhile (b), a 3-member knotting-up 1/2 interchange in *m, n, d,* jointed at 2—3 ("mindes / Admit impediments") also suggests a check at "Admit", in this case followed by a headlong topple in the polysyllabic last word. A hobbling effect of obstacles is pro-

> duced by (c), a species of double interchange, headed and tailed, of 4 members in *m, i/y, n, d/t* ("true mindes / Admit impediments", with "mindes" as [məɪndz] or /məindz/), of which the inner two members lack *n*. The interchange and syllable-doubling in (d) ['məɪndz, –ɪ,mənts] also give the impression of an onward progress (member 1) reduced to zigzag courses. A switch-headed loosening bracket (e) in *d, i, t,* here also suggests a "reversal" or headlong topple. Finally (f) the dissonant pair "let . . . . not" emphasize the rhetorical refusal of the poet, an effect continued by further modulation and interchange (plus element *d)* in the rest of the line. (pp. 288–89)

Only a regular contributor of similar articles in *Neophilologus* is likely to be prepared to take meaning from such a paragraph. Masson has probably caught himself up so far in technical jargon as to bar himself from those of his potential audience to whom he has most to say, the part of his audience concerned with the sonnets rather than the sciences of speech and hearing. Moreover, unless I overestimate the influence of an elegant slur in a general survey like Nejgebauer's, future Shakespearean scholars will probably consider themselves excused from attempting Masson's article at all. It is a shame. Masson's error is grandly but purely tactical. Buried in his article is a long step in the slow progress toward an understanding of the contribution made by the phonetics of a sonnet to its general effect.

Note 4. Further examples of definable identity in the first two lines of Shakespeare sonnets (see Chap. 3, n. 5):

The next-to-last syllables of lines 1 and 2 of Sonnet 78 are identical (see also 53):

> So oft have I invoked thee for my Muse
> And found such fair assistance in my verse

Here the alliteration of the voiced and unvoiced *f* sound in *oft, invoked, for, found, fair,* and *verse,* and the identical final *s* sound in *Muse* and *verse,* give an additional sense of unity and wholeness to the lines in direct contradiction both of the incompleteness of the quatrain rhyme scheme and of the manifest incompleteness of the syntax. Much the same is true of the first two lines of 94, where the penultimate syllables of the first two lines are also identical, and where, again as in 78, the necessities of syntax and rhyme deny whatever completeness the lines have phonetically. In 79 the third and fourth syllables of the first two lines are identical and their sixth syllables rhyme:

> Whilst I alone did call upon thy aid,
> My verse alone had all thy gentle grace

Similarly, the words *that I* are in exactly parallel metrical positions in the first two lines of 136:

> If thy soul check thee that I come so near,
> Swear to thy blind soul that I was thy Will

In the first two lines of 87, *my* and *thy* rhyme, balance each other logically, and are in parallel metrical positions before the assonant words *possessing* and *estimate:*

> Farewell: thou art too dear for my possessing,
> And like enough thou know'st thy estimate.

The last words of the two first lines of sonnet 6 are balanced logically and are also alliterative:

> Then let not winter's ragged hand deface
> In thee thy summer ere thou be distilled

In sonnet 83, *painting* is in the same metrical position in both of the first two lines, and the logical balance between the lines themselves evokes the same general sense of completeness and finality that is evoked by similar constructions in the previous examples:

> I never saw that you did painting need,
> And therefore to your fair no painting set

In this case there is an additional self-contained pattern in the lines: *therefore* and *your fair* are scrambled phonetic images of each other. The two *r* sounds and the *f* sound are in the same position in both pairs of syllables. The first vowel sound of *therefore* is the second of *your fair;* and intervening between the rhyming *there* and *fair* are three different kinds of *o* sound in series.

The self-contained phonetic nugget *therefore to your fair* is a particularly complicated example of a reasonably common phenomenon from which a sense of the wholeness of the opening lines of several other sonnets results. Sometimes that sense of separate identity corresponds with a syntactical unity of the two lines; sometimes it doesn't. It is always, of course, at variance with the rhyme scheme, which at the end of the second line is obviously incomplete. The one exception, 126, is not a sonnet in any technical sense, but six couplets. Inside the first couplet, however, is the ostentatious internal rhyme *fickle-sickle*.

At the end of line 2 of sonnet 31 the reader cannot feel that what he has read is whole in itself. Obviously there are twelve more lines on the page before him. Scarcely less obvious is the reader's need to go on to satisfaction in the completion of the quatrain rhyme scheme. However, although line 3 begins with a copula signaling that the preceding clauses are not completely self-sufficient, there is a momentary sense of finality at the end of line 2. This is the first quatrain of 31:

> Thy bosom is endearèd with all hearts
> Which I by lacking have supposèd dead;
> And there reigns love, and all love's loving parts,
> And all those friends which I thought burièd.

The first two lines are potentially self-contained syntactically. The real source of their unity, however, is the quasi rhyme of the final, unaccented, but pronounced *ed* of *endearèd* and *supposèd*. If there is a pause in line 1, it is a slight one after *endearèd*. Probably the main pause in line 2 is after *lacking*. A slight pause between the rhyming *I* and *by* is also possible. Another slight pause is inevitable from the mechanical necessity of placing the tongue and lips to pronounce *dead* after pronouncing the final *ed* of *supposèd*. The pauses and the rhymes on the unaccented *ed* sound give the lines a separate and metrically illogical rhythm of their own. It is unobtrusive but audible. The last word of line 2, *dead,* rhymes with *endearèd* and *supposèd,* and clinches a fleeting but real phonetic sense that the two lines, which are a sort of topic sentence for the poem, are set apart in a heading-like relationship to all that follows.

Something of the same sort occurs in 39, where the internal

rhyming of the unaccented word *art* with the accented word *part* in the second line results in an extrametrical rhymthmic unity of lines 1 and 2:

> O, how thy worth with manners may I sing
> When thou art all the better part of me?

The scarcely perceptible rhyme of *art* and *part* gives the reader a sense that *of me,* the last foot of line 2, is a resumption and completion of the alliteration in *m* in line 1. The phonetic unity of the two lines gives in a quiet and less final way the sort of extralogical support to the syntactical unity of the two lines that is more bluntly given by end-rhymes. See also the phonetic patterns in the second lines of 40 and 130, the near rhyme of *to see . . . do deeds* in 37, and especially the jingling abstract of the first two lines of sonnet 1 that is made by the assonance and rhyme of *creatures . . . increase . . . thereby . . . never die.*

The first two lines of 65 are dominated by the sound *or,* which is gradually drawn out in the second line through *mortality,* to *o'ersways,* to a culmination in the long single syllable *power:*

> Since brass, nor stone, nor earth, nor boundless sea,
> But sad mortality o'ersways their power

The opening pairs of lines in some of the sonnets have the kind of unobtrusive phonetic identity and the accompanying sense of unassailable truth that is found in proverbs like "Don't cry over sp*ilt* m*ilk*" and "Do*n't* cou*nt* your *ch*ickens before they're hat*ch*ed." Often such asymmetrical sound patterns are in conjunction with polyptoton. In 84, phonetic unity is achieved in the first two lines by internal rhyme, polyptoton, and extrametrical prose rhythm; in 54 there is phonetic wholeness from polyptoton, repetition of the double *e* sound in *seem* and *sweet,* unvoiced *th,* and *or*. In 77 the principal device is anaphora:

> Thy glass will show thee how thy beauties wear,
> Thy dial how thy precious minutes waste

Here both anaphora in the first syllables and the echo of *beauties wear* in *minutes waste* reinforce the logical coupling of the two simultaneously similar and different functions of *glass* and *dial.* In these opening lines of 77 the syntax and the sounds demonstrate similarity, and the substance of the lines demonstrates difference. That is the usual prose use of such constructions. It is more usual in lines linked by anaphora at the beginning of Shakespeare's sonnets for both logic and syntax to indicate difference. In the opening lines of sonnet 81, for example, the blunt parallelism of the *or I . . . or you* construction is sustained by the alliterating *v* in the fourth syllable of both lines, but after the second syllable the syntax of line 2 is totally different from that of line 1:

> Or I shall live your epitaph to make,
> Or you survive when I in earth am rotten.

In 96 the first six syllables of line 2 are, except for the replacement of *grace* for *fault,* identical with the first phrase of line 1:

> Some say thy fault is youth, some wantonness;
> Some say thy grace is youth and gentle sport

Note 5. Further examples of pulsating alliteration in the sonnets (see Chap. 4, n. 1):

I have already described David Masson's work on phonetic patterns in his "Free Phonetic Patterns in Shakespeare's Sonnets" (*Neophilologus, 37,* 277–89). In the course of illustrating larger and far more complicated effects, Masson demonstrates incidentally some excellent examples of pulsating alliteration. For example, he points out (p. 284) the division and then the unification of the sounds of *praise* in the couplet of sonnet 106:

> For we, which now behold these *p*resent d*ays,*
> Have eyes to wonder, but lack tongues to *praise.*

In the same sonnet he demonstrates a concurrent pattern which expands at the same time that the *praise* pattern contracts: *b* and *pr* appear close together in *but prophecies* (line 9), far apart in *behold these present* (line 13), and still farther apart in *but lack tongues to praise* (line 14). Masson also points out (p. 283) a contraction and expansion of *pr* and *ayze* in lines 2–4 of sonnet 85: *praise* (line 2) is split into *precious phrase* (line 4). Also in 85 Masson describes (p. 286) a pattern of division and contraction complicated by chiasmus in line 6: *And, like unlettered clerk, still cry 'Amen.'* The *l* and *k* sounds, separated by a vowel in *like,* are much farther separated and then brought closer together again in *unlettered c/lerk.* In *still cry* the *l* and *k* sounds are divided only by the intersyllabic pause. In line 3 of sonnet 107 Masson demonstrates (p. 285) a contraction of the phonetic essence of the whole line into its last word: *Can yet the lease of my true love control.* The grammatical relations cut across the patterning, but the argument, like the sound, knots up the phrases *Can yet, the lease of,* and *my true love* into *control.* Moreover, internally the line contains a contraction of the *l* and *ov* sounds of *lease of* into *love.*

Quatrain one of sonnet 32 is densely patterned in *l* sounds in various combinations with *t* and *d:*

> If thou survive my well-contented day
> When that churl Death my bones with dust shall cover,
> And shalt by fortune once more resurvey
> These poor rude lines of thy deceasèd lover

In *well-contented day* the *l* sound appears separated by the length of a syllable from the first of four stopped dentals. The pattern appears twice in the phrase *that churl Death:* chiasmically in *that churl,* where the *l* and *t* are again separated by a syllable, and in *churl Death,* where *l* and *d* are separated only by the pause between syllables. At the end of line 2 the *d* and *t* sounds of *dust* are again separated from the *l* sound of *shall.* In line 3 the two sounds come tightly together in *shalt,* only to be separated again by intersyllabic pauses when they reappear at the end of the quatrain in *rude lines* and *deceasèd lover.*

One of the commonest patterns of pulsating alliteration is in *b* or *p* (the voiced and unvoiced forms of the same sound), in combination with a variety of *r* sounds. Besides the example already noticed in sonnet 12 and the instance cited by Masson, there are excellent examples in 28.2–3 *(debarred, benefit of rest, oppression),* 32.11–13 *(birth, brought, better, prove),* 55.1–4, 6–7, 10–11 *(marble, princes, pow'rful, bright, besmeared; broils, burn; pace forth, praise, posterity),* 70.8 *(present'st, pure, prime),* 80.2–8, 10–12 (with pattern augmented by *s—better spirit, praise thereof spends, speaking of your, But since your, proudest sail doth bear, saucy bark, broad, appear; soundless deep doth ride, being wracked, worthless boat, pride),* 86.1–3, 5–7 *(proud, Bound for, prize, pre-*

cious, ripe, brain; spirit, spirits, mortal pitch, compeers), 152.2–6 *(But thou art, bed-vow broke, bearing, breach, break, perjured),* and, finally, 151, which, because positioning is important, particularly in the case of the expansion of *betray* (line 5) into *body's treason* (line 6) and then into *body that he may/triumph,* I quote entire; the patterning sounds *(br/pr* throughout, *btr/ptr* in lines 5 through 9, and *prd* in lines 10 and 11), are indicated by italics:

Love is too young to know what conscience is;
Yet who knows not conscience is *b*o*r*n of love?
Then, gentle cheater, urge not my amiss,
Lest guilty of my faults thy sweet self *pr*ove.
For, thou *b*e*tr*aying me, I do *b*e*tr*ay
My nobler *p*ar*t* to my gross *b*ody's *tr*eason;
My soul doth tell my *b*ody that he may
*Tr*iumph in love; flesh stays no farther reason,
*B*ut, *r*ising at thy name, doth point out thee
As his triumphant *pr*ize. *Pr*ou*d* of this *pr*i*d*e,
He is contented thy *p*oo*r* *d*rudge to be,
To stand in thy affairs, fall by thy side.
  No want of conscience hold it that I call
  Her 'love' for whose dear love I rise and fall.

In Chapter 4 I talked about the contraction and expansion of combinations of *f* and *r* and of *f* and *l* in sonnet 33. There is another good example of the pattern in *f* and *l* in 109. The two sounds appear separated in *false* (line 1), then together in *flame* (line 2). In *qualify* (line 2) they are in reverse order and separated; they come together again in *myself* (line 3) and spread far apart in *from my soul* (line 4). They spread farther apart and then come closer together in *lie/ That is my home of* (lines 4–5) and *love* (line 5), in both of which the *f* sound is voiced *(v)*. In *travels* (line 6) the *v* and *l* sounds are reversed but still separated; the sounds come together in *myself* (line 8) and separate into the *l* and *v* of *believe* (line 9). They are further separated in *frailties,* and still further separated and then brought closer together in the two combinations *(all kinds of* and *of blood)* within the phrase *all kinds of blood.* They come relatively close together in *leave* (line 12) and then spread apart again in *all thy sum of* (line 12) and *universe I call* (line 13). In the last line of the poem the two sounds appear in *Save* and *all,* separated by the whole length of the line:

O, never say that I was false of heart,
Though absence seemed my flame to qualify;
As easy might I from myself depart
As from my soul, which in thy breast doth lie.
That is my home of love: if I have ranged,
Like him that travels I return again,
Just to the time, not with the time exchanged,
So that myself bring water for my stain.
Never believe, though in my nature reigned
All frailties that besiege all kinds of blood,
That it could so preposterously be stained
To leave for nothing all thy sum of good;
  For nothing this wide universe I call
  Save thou, my rose; in it thou art my all.

Running through sonnet 109 concurrently and often in the same words and phrases with the pattern in *l* and *f/v* is a pattern in which combinations of *r* and *f/v* also contract and expand: *never, false of heart, myself depart, from, if I have ranged, travels, myself bring, for, Never, frailties, for, For, universe, Save thou my rose*. The pattern in *r* and *f/v* is as common in the sonnets as the pattern *r* and *b/p*. The pattern of English syntax makes phrases like *from far, far from,* and *farthest from* almost inevitable. The combination *far from* appears ten times in the sonnets (27.5, 28.8, 44.4, 44.6, 50.4, 61.6, 61.14, 76.2, 117.8, 124.5), and, except where it is sustained (as in 76.1–2, where *far from* is preceded by *verse* and followed by *variation),* the resulting sense of pulsation can be written off as an automatic dividend of English syntax, open equally to every writer and speaker of English, and no evidence for the fineness of Shakespeare's ear. On the other hand, the evidence of Shakespeare's use of the word *for,* which appears in 165 lines in the sonnets, is not so easy to discount. In 151 of those 165 lines the *f* and *r* sounds of *for* are a contraction or an expansion of a combination of *f* or *v* and *r* earlier in the same line or in the line immediately preceding, or else are contracted or expanded in a combination of those sounds later in the same line or in the line immediately following.

The details of the 151 instances in which *for* appears in a pulsating pattern in *f*/*v* and *r* are as follows. (Since I put such emphasis on *for,* I may seem to be more impressed by these statistics than I am or should be. In Shakespeare's sonnets *for* appears in a pulsating pattern in *f*/*v* and *r* 92 per cent of the time; 69 per cent of the time the same is true of *Astrophel and Stella.* I consider the statistics more important in Shakespeare's sonnets than in Sidney's largely because in Shakespeare's sonnets the pattern appears among so many other similar phenomena.) In 25 lines *for* presents the sounds *f* and *r* farther from one another than they are in a combination of *f* and *r* or *v* and *r* earlier in the line or in the line immediately preceding (parentheses indicate lines in which *for* presents the preceding or following combination of *f* or *v* and *r* chiasmically): 5.5; (11.13); 21.3; 25.12; 29.13; 33.13; 42.8; 44.7; 52.4; 61.12; 62.13; 72.6; (75.10); 86.2; 97.11; 99.4; 104.2; 120.2; (120.5); (121.5); 134.6; 134.11; 140.9; 147.13; 149.4.

In 50 lines *f* and *r* are contracted in *for* from a preceding looser combination of *f* and *r* or *v* and *r:* 6.8; 9.10; (10.13); 22.10; 23.11; 24.10; 25.4; 25.9; (32.7); (32.14); (34.7); 37.5; (40.6); (41.4); 42.7; 42.12; (45.5); 47.11; 48.14; 51.12; 53.14; 54.4; 57.6; 60.12; (61.12); 62.3; 63.9; (67.11); (70.7); 71.6; 72.4; (72.10); 72.13; 74.4; (79.13); 83.9; 83.14; 87.1; 99.6; 106.11; 106.13; 112.3; 124.2; (134.7); 136.4; 147.2; (151.14); 153.10; 153.13; 154.12.

In 75 lines the *f* and *r* of *for* appear later in the same line or in the following line in a looser combination of *f* and *r* or *v* and *r:* 3.5; (4.9); 6.7; 6.8; 6.13; 9.1; (10.1); 10.2; 10.5; 11.9; 20.13; 21.3; 23.5; 24.5; 24.9; 25.4; (27.2); 35.9; 38.4; (40.5); 41.4; 43.2; (45.5); (47.3); 47.11; (48.14); 50.13; 59.3; 62.7; 66.1; (67.11); 68.13; (70.7); 72.10; 75.3; 78.1; 82.11; 83.11; 85.13; 88.10; 88.14; (89.13); (89.14); 90.4; (92.2); 92.4; 93.5; 94.13; 96.8; 99.12; 101.2; 104.13; 106.11; 106.13; (111.1); 111.3; 113.9; 120.5; (121.5); 124.2; (125.3); 125.7; 125.12; 127.5; 131.3; 133.13; (141.2); 147.13; (151.14); 152.7; 152.9; 152.13; 153.10; 153.13; 154.13.

In 32 lines *for* is followed in the same or the next following line by *f* and *r* or *v* and *r* in tighter combination than that in *for:* 5.5; 15.13; 20.9; 22.5; 25.8; 27.5; 29.13; 30.6; (39.5); 42.12; 44.3; 51.12; 54.9; 60.12; 61.13; 62.13; 70.2; 87.5; 87.6; 95.10; 97.11; 103.11; 104.2; 108.12; 109.8; 109.12; 109.13; 113.5; 132.11; 133.2; (147.2); 149.4.

(In lines where *for* is in the middle of a pattern of pulsation that continues from a preceding word or phrase into a following word or phrase, the line number appears in both of the relevant lists —e.g. 5.5).

Note 6. Antanaclasis in *with* and *but* in the sonnets, and examples of similar uses of *of, to, so,* and *in* (see Chap. 4, n. 12):

The *OED* gives 40 different uses of the preposition "with"; many of them are so nearly identical that, except for purposes of grammatical description, the differences are negligible. I have therefore restricted the basis of my distinctions to the three broad categories under which the more precise variations are ranged. The three major categories of meaning are: (1) "with" indicating opposition; (2) "with" indicating personal relation, association, accompaniment; (3) "with" indicating instrumentality, causation, agency. (Such a limitation perforce ignores meaningful distinctions in usage within a broad category. For example, both uses of *with* in sonnet 4 fall under category 2, but in line 9—*For, having traffic with thyself alone—with* indicates transaction, while in line 13—*Thy unused beauty must be tombed with thee—with* means "accompanied by." See also 21.1,4; 63.2,4; and 136.6,7.)

Even after the basis for distinction is restricted, there are, in the 47 sonnets where the word is repeated, still 20 instances of unobtrusive but perceptible antanaclasis in *with* (5.7,11; 7.4,9; 8.2,4; 12.4,8; 15.11,13; 20.1,4; 23.2,3; 29.1,3,6,8; 32.2,5; 33.4,6,8,10; 45.2,4,7,8; 47.4,5; 67.1,2; 71.12,14; 75.7,9; 128.10,11; 139.3,4; 141.5,8; 149.2,8; 150.2,12). Here are three examples; in the last of them a complex anaphora between the first two lines and lines 11 and 12 stresses the simultaneous likeness and difference of the two uses of *with:*

> Sweets with sweets war not, joy delights in joy:
> Why lov'st thou that which thou receiv'st not gladly,
> Or else receiv'st with pleasure thine annoy? (8.2–4)
>
> The other two, slight air and purging fire,
> Are both with thee, wherever I abide;
> The first my thought, the other my desire,
> These present-absent with swift motion slide.
>
> . . .

My life, being made of four, with two alone
Sinks down to death, oppressed with melancholy (45.1–4, 7–8)
O, from what pow'r hast thou this pow'rful might
With insufficiency my heart to sway?

. . .

O, though I love what others do abhor,
With others thou shouldst not abhor my state (150.1–2, 11–12)

The word *but* appears more than once in 45 sonnets. In 34 of those it appears first with one meaning and then with another. Discounting the sonnets in which the two uses are too widely separated to be even minutely effective, there are 24 instances in the sonnets of antanaclasis in *but* (1.3,5; 5.13,14; 9.10,11; 15.2,3; 22.3,6,10; 32.9,13; 34.11,13; 42.13,14; 44.9,11,14; 45.11,13; 51.6,12; 74.1,7; 78.11,13; 84.7,9; 93.9,12; 94.8,11; 99.12,15; 102.5,11; 106.11,14; 125.10,12; 133.4,10; 134.5,7; 139.3,5; 152.5,7). The commonest alternation is between *but* meaning "on the contrary" or "however" and *but* meaning "only" or "except." The first three instances in the 1609 sequence will serve as examples:

That thereby beauty's rose might never die,
But as the riper should by time decease,
His tender heir might bear his memory;
But thou, contracted to thine own bright eyes,
Feed'st thy light's flame . . . (1.2–6)

But flowers distilled, though they with winter meet,
Leese but their show; their substance still lives sweet. (5.13–14)

Look what an unthrift in the world doth spend
Shifts but his place, for still the world enjoys it;
But beauty's waste hath in the world an end (9.9–11)

This welter of particulars is intended to demonstrate that the quotations in the text are not isolated examples and that the insignificant and unobtrusive word play I'm talking about is very common in the sonnets. I hope the point is made. I doubt that further exhaustive documentation would serve any purpose. I could make similar lists for *of, to, in,* and so on; but I hope that my reader will be grateful to be spared further apparatus and will accept the following random examples as given in good faith.

In each of the following examples I give the word played upon in italics:

Will be a tottered weed *of* small worth held:
Then being asked where all thy beauty lies,
Where all the treasure *of* thy lusty days (2.4–6)

Be scorned, like old men *of* less truth than tongue,
And your true rights be termed a poet's rage
And stretchèd meter *of* an antique song.
  But were some child *of* yours . . . (17.10–13)

Of public honor and proud titles boast,
Whilst I, whom fortune *of* such triumph bars (25.2–3)

Was it the proud full sail *of* his great verse,
Bound for the prize *of* all-too-precious you

. . .

As victors, *of* my silence cannot boast;
I was not sick *of* any fear from thence (86.1–2, 11–12)

How have mine eyes out *of* their spheres been fitted
In the distraction *of* this madding fever!
O benefit *of* ill . . . (119.7–9)

To thee I send this written ambassage
To witness duty, not to show my wit (26.3–4)

Where thou art forced *to* break a twofold truth:
  Hers, by the beauty tempting her *to* thee,
  Thine, by thy beauty being false to me. (41.12–14)

That you yourself may privilege your time
To what you will; *to* you it doth belong
Yourself *to* pardon of self-doing crime.
  I am *to* wait . . . (58.10–13)

On newer proof, *to* try an older friend,
A god in love, *to* whom I am confined.
  Then give me welcome, next my heaven the best,
  Even *to* thy pure and most most loving breast. (110.11–14)

Like as *to* make our appetites more keen,
With eager compounds we our palate urge;
As *to* prevent our maladies unseen,
We sicken *to* shun sickness when we purge:
Even so, being full of your ne'er-cloying sweetness,
To bitter sauces did I frame my feeding;
And, sick of welfare, found a kind of meetness
To be diseased ere that there was true needing.
Thus policy in love, *t'*anticipate
The ills that were not, grew *to* faults assured,
And brought *to* medicine a healthful state
Which, rank of goodness, would by ill be cured.
But thence I learn, and find the lesson true,
Drugs poison him that so fell sick of you. (118)

So shall I live, supposing thou art true,
Like a deceivèd husband; *so* love's face
May still seem love to me though altered new,
Thy looks with me, thy heart *in* other place.
For there can live no hatred *in* thine eye;
Therefore *in* that I cannot know thy change;
In many's looks the false heart's history
Is writ *in* moods and frowns and wrinkles strange:
But heaven *in* thy creation did decree
That *in* thy face sweet love should ever dwell (93.1–10)

And *in* themselves their pride lies burièd,
For at a frown they *in* their glory die. (25.7–8)

In sequent toil all forwards do contend.
Nativity, once *in* the main of light (60.4–5)

From you have I been absent *in* the spring,
When proud-pied April, dressed *in* all his trim,
Hath put a spirit of youth *in* everything (98.1–3)

Note 7. Further examples of sonnets in which quatrains 2 and 3 are a distinct eight-line entity (see Chap. 4, n. 13):

In sonnet 25 *(Let those who are in favor with their stars)* quatrains 2 and 3 have a substantive unity; both are concerned with the instability of public honor. The overall substantive pattern of the poem is 2, 2, 8, 2: two lines on public men, two lines on the speaker, eight lines on public men, and two more lines on the speaker. Sonnet 124 *(If my dear love were but the child of state)* also has second and third quatrains unified and differentiated from the rest of the poem by common subject matter. Quatrain 1 concerns itself with a state contrary to fact; quatrain 2 begins *No;* and quatrain 3 continues the same denial of mutability: *It fears not Policy* . . . .

Sonnet 30 *(When to the sessions of sweet silent thought)* is complicated by the superimposition of the pattern 4, 8, 2 upon an almost perfect alignment of syntactical and formal units. Each quatrain is a separate syntactical unit, as is the couplet, but quatrain 1 begins *When,* and both quatrains 2 and 3 begin *Then;* the couplet begins *But.* As the syntactical steps from *When* in quatrains 1 and 2 to *Then* in quatrain 3 gives identity to an octave in sonnets 12 and 15, here the step from *when* to *then* after quatrain 1 and the repetition of the *then* construction in quatrain 3 gives a similar identity to lines 5 through 12.

The first quatrain of sonnet 34 *(Why didst thou promise such a beauteous day)* is a question. Quatrain 2 begins *'Tis not enough that* . . . . Quatrain 3 continues the negative statement, thus pulling lines 5 through 12 together in opposition to the formal division between quatrains.

In sonnet 48 *(How careful was I, when I took my way)* the 4, 8, 2 pattern coexists with an octave. The identity of the octave is established by a change at line 9 from the positive statements of the first two quatrains to the negative statement of the third. At the same time, however, an equally valid division exists between the subject matter (material possessions) of quatrain 1 and that of the next two quatrains, which are concerned with the beloved. (What I call a 4, 8, 2 pattern might in this sonnet and in several of those discussed below be just as well called 4, 10. Here, for example, the subject matter of lines 5 through 12 is continued in the couplet, so that the last ten lines of the poem are substantively distinct from the first four. I talk about an eight-line rather than a ten-line unit because the formal division between the three quatrains and the couplet is so nearly total as to obliterate all sense of continuity except that of the logical relevance of one distinct section of a poem to the rest of the same poem.)

The tone and syntax of quatrain 2 of sonnet 59 *(If there be nothing new, but that which is)* break it sharply from quatrain 1. The tone of the second quatrain is continued in quatrain 3, which is also a syntactically incomplete appendage of the sentence begun in line 5.

The second quatrain of sonnet 80 *(O, how I faint when I of you do write)* begins with *But* and introduces a metaphor of ships and sailing which runs over quatrains 2 and 3.

Each of sonnets 96 through 100 in the 1609 order exhibits a unifying factor linking together the second and third quatrains. Sonnet 96 *(Some say thy fault is youth, some wantonness)* begins with a four-line statement of the problem of the poem. The second quatrain is made up of a two-line simile followed by a two-line application. That pattern is duplicated in quatrain 3—a two-line metaphor followed by a two-line application.

The second and third quatrains of both sonnet 97 *(How like a winter hath my absence been)* and sonnet 98 *(From you have I been absent in the spring)* are linked by a muted anaphora in lines 5 and 9. In sonnet 97 quatrain 2 begins: *And yet this time,* and quatrain 3 begins: *Yet this abundant issue.* In sonnet 98 a similar repetition of *nor* has a similar effect.

Sonnet 99 is fifteen lines long; the extra line is the fifth. The next eight lines are two regular quatrains made inseparable by a logical unit that begins in lines 3 and 4 of quatrain 2 and runs into quatrain 3:

> The roses fearfully on thorns did stand,
> One blushing shame, another white despair;
> A third . . . .

Sonnet 100 is made up of seven two-line sentences. Those in quatrain 1 are interrogative. Line 5 begins with an imperative: *Return, forgetful muse.* The next sentence also begins with an imperative: *Sing.* The pattern continues across the formal division between quatrains; quatrain 3 begins *Rise, resty muse* . . . .

Note 8. Informal sound patterns in sonnet 15 (see Chap. 7, n. 4):

The first line, a metrical unit as well as a physical unit on the page, is divided by a pause between *When I consider* and *every-*

thing that grows. It is unified by phonetic patterns that override the rhythmic break: vowel plus *n* in *when, con–* in the first half-line, and *everything* (presumably pronounced "everythin") in the second; the sound of *k,* distant from *r* in *consider,* in the first half-line, and the similar sound of the *g,* in combination with *r* in *grows,* in the second. In the lines that follow, the sound patterns that bridge the internal rhythmic pause range from the light and simple patterning of line 2 *(Holds in perfection but a little moment)* to the heavy and complex patterning of line 6, which demonstrates phonetically a contrariety of actions comparable to those it describes *(Cheerèd and checked even by the selfsame sky).* In line 2 a pattern in combinations of *l* plus dental in *Holds* and *little* runs across the internal pause as does the pattern in vowel and *n* in *in, perfection,* and *moment* (that pattern, which also appeared in line 1, runs across and takes in most of the other systems in the poem: the rhyme scheme—*moment, comment*—the syntactical pattern in anaphora—*When, When, Then*—and such substantially vital words as *increase, inconstant,* and *ingraft).* In line 6 the repetition of *ch* sounds and dental endings cuts *Cheerèd and checked* off from *even by the selfsame sky,* to which heavy alliteration in *s* gives independent identity almost as great as that of the first phrase. The division between the two parts of the line is partially countered by the vowel/*n* pattern in *and* (probably pronounced simply as syllabic *n)* and *even,* and by the *k* sound in *checked* and *sky,* the final syllables of the two distinct parts of the line. More interestingly, the two half-lines, which are syllabically, grammatically, rhythmically, and alliteratively unequal, give an illusion of similarity from an equation of differently achieved balanced constructions: the balance of *Cheerèd and checked* is matched in the rhyming jingle *even by/the selfsame sky.*

On a larger scale, the formal division between lines is countered at the beginning of line 2, where the first word, *Holds,* echoes the vowel sound of *grows,* the last word of line 1. Similarly, when the division between lines is accentuated by the dissimilarity of the *b* rhyme in *moment* to the *a* rhyme in *grows,* that difference and division is partially offset by the reappearance in the first syllable of *moment* of approximately the *o* sound of *grows;* the same thing happens in the other two rhyme words of the quatrain, *shows* and *comment.*

Throughout the poem informal sound patterns arise to counter the various different kinds of division.

As the first and second quatrains are at once divided by the sonnet form and linked by the reappearance of *When I*—the first words of quatrain 1—as the first words of a substantially similar statement in quatrain 2—so the stronger division between "when" and "then" at line 9 is in part denied by the similarity between *conceit,* the third and fourth syllables of line 9, and *consid–,* the third and fourth syllables of line 1.

The third quatrain is also tied to the second: the second vowel sounds of the identically placed *conceit* (line 9) and *perceive* (line 5) are identical.

Perceive in the first line of quatrain 2 is also linked with the formally alien second line of quatrain 1: the third syllable of line 2, *per–* in *perfection,* is the same as the third syllable of line 5, *per–* in *perceive.*

Lines 7 and 8 are divided by rhyme and united by possession of a third syllable, *their,* in common.

Lines 10 and 12, physically separated by an intervening line, are linked not only by formal rhyme but by a common sixth syllable, *youth.*

Nothing is common to lines 4, 8, and 11 except a substantially irrelevant repetition at the beginning of the lines of nearly identical sounds in *Whereon, And wear,* and *Where.* That pattern is continued in a variation on it, *war,* in line 13, and thereby helps counter the formal division between quatrains and couplet.

Even less obtrusive than *Whereon, wear* and *Where* are the repetitions of incidental indicators of relationship in different meanings: *but* appears in line 2 meaning "only"; it reappears in line 3 meaning "except." Similar examples are *in perfection* (line 2) and *in secret influence* (line 4), and *To change* and *to sullied night* beginning the two halves of line 12.

Lines 11 and 12, divided by rhyme, are united by the word *day* in the middle of line 12:

> Where wasteful Time debateth with Decay
> To change your day of youth to sullied night

Day is a contraction of dominant sounds in the preceding half-line; moreover, it rhymes with *Decay.* The meaning of *day* is contrasted to the meaning of *night,* the word that in the rhyme scheme pointedly fails to be like *Decay.* All in all, the two lines present a paradigm of the action of the multiple patterns I describe: *Decay* and *sullied night* are drawn together by a chiasmic echo of the first syllable of *Decay* in the second of *sullied;* they are alike in position and in both denoting something undesirable. On the other hand, they are unlike, and so separated, in that they do not rhyme. *Decay* and *sullied night* are set against each other formally but not logically. *Day,* the logical opposite of *night,* however, does rhyme with *Decay. Day* and *sullied night* are set against each other logically but not formally; even the syntactical constructions are different: the opposition between day and night is presented not in the metrically possible "youthful day"/"sullied night" but in *day of youth/sullied night.* In these two lines the various patterns so densely overlay each other and pull in so many different directions that the two lines are as I say the whole poem is: they are so intensely and unobtrusively demanding of mental energies that in the momentary, but real and successful, exercise of its powers of comprehension the reader's mind performs almost as it would if it actually had the capacity to know greater complexities than a human mind can bear.

Informal sound patterns do not only act to counter the unifying or dividing actions of other patterns; they can also be patterns of unification and division in their own right. Of the two consonantal patterns I pointed out in line 1, I have already talked about the continuing presence of the vowel/*n* pattern. The other pattern that unifies line 1, that indicated by *c* and *r* in *consider* and by *g* and *r* in *grows,* also spans the various divisions of the poem. The relationship of the *k/g* sound to the *r* sound changes constantly; sometimes the two are together, sometimes apart. (In the following articulation of the *k/g-r* pattern, I indicate the relevant sounds by capitals; everything else is in lower case for clarity: *ConsideR; GRows;* chiasmically in *peRfeCtion; seCRet; Comment/when i peR–; inCRease;* chiasmically in *cheeRed and checKed; sKy/vaunt in theiR; deCRease;* chiasmically in *memoRy/then the Con–; inConstant stay/sets you most Rich; deCay/to change youR;* chiasmically in *taKes fRom; inGRaft.* As the list indicates, *k/g* and *r* are widely separated throughout most of the second half of the poem, one appearing regularly in one of the last syllables of a line, and the other appearing in the third or fourth syllable of the next. In the last line, however, they come close together in *takes from,* and then meet in *ingraft,* whose sound like its sense renews the condition of *grows* in line 1.)

A similarly pulsating pattern in *s* sound and dental behaves in much the same way: it begins in line 1 in the second syllable of *consider,* and it too runs across the whole of the sonnet. As the poem continues, the two sound-types of the *s*-dental combination, like those of the *k/g-r* combination, act in relation to various rhythmic, formal, and logical divisions; in relation to the whole, which their density helps to unify; and in relation to each other as the two sounds come together and separate over and over again.

Such networks of sound pattern help the sonnet achieve the sense it gives its reader of the relevance of all things to all other things. I have said that Shakespeare's couplets ordinarily give the reader a sense of diminished complexity that results from a tendency in the multiple patterns to coincide at the ends of sonnets and to work in a single direction. It is typically paradoxical that this coming together of the various organizations occurs in the couplet, at the point of the largest formal division in the sonnet—the break between quatrains and couplet. The phonetics of the couplet of sonnet 15 demonstrate such a coming together as well as a phonetic example of another paradox of the nature of Shakespeare's sonnets: this couplet achieves an effect of triumphant simplicity and clarity by means of the greatest phonetic complexity in the poem:

> And, all in war with Time for love of you,
> As he takes from you, I ingraft you new.

The most noticeable sound pattern here is the formally accentuated couplet rhyme, *you/new,* in which the promised renewal is capsuled. That rhyme pair and the couplet proportion also exist in two other pairings, both of which include the last word of the poem. As the two lines of the couplet are to each other, so are the two halves of line 14; they balance each other and rhyme: *As he takes from you/I ingraft you new.* Similarly, the last two words duplicate both of the patterns that contain them: *you new.*

In these last lines the poem still demands mental activity from the reader (for example, the balanced contrast in line 14 between the action of time and the action of the speaker is presented in a pair of logically nonparallel constructions), but the formal neatness of the couplet has the sound of a simplification, and it makes a simple assertion. There are a great number of simultaneous actions in the couplet, but, as is common in Shakespeare's couplets, they tend to duplicate each other in general effect; indeed, all the patterns of this couplet are contrasting pairs. They range from the simple alliterative pairs and rhyme pairs inside line 13 *(war with, 'n' . . . in, war . . . for, love of)* to the complicated balances inside line 14, where sound pairs constant to the whole poem reappear in patterns that take in the substantially vital word *ingraft* (in the examples that follow I indicate the relevant sounds by capitals): the pattern in *k/g* and *r* in *taKes fRom* and *inGRaft;* the pattern in *s* and dental in *aS . . . TakeS . . . ingrafT;* and a pattern in *t* and *f* which, in *Takes From* and *ingraFT,* mirrors the contrary action the line describes.

An Index of Sonnets Discussed

Detailed analyses are indicated by figures in italics.

Herbert, George, "My God, where is that ancient heat towards thee," 178

Shakespeare, William

Sonnet 1: 2, 11, 42–43, 44 n., 110, 150 n., 165, 184, 198, 205
Sonnet 2: 206
Sonnet 3: 41, 44 n., 203
Sonnet 4: 36 n., 159, 203 f.
Sonnet 5: 41, 43, 203 ff.
Sonnet 6: 11, 36 n., 94 n., 96, 196, 203
Sonnet 7: 13, 41, 42 n., 72 n., 204
Sonnet 8: 43–45, 110 n., 204
Sonnet 9: 42, 72 n., 203, 205
Sonnet 10: 41, 94, 203
Sonnet 11: 55 n., 72 n., 94, 184, 203
Sonnet 12: 27, 42, 45 n., *64–66*, *69–84*, 87, 98, 132 n., 200, 204, 208
Sonnet 13: 43
Sonnet 14: 42 n., 43, 45 n.
Sonnet 15: 3, 11, 42, 44 n., 45 n., 55, 66, *174–86*, 203 ff., 208, *209–14*
Sonnet 16: 3, 44 n.
Sonnet 17: 2, 3, 11, 43, 44 n., 110, 165, 206
Sonnet 18: 3, 42 n., 43, 72 n., 161 n.
Sonnet 19: 20, 43
Sonnet 20: 39, 94 n., 96 n., 104, 110, 180, 191, 203 f.
Sonnet 21: 39, 43, 72 n., 192–93, 203 f.
Sonnet 22: 41, 43, 72 n., 100, 203, 205
Sonnet 23: 38–39, 43, 94 n., 100, 190, 203 f.
Sonnet 24: 41, 43, 94 n., 95 n., 100, 111 n., 203
Sonnet 25: 36 n., 72 n., 94 n., 95 n., 203, 206 f.
Sonnet 26: 39, 192, 206
Sonnet 27: 3, 11, 41, 43, 44 n., 72 n., 94 n., 95 n., 100, 111, 202 f.
Sonnet 28: 3, 11, 41, 43, 111, 200, 202
Sonnet 29: 17, 39, 44 n., 45 n., 47, *48–49*, 192, 203 f.
Sonnet 30: 20, 36 n., 72 n., 203, 208.
Sonnet 31: 36 n., 197
Sonnet 32: *38–39*, 94, 189, 190, 200, 203 ff.
Sonnet 33: *3–12*, 14, *39–41*, 45, 55, *88–90*, 131 n., 191, 201, 203 f.

Sonnet 34: *3–12,* 14, 20, 36 n., 203, 205, 208

Sonnet 35: *3–12,* 14, 35, 36 n., *58–59,* 72 n., 111, 203

Sonnet 36: *8–12,* 14, 72 n., 111–13

Sonnet 37: *9–14,* 41, 112–13, 123 n., 198, 203

Sonnet 38: 11, 36 n., 72 n., 94 n., 95, 203

Sonnet 39: 41, 44, 45 n., 113–14, 197–98, 203

Sonnet 40: 11, 36 n., 54 n., 66, 94 n., 95 n., 114 n., 198, 203

Sonnet 41: 11, 42 n., 44, 114 n., 203, 206

Sonnet 42: 11, 20, 36 n., 94, 114, 203, 205

Sonnet 43: 43, 203

Sonnet 44: 3, 42 n., 44, *47–48,* 94, 111, 202 f., 205

Sonnet 45: 3, 41, 72 n., 111, 131 n., 203 ff.

Sonnet 46: 42, 44, 46, 111

Sonnet 47: 38–39, 45 n., *53–54,* 55, 111, 189–90, 203 f.

Sonnet 48: 42–43, 44 n., 45 n., 94 n., 95, 203, 208

Sonnet 49: 11

Sonnet 50: 45 n., 202 f.

Sonnet 51: 36 n., 203, 205

Sonnet 52: 44 n., 203

Sonnet 53: 11, 36 n., 44 n., 66, 72 n., *96–110,* 195, 203

Sonnet 54: 42 n., 45 n., 94 n., 95 n., 198, 203

Sonnet 55: 44, 200

Sonnet 56: 43, 45 n.

Sonnet 57: 3, 11, 36 n., 203

Sonnet 58: 3, 11, 44, 206

Sonnet 59: 36 n., 203, 208

Sonnet 60: 11, 20, 36 n., *130–43,* 144 f., 203, 207

Sonnet 61: 43, 72 n., 94 n., 96 n., 202 ff.

Sonnet 62: 42 n., 94 n., 95, 113 n., 203

Sonnet 63: *37–38,* 44, 203 f.

Sonnet 64: 36 n., 54 n., 72 n., 131 n.

Sonnet 65: 44, 166, 198

Sonnet 66: 36 n., 203

Sonnet 67: 36 n., 57 n., 203 f.

Sonnet 68: 39, 43, 45 n., 191, 203

Sonnet 69: 36 n., 113 n., 130 n.

Sonnet 70: 44 n., 72 n., 94, 200, 203

Sonnet 71: 43–46, 72 n., 203 f.

Sonnet 72: 39, 45 n., 94 n., 95 n., 192, 203

Sonnet 73: 17, 36 n., 72 n., *118–30,* 131 f., 144

Sonnet 74: 57, 132 n., 203, 205

Sonnet 75: 36 n., 57, 203 f.

Sonnet 76: 43, 45 n., 60, 66, 202

Sonnet 77: 66, 72 n., 198–99

Sonnet 78: 72 n., 195–96, 203, 205

Sonnet 79: 44, *56–57,* 72 n., 196, 203

Sonnet 80: 36 n., 200, 209

Sonnet 81: 60, 123 n., 199

Sonnet 82: 44, 45 n., 203

Sonnet 83: 41, 196, 203

Sonnet 84: 20, 198, 205

Sonnet 85: 44 n., 72 n., 94, *145–48,* 199, 200, 203

Sonnet 86: 20, 36 n., 147 n., 200–01, 203, 206

Sonnet 87: 36 n., 41, 94 n., 95 n., 159, 196, 203

Sonnet 88: 94 n., 95 n., 203

Sonnet 89: 36 n., 72 n., 91–94, 203

Sonnet 90: 42, 44, 45 n., 203

Sonnet 91: 20, 41

Sonnet 92: 20, 36 n., 94 n., 95, 153 f., 203

Sonnet 93: 36 n., 153 f., 159, 165, 167 n., 203, 205, 207

Sonnet 94: 43, 45 n., 38 f., *152–67*, 190, 196, 203, 205

Sonnet 95: 36 n., 131 n., 154, 159, 203

Sonnet 96: 36 n., 154, 159, 199, 203, 209

Sonnet 97: 36 n., 41, 203, 209

Sonnet 98: 36 n., 207, 209

Sonnet 99: 15, 94 n., 96 n., 203, 205, 209

Sonnet 100: 36 n., 132 n., 209

Sonnet 101: 36 n., 72 n., 203

Sonnet 102: 44 n., 66, 205

Sonnet 103: 36 n., 203

Sonnet 104: 45 n., 72 n., 94 n., 203

Sonnet 105: 36 n., 44 n.

Sonnet 106: 38 f., 45 n., 54 n., 94, 130 n., 136, 190, 199, 203, 205

Sonnet 107: 44 n., 45 n., 200

Sonnet 108: 36 n., 130 n., 203

Sonnet 109: 44 n., 45 n., 94 n., 95, 201–03

Sonnet 110: 43, 206

Sonnet 111: 36 n., 72 n., 94 n., 96 n., 203

Sonnet 112: 36 n., 203

Sonnet 113: 36 n., 94, 111 n., 203

Sonnet 114: 39, 43, 191–92

Sonnet 115: 42 f., 130 n.

Sonnet 116: 36 n., 131, 132 n., 161 n., 184, 194–95

Sonnet 117: 39, 44, 46, 191, 202

Sonnet 118: 38 f., 190, 206–07

Sonnet 119: 43 f., 206

Sonnet 120: 3, 11, 41, 44 n., 94 n., 95 n., 203

Sonnet 121: 41, 44, 46, 203

Sonnet 122: 39 n.

Sonnet 123: 42, 131 n., 132 n.

Sonnet 124: 36 n., 56, 94 n., 130 n., 131 n., 202 f., 207–08

Sonnet 125: 43, 203, 205

Sonnet 126: 15, 132 n., 197

Sonnet 127: 41, 44 n., 72 n., 158, 203

Sonnet 128: 38 f., 190, 204

Sonnet 129: xiv, 39, 44 n., 131 n., *148–51*, 191

Sonnet 130: 36 n., 66, *144–45*, 180, 198

Sonnet 131: 20, 36 n., 54 f., 150 n., 203

Sonnet 132: 36 n., 41, 203

Sonnet 133: 20, 36 n., 94 n., 114 n., 203, 205

Sonnet 134: 36 n., 94 n., 95 n., 114 n., 203, 205

Sonnet 135: 36 n., 92

Sonnet 136: 36 n., 92, 94 n., 95 n., 196, 203 f.

Sonnet 137: 36 n.

Sonnet 138: 42 n.

Sonnet 139: 11, 20, 44 n., 111, 130 n., 204 f.

Sonnet 140: 36 n., 203

Sonnet 141: 20, 42 n., 57–58, 203 f.

Sonnet 142: 39 n.

Sonnet 143: 10, 38 f., 190

Sonnet 144: 36 n., 180

Sonnet 145: 15, 37, 44, *51–53*, 72 n.

Sonnet 146: 43

Sonnet 147: 36 n., 94 n., 203

Sonnet 148: 44

Sonnet 149: 11, 36 n., 203 f.

Sonnet 150: 36 n., 204 f.

Sonnet 151: 36 n., 42 n., 180, 201, 203

Sonnet 152: 36 n., 72 n., 94, 201, 203, 205

Sonnet 153: 39, 42 n., 44, 46–47, 192, 203

Sonnet 154: 35, 37, 44, 47, *49–50*, 94 n., 96 n., 203

Sidney, Philip
"It is most true, that eyes are form'd to serve," 179
"Not at first sight, nor with a dribbed shot," 34–35
"What length of verse can serve brave *Mopsa's* good to show," 179–80

Surrey, Henry Howard, Earl of
"Ffrom Tuscan cam my ladies worthi race," *30–32*
"When Windesor Walles sustained my wearied arme," *32–34*, 50

Wordsworth, William
"Nuns fret not at their convent's narrow room," 186
"Scorn not the Sonnet; Critic, you have frowned," 174